The
COMMERCE
of the
SACRED

The
COMMERCE
of the
SACRED

Mediation of the Divine among Jews
in the Greco-Roman World

Jack N. Lightstone

WITH A FOREWORD TO THE NEW EDITION BY
WILLI BRAUN

AND AN UPDATED BIBLIOGRAPHY BY
HERBERT W. BASSER

Columbia University Press · *New York*

Columbia University Press
Publishers Since 1893
New York, Chichester, West Sussex
First Printed 1984 by Scholars Press for *Brown Judaic Studies* (Number 59)
New Material Copyright © 2006 Columbia University Press

Library of Congress Cataloging-in-Publication Data

Lightstone, Jack N.
The commerce of the sacred : mediation of the divine among
Jews in the Greco-Roman world / by Jack N. Lightstone ;
with a foreword to the new edition by Willi Braun
and an updated biliography by Herbert W. Basser. — New ed.
p. cm.
Includes biliographical references and index.
ISBN 0–231–12856–8 (cloth : alk. paper) — ISBN 0–231–12857–6
(pbk. : alk. paper) — ISBN 0–231–50276–1 (electronic)
1. Mediation between God and man—Judaism
2. Judaism—History—Post-exilic period, 586 B.C.–210 A.D.
3. Judaism—Relations—Christianity.
4. Christianity and other religions—Judaism.
I. Basser, Herbert W. II. Title.
BM645.M37L53 2006
296.09'015—dc22 2005031784

Columbia University Press books
are printed on permanent and durable acid-free paper

Printed in the United States of America

c 10 9 8 7 6 5 4 3 2 1
p 10 9 8 7 6 5 4 3 2 1

Contents

Contents

Foreword

Willi Braun

There is dissatisfied restlessness in the world of comparison
—Pramoedya Ananta Toer[1]

The disciplined study of any subject is, among other things,
a disciplined assault on self-evidence, on matters taken for granted,
nowhere more so than in the study of religion
—Jonathan Z. Smith[2]

One could be excused for thinking that Stephen Jay Gould, the late Harvard paleontologist and historian of science, had consulted *Commerce of the Sacred* and found there a confirming nod for his claim concerning "the subtle and inevitable hold that theory exerts upon data and observation." "The greatest impediment to scientific innovation," Gould aphoristically states, "is usually a conceptual lock, not a factual lack."[3] Half a decade before Gould's oft-forwarded aphorism appeared, Jack Lightstone introduced his *Commerce of the Sacred* with a similar announcement of his approach toward an understanding of Jewish communities outside Palestine in the various cities of the Greco-Roman world. He states that readers should not expect "fresh evidence relevant to better understanding Hellenistic Judaism" (p. xviii). "I announce no new discoveries," he continues, "nor can I contribute better editions or translations of existing texts" (p. xviii).[4]

This promise of nothing new, however, is not by any means a negative way of promising yet another recitation of an old narrative of Jewry in the Greco-Roman diaspora, whether the old is understood as a paraphrastic replication of apologetic or polemic self-representations in the ancient sources or as a humming of the ethnocentric historiographical tune that marks much historical scholarship on the ancient sources that are in Lightstone's view.[5] Nor is the "nothing new" disclaimer a devaluation of new discoveries, better text editions and translations, and exegetical sophistication: all the venerable trade crafts that have produced such swelled storehouses of information about early Judaisms, Christianities, and other religious formations in Greco-Roman antiquity. Lightstone knows the importance of these traditional philology-based labors and plies the appropriate tools as ably as the best scholars in the field.

So, "nothing new" on this front is a directional device of the utmost importance, a pointer that asks us to attend to *Commerce of the Sacred* as a work of the productive theoretical imagination, rather than as a conveyor of reproduced tidbits of exotic or quotidian ancient Jewish doings of self-disclosing or self-evident significance. And it is in the first place as a work of the productive theoretical imagination that *Commerce of the Sacred* is a signal work, not only within the realm of scholarship on ancient Mediterranean Jewry, but also for historians of religious and other social practices in general. Why so and how so?

The study of religion has long been excited by the presumption that its object consists of a privileged stratum of facts and phenomena that "stand on their own feet" as religious, just as the scholar's recognition of self-evidently religious matters "stands on it own feet." This kind of foundationalism, assigned both to a class of facts and—on some (usually implicit) postulation of a unity of "human" and "religion" across time and cultures and by eliding the difference between first-person authority (the level of our data) and the relationship of the scholar to that authority (at the level of explanation)[6]—also to the manner of knowing those facts, Wilfrid Sellars has called the epistemological "framework of givenness" or the "myth of the given."[7] Lightstone's first chore thus is a removal exercise, one that sets aside the "myth of the given" or, as he calls it, the self-evidence of scholarly categories, themselves often items of vocabulary native to the tradition under study that are transplaced into scholarly discourse by force of socialized habit (p. 1), as "monkeys riding on a variety of exegetes' backs" (p. 58) or, when done quite self-consciously, on the presumption of the untranslatability of certain native terms into analytically useful scholarly terms.[8]

We use words like "magic" and "religion," "Christian" and "Jew," "Christianity" and "Judaism," as if their appropriate referents are self-evident. And to the extent that we feel so, the classification of data accordingly represents *less analytic judgment, than a prejudicial restatement* of our own cultural categories (pp. 1, emphasis added).

Making place for "analytic judgment," which is Lightstone's aim, entails displacing "prejudicial restatement" by deliberate, thoughtful refusal on two related matters: waiting passively for the historical source fragments that provide evidence of the phenomena in which he has an interest to appear to him with an announcement of their own significance, and agreeing to the self-declared significance in the data, when such declaration is present, as it usually is, especially in textual documents. "We must treat documents as data, not sources," Lightstone aphoristically condenses the point (p. 5). And, what counts as data for the "Jewry" about which he is curious, and for what purpose the data will be adduced, are matters that are for him, for any scholar, to stipulate, so as not to obscure his own analytic purposes by disguising them and the cognitive procedures appropriate to them in the "network of [a] religion's own terms, categories, and understandings."[9] Lightstone articulates this refusal as not being beholden to his subjects' own classifications by which they order their worlds:

> To wholly adopt the subjects' classifications, unable to move beyond them in acts of interpretation, is to become a member of the group [under study], bound by its framework. To explain and to interpret, and thus to transcend, the world-view of the subject matter entails appealing to categories beyond [those native to the subject group] (p. 4).

Lightstone here points to a circularity, a "magic circle" he calls it (p. 4), that leads to scholarship with little more than paraphrastic, self-validating, and tautologous results, even though it may intend and claim to produce second-order (explanatory) knowledge. This is a persistent Lightstonian worry that comes into sharper view in his more recent work on the social formation of the early rabbinic guild.[10] Remarking on the scholarly reconstructions of the history of rabbinism, and drawing on Burton Mack's programmatic attempt to rectify the study of early Christian associations, Lightstone points out:

in the main what one has is a scholarly refinement of rabbinic literature's own account of its own literary history. This account, distilled and re-fined, becomes the [modern scholarly] description of the early rabbinic and proto-rabbinic social formation, in terms of which the literary his-tory and character of the early rabbinic documents are explained, and in which framework their meaning is elucidated. "Catch-22!"[11]

For this reason he argues for a double relation of difference as a way of squeezing himself out of the magic circle: difference with re-spect to the emic categories of the historical data in question; differ-ence with respect to the classifications of scholars who have not taken care to translate the historical subjects' self-descriptions into second-order *taxa*. Various persistent extra- or pseudo-historical descriptive and classificatory categories that have marked the *Wissenschaft des Judentums* thus must be invited to leave their seats of self-evidence and privilege—and Lightstone's workshop. "Normative" and "au-thentic," prevalently identified with "Pharisaic-Rabbinic Judaism," often further distinguished as "rational" over against presumably nonrational Judaisms, are out (p. 2).[12] Out also is the familiar dis-tinction between Palestinian and Hellenistic Judaism, especially the privilege that scholarship has accorded Philo Judaeus's writings as the measure of Hellenistic Judaism (pp. 119–29). Too, insofar—and it is far indeed—as the Judaisms in the Hellenistic period have been described for the purpose of worrying about "another problematic altogether, whence early Christianity" (pp. 2, 137 n. 6), we should be wary.[13]

Finally, Lightstone is critical of a historiography that (usually quite unwittingly but passionately) looks to the past to legitimate stances within and responses to contemporary social, cultural, and political realities. What one holds dear and wants to preserve as normative, in-tramurally and extramurally, in a given socio-religious formation, say nineteenth-century European Jewish communities who "faced major questions regarding their place and future in an 'open' society" (pp. 2, 137 n. 7), may be authorized by means of inscribing current inter-ests on the past as what has always been the case, thus a given. Or, what is in the present considered a corrosive invention intramurally or an abjured set of conditions and practices extramurally may be excoriated by means of rhetorically erasing intolerable aspects of the present from the register of the historical givens. This management of the past to validate or invalidate present preferences is familiar to historians, though the relationship of "then" and "now" may of course be parsed in different ways. As Eric Hobsbawm, among many others, has reminded us: "History is the raw material for nationalist or ethnic or fundamentalist ideologies, as poppies are the raw material for heroin addition. The past is an essential element, perhaps *the* essential element" in ideology formation, just as ideology formation, in turn, is necessary for rationalizing social identities, arrangements, and preferences.[14]

Lightstone recognizes clearly the almost irresistible temptation by social formations, especially, but not only religious ones, to draw maps of the past for use in navigating social territories in the present, something that in effect "derealizes" the past as territory and replaces it with the sign, the map, even a simulacrum, of the past—in a kind of "retro-process" steered by a delirious nostalgia for Origin,[15] seen most remarkably in the American cultural and scholarly "historical Jesus hoopla" that is deeply embedded in problematics related to contemporary identity construction.[16] When Lightstone nonetheless holds out for the possibility of letting the "other" live, both socially and historically, he does so, as he must, by rethinking fundamental theoretical issues in classification, comparison, and historical reconstruction in order to position Greco-Roman "Jewry" within the realm of verifiable hypotheses that also have utility for a general comparative study of religions' structures and histories—"a state of affairs," he rightly says, "too uncommon in religious studies" (p. 5).

The first step toward rectification is what he calls "the dismemberment of a particular beast, Judaism in the Greco-Roman age" (p. 5) to allow for a classification of Judaism that is not encumbered by the multifaceted myth of the given. If one may introduce some terms that Lightstone does not use but that elucidate his "dismembered" Judaism: take the term "Judaism" at least as a multivariate category, a plural entity perhaps better explicitly pluralized as "Judaisms" despite the inelegance of this pluralized abstract noun. Since a monothetic definition of Judaism has no cognitive or explanatory advantage and tends, moreover, to be tightly allied with apologetic and theological agenda, why not opt for a polythetic definition of Greco-Roman Judaism? Polythetic classificatory thought was influentially introduced into biology by Morton Beckner, into anthropology by Rodney Needham, and for the study of religion,

using the exemplum of Judaism of the very period that is in Lightstone's view, by Jonathan Z. Smith.[17] Coarsely stated, the polythetic
principle posits a relationship of resemblance and difference among
members of a class such that the relationship is not based on the
notion of an "essence" or *sine qua non*, as the older Aristotelian notion of what constitutes a class had it. Rather, admission to a class is
based on possessing a stipulated number, even a large one, as Beckner and Smith recommend,[18] of a stipulated set of characteristics or
properties—social, ritual, doctrinal, moral, dietary preferences, body
markings, and so on—that defines a class. It is neither necessary for
all members of a class to share all the properties nor necessary to admit some people who possess one or a few of the properties into the
class. "Real people—even Jews!—have different views and behave in
multiple ways"[19] without jeopardizing their membership in the class
"Jew." Just so, real people have views and behave in ways shared by
some Jews without thereby having membership in the class "Jew."
Greco-Roman Jews were neither wholly other, thus unique and in-
comparable with respect to their Gentile neighbors, nor must all Jews
be pigeonholed into being Jewish "just so" if they are to be reckoned
as members of Jewry. The polythetic classificatory principle makes
possible both intramural and extramural comparison with respect to
specified practices, beliefs, rituals, worldviews.

The advantage of a polythetically defined Greco-Roman Jewry for
Lightstone is startling in what it allows him to bring in as historical data and what the data allows him to claim. It would be impo-
lite for me to steal Lightstone's thunder here on the former, but note
as important examples: his claim (chapter 2) that "Diaspora Jews
. . . remain demon believers and exorcists throughout" (p. 37); his
demonstration of a thriving cult of the dead in which tomb replaces
Temple altar among Diaspora Jewish communities (chapter 3); his
argument that Torah was seen as a relic, a portable locus of the sacred, that functioned efficiently in decentralizing and denationalizing
the locus of mediation between the mundane and the supra-mundane
worlds (chapter 4); the argument that, contrary to the rabbinic claim
that the synagogue was a substitute "small Sanctuary," it appears to
have been no such thing (chapter 5)—"Synagogues in themselves are
not holy places; they can become holy places only by bringing within
them some sacred object which itself is a portable locus of the sacred
and link between the realms" (p. 115); Torah did not define a "comprehensive 'system' of cosmic order" (p. 116); Diaspora Jews and

Gentile Christians lived deeply intertwined in shared practices and mutual recognitions for the first three and a half centuries (chapters 6 and 7).[20]

A second step consists in reassembling the data for the purpose of comparing and explaining various Judaisms with reference to each other and with reference to analogous socioreligious formations in the Greco-Roman cultural mix generally. Here Lightstone relies on two conceptual propositions from "the anthropology of knowledge," so called by Lightstone in a most general sense.[21] From the tradition of Durkheimian sociology, mediated to him most influentially by the work of Mary Douglas, he posits the idea of "homological structures" and "homological relations" within these structures (pp. 5–11; cf. pp. 112–14).[22] That is, layers of classificatory schemas are integrated into a totality that bring coherence to the various taxonomic regimes that make up a society's "universe" or "world." In Lightstone's terms: "Cultures are comprised of numerous classificatory structures rendering ordered and meaningful various facets of their universe. The homologous relationship among these substructures of a culture makes each taxonomy a reflection, on the one hand, and a representation, on the other, of all systems of classification operating in the society's 'universe'" (p. 113).[23]

The second proposition, demonstrated more in procedure than by long statement, is that rather than comparing "homologous structures" as wholes, Lightstone is much more interested in making comparisons of subelements to other subelements in homologous wholes, specifically the homologous structure of the national cult in ancient Israel, the Yahweh cult of the Greco-Roman Diaspora, and (less so) rabbinic religion. "It is in the comparison of disparate content of comparable structures that the act of interpretation (explanation?) lies" (p. 4). The result of all this generates remarkable insights and brings to light a shamanistic Jewish "world" that is as plausible as it is unimagined and unimaginable in an earlier (though partially convergent) temple-cultic "universe," and that was as real as it "feels" out of step with a later (though partially convergent) rabbinic "world."

There are too few signs that *Commerce of the Sacred* has been read widely, much less with attention and hospitality of mind. For some of us, however, trying to find our way out of similar "magic circles," this book and Lightstone's later work is not only an important guide

for reimagining Greco-Roman Judaisms and their "proximate others," foremost among them Greco-Roman Christianities, but a signal
theoretical proposal for how to do "history of religion(s)" that understands itself as a small-a anthropological and comparative work in the
academy.[24] Commerce with the sacred is, after all, entirely a matter of
human doing.

Preface to the New Edition

This new edition of *The Commerce of the Sacred* is the result of an initiative undertaken by Columbia University Press, and specifically Ms. Wendy Lochner, who approached me several years ago with the proposal to reissue the work in an updated version. While intrigued (and, I must admit, flattered) by Columbia's offer, I was also ambivalent about the project for several reasons.

First, as I was heavily involved in my current research and writing projects, it seemed counterproductive to drop what I was doing in order to reenter the world of a work I had written some twenty years before. Second, the Press wanted the new edition in part to resituate the original edition within the scholarship of the intervening two decades, not only by providing an updated bibliography, but also by assessing what *The Commerce of the Sacred* has had to say, or still has to say, to that scholarship. I strongly felt that the latter was a task better left to someone else, someone with a little more distance and objectivity than the author. In the end, Ms. Lochner asked Professor Willi Braun of the University of Alberta to compose a foreword to the new edition to (re)situate *The Commerce of the Sacred*'s perspective and contribution, and she commissioned Professor Herbert W. Basser of Queens University to provide an updated bibliography.

I am grateful to Professors Braun and Basser for their contributions, without which this new edition by Columbia University Press would not have seen the light of day. I should like to thank Wendy Lochner of the Press, who initiated and saw to completion this project, and Christine Mortlock and Leslie Bialler, also of the Press, for their help in preparation of the final copy of the maniscript. Loredana Carbone at Concordia University retyped the book from the original printed edition, an onerous task, for which I am grateful.

Preface to the New Edition

The original edition of *The Commerce of the Sacred* was published in 1984 by Scholars Press for *Brown Judaic Studies,* in which series it appeared as number 59. This new edition of *The Commerce of the Sacred* is printed with the permission of the current editors of *Brown Judaic Studies.* They have been most gracious and cooperative.

Jack N. Lightstone,
Concordia University,
Montreal, Erev Shavout,
5765 AM, June 2005.

Preface to the Original Edition

This work evolved out of the clash of three discrete goals. For the first, and generative one, I owe a debt of gratitude to Professors S. Wilson (Carleton University) and G. P. Richardson (University of Toronto). The second originated in me as a reaction to the former. The third goal the evidence itself imposed upon me.

Wilson and Richardson kindly invited me to prepare a short paper on the early rabbinic reaction to Christianity and its anti-Judaism, this for the last of a five-year-long seminar on early Christian anti-Judaism sponsored by the Canadian Society for Biblical Studies. After some reflection upon the invitation I foisted upon them a different theme—the Judaic context of Early Christianity and its anti-Judaism—because of a conviction that the tannaitic rabbinate had little to say about Christians and went about their work in (feigned perhaps) ignorance of the followers of Jesus. To be sure, this flies in the face of a long scholarly tradition, including much of the work of Moore and Lauterbach, to name a few. But the work on rabbinic reactions to Christianity seemed singularly beside the point and methodologically antiquated.

The Judaic Background of Early Christianity, my choice of topic, evolved, however, in directions at first not fully expected. Here too the adducing of rabbinic materials in order to elucidate the conceptions and praxis of early Christianity has a formidable history of modern scholarship. But rabbinic evidence impressed upon me a profound sense of distance from the world-views and life of the Early Church. New Testament and Early Patristic literature appear far removed in character and geography from the writings of the tannaitic rabbinate. The Jews whom the early Christian writers knew, whose religion posed the threat of judaizing the Church, against whom they strove for self-definition, and from whom they were most likely to borrow were the Jews outside of Palestine in the Hellenistic world. What follows, then, lays out the data such as it is for those Jewish communities that ringed the Mediterranean basin, beyond rabbinic control or influence. The study strives to describe the structure of their "world," define the religious problematic as seen by these Jews, and elucidate the patterns of their solutions.

I cannot claim to have contributed fresh evidence relevant to better understanding Hellenistic Judaism. I announce no new discoveries, nor can I contribute better editions or translations of existing texts. This study, nevertheless, does in my view shed further light on the data in question, by strength of asking different questions. Whether I have properly perceived the relevant questions and responsibly answered them, my readers will have to judge.

Below, then, follows an exercise within the History of Religions. That is to say, we attempt to shed light upon the developments within a particular religious tradition and in so doing appeal to both data and analytical agenda that transcend the literature under study. But more important, I have turned the concerns of the History of Religions itself in somewhat of a new direction, namely, toward the social anthropology of knowledge, of shared cultural perceptions. The results should vindicate the method. There are many who deserve my thanks beyond Professors Wilson and Richardson. My colleagues, Professors F. Bird, C. Davis, M. Despland, and L. Rothkrug, Rabbi Howard Joseph, and Mrs. Norma Joseph, all of Concordia University; Professor William Scott Green of the University of Rochester, and Professor Jacob Neusner of Brown University commented extensively upon this work during its various stages. If I have at times failed to heed their counsel, I have only myself to blame.

The study saw completion during a sabbatical leave from Concordia University and during the tenure of a Leave Fellowship from the Social Sciences and Humanities Research Council of Canada; their generous support proved instrumental to the project at hand. This book is published with the aid of the Max Richter Foundation.

I acknowledge my use of the Revised Standard Version and R. H. Charles, *Apocrypha and Pseudepigrapha of the Old Testament* (both in editions by Oxford University Press) for renderings of biblical texts and passages from the Apocrypha and Pseudepigrapha respectively.

Where, however, I have had reason to do so, my own translations appear. References to other editions and translations are given in the body of the text or in footnotes.

Jack N. Lightstone,
Concordia University,
Montreal,
Erev Yom HaKippurim,
5744 AM, September 1983.

Abbreviations and Transliterations

ANRW: Temporini, H. and W. Hasse, eds., *Aufstieg und Niedergang der römishen Welt*. Berlin: de Gruyter, 1972-present.

b.: Babylonian Talmud, Vilna Edition, 1888.

Deut.: Deuteronomy

EJ: *Encyclopedia Judaica*. Jerusalem: Keter, 1972.

Ex.: Exodus

Ezek.: Ezekiel

Gen.: Genesis

Goodenough, *Light*: Goodenough, E. R. *By Light, Light*. New Haven: Yale University Press, 1935.

Goodenough, *Symbols*: Goodenough, E. R. *Jewish Symbols in the Greco-Roman Period*. 13 vols. New York: Pantheon-Bollingen, 1956–1968.

IEJ: *Israel Exploration Journal*

Is.: Isaiah

JAAR: Journal of the American Academy of Religion

JJS: Journal of Jewish Studies

JSJ: Journal for the Study of Judaism in Persian and Hellenistic Times

Josh.: Joshua

LCL: Loeb Classical Library

Lev.: Leviticus

M.: Mishnah, Albeck Edition, 1956

Matt.: Matthew

PGM: Preisendenz, K. and A. Henricks eds., *Papyri Magicae Graecae*. 2nd edition. Stuttgart: Teubner, 1973–74.

Ps.: Psalms

Smith, *Jesus*: Smith, Morton. *Jesus the Magician*. San Francisco: Harper and Row, 1978.

Stern, *Greek and Latin:* Stern, Menahem ed., *Greek and Latin Authors on Jews and Judaism.* 2 vols. Jerusalem: Academic Press, 1974–78.

T.: Tosefta

y.: Palestinian Talmud, Vilna Edition, 1888

TRANSLITERATIONS

א = '	מם = m
ב = b	נן = n
ג = g	ס = s
ד = d	ע = '
ה = h	פף = p
ו = w	צץ = ṣ
ז = z	ק = q
ח = ḥ	ר = r
ט = ṭ	שׁ = š
י = y	שׂ = ś
כך = k	ת = t
ל = l	

The
COMMERCE
of the
SACRED

Introduction

This work relocates data concerning Judaism of the Greco-Roman diaspora within a different interpretive context than is usually the case. Our contribution lies not in uncovering new evidence; rather, what follows emerges from querying the way scholars have organized, and so interpreted and explained, the data for Greco-Roman Judaism. That reorientation shifts the classification of materials analyzed and the problematic addressed into the sphere of the social anthropology of knowledge. To detail how so and with what results introduces the parameters and substance of our study.

I. PROBLEMATIC, THEORY AND METHODOLOGY

The scholarship of culture shares with cultures themselves the goal of rendering meaningful the ""raw materials"" with which it works.[1] Students of culture "create" order out of chaos. They do so in the same manner as cultural systems, namely, by (initially) making judgments about what phenomena evince substantive similarities over against other "classes" of data. The work of scholarship, therefore, begins in, even if it is not exhausted by, systems of taxonomy.[2] And to a large degree such systems are implicit in our very terminology,[3] a terminology into which most scholars are "socialized" and experience as "givens," as "the way things evidently are." We use words like "magic" and "religion," "Christian" and "Jew," "Christianity" and "Judaism," as if their appropriate referents are self-evident. And to the extent that we feel so, the classification of data accordingly represents less an analytic judgment than a prejudicial restatement of our own cultural categories.

With regard to Late Antique Judaism, the *taxa* of scholars have skewed the descriptive and interpretive task considerably—and for a number of "reasons." First, for "Pharisaic-Rabbinic" Judaism was claimed not only normative status—a historical assertion—but also "authenticity"—a pseudo-historical (theological) position.[4] Second, Judaic religion, especially rabbinic religion, was viewed as essentially "rational," in both the Enlightenment and Weberian senses of the word.[5] Third, much of the study of Late Antique Judaism was carried out in service to another problematic altogether, namely, whence early Christianity, particularly the theology of the New Testament.[6] A fourth factor of a different order also intervened, namely, the peculiar social and cultural context of the *Wissenschaft des Judentums;*[7] Jews in the West during the nineteenth (and twentieth) centuries faced major questions regarding their place and future in an "open" society—historians of Judaism no less so. They looked to the past in formulating appropriate responses to their contemporary situation. And they expected that past to legitimate contemporary policies. All four factors, operating independently and in combination, acted upon the scholarly task and specifically upon the "parceling" of the data for description and interpretation.

Premises that informed scholarly *taxa* may fail today to satisfy. Still the classifications themselves, by which scholars "made sense" of their "world" of data, have not undergone general reformulation. Cultural perceptions and symbolic patterns persist, even after the abandonment of those more abstract ideologies and views, because the *self-evident* appropriateness of the former depends less upon "logical" premises than upon a total social context of knowledge and of shared perceptions.[8] Academics are socialized into patterns of scholarship and categories that retain their plausibility even apart from their (supposedly) generative underpinnings. Scholars may abandon claiming for early Rabbinism normative status but continue to allow their research agenda to be governed by concerns reflecting that claim. They may still brand data as "mere magic and superstition" or as "pagan," because this or that behavior is foreign to "Judaism." Once historical claims and analytic principles were adduced for such classificatory edifices, but these distinctions now amount to question begging, ruling out directions of inquiry, not merely *a priori*, but for no reasons whatsoever.

No mere uninterest of students of Late Antique Judaism in such methodological questions underlies the problem at hand. Rather we have not been intent upon developing theories of cultural knowledge and perception, theories that embrace both ourselves and "others," without simply translating those others' "universe" into our own.

Understanding, via an anthropology of knowledge, why values, perceptions, and structured patterns of symbolic behavior have the ring of self-evidence for us and them provides a basis for two endeavors. (1) We may control for our perceptional world, no longer *a priori* in the strict sense. (2) We furnish ourselves with tools for equally understanding the complex of symbolic structures of other cultures and groups.[9] Let me spell this out, with specific reference to Judaism in the Late Antique diaspora.

If claims about how things really are have the ring of self-evident truth for those who would make them, then the context in which such claims abound has much to do both with what is said and why such views of the world retain their plausibility. That is to say, statements about reality remain appropriate and have meaning in terms of the larger cultural context of meanings. And that context of structured symbols will embrace not only verbal acts but also social organization and behavior.

This sense of the propriety of cultural knowledge rests on a consistency across taxonomic systems of meaning and order.[10] Cultures consist of numerous classificatory structures rendering ordered and meaningful various facets of their universe. The homologous relationship among these substructures of a culture makes each taxonomy a reflection, on the one hand, and a representation, on the other, of all other systems of classification operating in the society's "universe." To entertain notions or to engage in behavior that threatens to weaken this homologous and emotionally satisfying arrangement will be met, not with reasoned argument to the contrary, but with an affectively nuanced rejection of such claims or behavior, that is, an entirely *a priori* denial. So objects, claims, and behavior that defy or challenge the systems of classification will no doubt immediately be recognized and dealt with at the level of "gut reaction."

Such a theory pulls in its wake a number of correlative concerns of method and methodology. First, it focuses the student's attention upon "whole" cultural structures. Second the perspective asks that one identify the "lexical items," and the "grammar" and "syntax" governing the relationship among these items within the whole. Third, the scholar must gain a synoptic perspective upon the various structures constituting a culture's "universe." Fourth, no one such substructure may claim glorious independence and be viewed as interpretable within itself. And, finally, no set of lexical items within a structure *a priori* commands attention.

Scholars of religion, then, will describe the interpretive taxonomies of the group or document under study; and in this the data themselves remain primary signposts in one's operations. In the case of texts, the student will want to know a document's own divisions, subdivisions, agenda of concerns, consistencies of operation, and the like. In short, we must take documents as data, not sources. To translate these methodological concerns into the study of a historical group, beyond the parameters of a single text, presents, to be sure, problems foreign to the field anthropologist. The limitations of available evidence hamstring studies such as ours to some extent. There remains much about the social organization of Late Antique Jewry I should like to, but cannot, know. Still our theoretical and methodological desiderata will obtain.

Once, however, the analyst moves beyond description of taxonomic systems, the scholar's own (analytic) *taxa* must be other than those of the data. To wholly adopt the subjects' classifications, unable to move beyond them in acts of interpretation, is to become a member of the group, bound by its framework. To explain and interpret, and thus to transcend, the world-view of the subject matter entails appealing to categories beyond, yet still not foreign to, that particular framework (in a sense, a taxonomy of cultural systems).

Interpretive categories appropriate to the study of Late Antique Judaism ought, then, to have cross-cultural utility. That is to say, we may make sense of the data of Greco-Roman Judaism, insofar as we intend to transcend its "magic circle" of belief, by seeing it in terms of other comparable phenomena, other religious, even other Judaic, cultural systems. One will, at a certain level of analysis, "divide up the beast" in accordance with categories of value in the analysis of those other like "animals." It is in the comparison of disparate content of comparable structures that the act of interpretation (explanation?) lies. Significance, as in language, resides in the variety (within the allowable range) of transformations across (and within) various religious traditions. The meaning of a religious system seems bound up with what it permits as the range of content for a particular structural pigeon hole, viewed against the more broad allowable range as indicated by other cultures and systems.

II. DATA AND RESULTS

A social anthropology of knowledge provides, therefore, not only a "control" for our own "universe" of shared perceptions, but also methodological guidelines for both the description and interpretation of other cultures, including our own viewed as other. And such a perspective generates verifiable hypotheses, a state of affairs too uncommon in religious studies. With these concerns in view, this study attempts the dismemberment of a particular beast, Judaism in the Greco-Roman diaspora. To furnish the requisite comparative perspective, however, I first lay out alongside Greco-Roman Judaism the homological structures of its antecedent (and later contemporary) Judaic universe that centered in the Jerusalem Temple of the Second Commonwealth. I shall argue that Judaism of the Greco-Roman diaspora reflects a different configuration in appropriating and mediating the sacred, a shamanistic model in many respects. Removed first by distance (before 70 CE), and later (after 70) by the cult's demise, from the "socio-systemic" sacred order of the Temple, the Yahwehists of the Greco-Roman world depended upon various and varied local loci at which the sacred could be had—this to effect health, order, and prosperity in this lower realm.

a. The National Cult in Ancient Israel

"The Torah of Moses" has close generic ties with that form of Israelite social and cultic organization which emerged in Jerusalem in the fifth and fourth centuries BCE. There obtains a systemic relationship between the "idea" of Torah, that Deuteronomic-Priestly document, the Pentateuch, which emerges from those centuries and the socio-cultic form of organization of the community in question. Indeed the homological fit between these systems of meaning constitutes the "structural" problem that Late Antique Judaism (and early Christianity) subsequently face and variously address.

The Israelite social world of the early Second Commonwealth was a circumscribed one not unlike Hellenic and Ionic city-states.[11] Jerusalem (and immediate environs) had its law, its law-giver, its city God, its idiomatic cult, and its particular *ethnos*. In these were defined over and over again the shape of the Israelite universe in a series of mutually reinforcing symbolic structures.

The Books of Ezra and Nehemiah associate the term The Torah of Moses with the social configuration of Israelite world as "reestablished" by post-exilic colonizers of Jerusalem. That social map hardly reflects either earlier or contemporary Yahwehistic "landscapes." It withdraws legitimate society within the immediate confines of the city, limiting social intercourse according to strict rules within those boundaries. Or so the Books of Ezra and Nehemiah would have it. First, what sets apart the original colonists remains their unsullied bloodlines; the narrative provides genealogies for the colonists. Second, the overtures of the "people of the land" meet with rejection for two reasons: they worship other gods in addition to Yahweh; they have mixed blood. Ezra-Nehemiah assimilate this "mixed rabble" to the Assyrian importees of II Kings 17. But the polemical nature of the claim requires little argument. For the shortcomings of these "people of the land" have, on the one hand, a longstanding Israelite tradition behind them, and they quickly "(re)infect," on the other, the community of colonizers, priest and commoner alike. The policy, then, of the Books of Ezra and Nehemiah intends to effect a new Israelite social universe, a "pure" community defined largely in endogamous terms.

The other structures defining the Israelite world, as laid out in the Scriptures (the Torah of Moses) of that party, reinforce, and are reinforced by, that social configuration. The formal differentiation between the Torah of Moses and the (Former) Prophets intends to limit that which is canonical in the highest degree to the confines of Moses' life. But, in addition, there remains the impression that the "generation of the wilderness" represents a "pure" community in a manner distinct from either their parents or their progeny. They bear no contamination from Egypt and have not yet been subject to the contamination of the "nations of the Land," which they soon enter; to this generation YHWH, through Moses' agency, has completely revealed that which is Torah. The generation of the desert represents the paradigm of that "people living apart."

Such a reading of the formal cleavage in the Hebrew Canon between the narrative of desert sojourn and the conquest of the Land finds much to confirm it in the content of the Torah. We may take Deuteronomy as exemplary.

Deuteronomy replicates a covenant structure. Moses recounts the deeds of YHWH; YHWH's demands follow; the final sections provide adjurations of YHWH's subjects. Paramount in the center section of the document, YHWH's laws, seems a pronounced "xenophobia." Keep "their gods" away from me, says God. Destroy their cultic sites, and do not worship me there either. Do not give your daughters to them in marriage and do not take their daughters in marriage for your sons. And with regard to some of them, do not permit them entrance into the community, "even unto the tenth generation."

With some variation most of these themes find their way into the Pentateuch, the laws of Exodus and Numbers in particular. But in addition Numbers 1–10 depicts a similar notion of the sacred ordered world as entirely contiguous with, and constituted by, a bounded and internally configured Israel. After the census, the tribal encampments about the Tabernacle are delineated: the Sanctuary with its priests at the center; the Levites about it; the tribes of "commoners" still outermost; and, finally, all who are unclean (and foreigners?) outside the camp itself, outside both sacred ordered space and community. Outside the camp, therefore, there is no order, but ambiguity and anomaly.

This "socio-tectonic" definition of ordered world seems the exact counterpart of the architecture itself of the Temple of the Second Commonwealth, to return to our fifth and fourth century BCE setting. For, as we know it even in its rebuilt Herodian version, the layout of the Temple Mount formed a series of concentric circles about the Holy of Holies. These successive courtyards marked the boundaries of access to the cult's center for Gentiles, clean Israelite women, clean Israelite men, Levites, ministering priests and the High Priest respectively. Homologous relationships, therefore, obtain across the cultic architecture, the social configuration of the early Second Commonwealth and both the formal and substantive traits of the "Torah of Moses," a homological relationship carrying with it all the requisites imparting "gut level" plausibility to each of the parts of the whole, social, cultic, theological, and cosmological.

b. *The Cult of Yahweh in the Greco-Roman Diaspora*

The Jerusalemite community had considerably expanded its geographical and "moral" boundaries by the height of the Hasmonean Era. And the tight concentric model of the ordered (sacred) world came under increasing stress and strain. In contrast to the fifth century BCE, the Pentateuch will have come to take on a utopian air, describing a sacred reality that could exist "nowhere." The socio-cultic conditions of the Israelite world had far overrun the boundaries of Torah's model of world.

Thus Philo, living beyond any proximity to that concentric configuration of cosmic order on earth, writes (in Legatio 28lff, ed. LCL)

As for the holy city [Jerusalem], I must say what befits me to say. While she, as I have said, is my native city, she is also the mother city not of

one country Judaea but of most of the others in virtue of the colonies
sent out at divers times to the neighbouring lands . . . situated in every
region of the inhabited world. . . .

The passage includes a lengthy list of areas of "colonization."

Philo here describes not only a demography centered on Jerusalem
but also a social "universe" entirely inconsistent with that of the early
Second Commonwealth. Ordered "world" no longer is constituted of
concentric circles of humanity about the Temple. For in that earlier
paradigm, the order of persons, each category within its ring of space,
defined God's social, cultic and cosmic universe. That outermost ring,
where all people mixed, where categories were ignored, marked the
perimeter of ordered space.

Most Late Antique Jews, however, will have been relegated by such
a configuration to the regions of the chaotic or semi-ordered, devoid of
access to the sacred, under constant siege by the (anomalous) demonic
forces beyond the perimeter of the universe reflected in Torah. Philo
views the demography of the Judaic world not as one in which most
Jews inhabit a chaotic exile, but as a world studded with "colonies"
of that mother of all sacred space, Jerusalem. Here each community
is in itself a locus of sacred order, given birth by the home city, to be
sure, but also with independent access to order in the midst of chaos.
What Philo describes in geopolitical terms appears wholly consistent
with the evidence for the Yahwehistic cult in the diaspora.

Jews in the Greco-Roman diaspora, widely dispersed across numerous locales, constituted a minority within a larger non-Jewish society
with which they had seriously to deal. Hellenistic Jewry could not
avail themselves of the social-concentric model for creation of sacred
place, whatever their loyalties to Torah and Temple. For them, loci of
the sacred must remain diverse and diffuse. The diaspora cult identified a host of places, means, and persons that in each locale might
mediate the sacred, *just as* the Jews themselves must maintain ethnic
solidarity by mediating across wide geographical distances with their
co-religionists and have meaningful dealings with their Gentile and
Christian neighbors. Thus, as detailed in chapters 2 and 3, they posit
and value intermediaries in their various taxonomic systems. Greco-
Roman Jewry in the diaspora elevate the dead to the status of semi-
divine intermediaries, worship and commune with dead saints and
martyrs at their tombs, and have recourse to shamanistic Holy Men,
who make available the sacred life-giving power of heaven on earth.

Introduction

These Jews, we show in chapters 4, 5 and 6, welcome into their synagogues (and courts) Gentiles and Christians, who, while having no intention formally to convert to Judaism, selectively practice Judaic ritual and participate in the liturgy of the synagogue, a liturgy that itself seems a communal incantation.

Again homological relations obtain across the various materials. Intermediaries, that is, those persons who cross defined boundaries in order to effect the exchange of goods and services, appear throughout. Tombs link heaven and earth. Holy Men dispense heavenly benefits, because these shamans straddle humanity and divinity. The dead assume semi-divine status, having dispensed with their earthly garb of flesh. So too, at the social level, Jews must have commerce with non-Jews, and Gentiles find themselves welcome in the synagogue. This replication in various spheres of the same configuration provides the social context of knowledge in which Torah too becomes *another* link between heaven and earth, now as the *relic* of YHWH's word. The presence of the Torah Scrolls in the synagogue makes the latter an efficacious place for communal prayer—like the tombs of the dead.

From at least the first century CE on we possess clear attestation to the synagogue as a place of community prayer and locus of other forms of divine mediation. But the synagogue, even at those moments when the community was at prayer, could never replicate the Deuteronomic-Priestly cult, not while the Temple stood, to be sure, nor after its demise. No synagogue could effect the systematic ordering of people that was possible in the Temple courts. No synagogue remains of the period evince a Temple-like arrangement. To be sure, no synagogue could view itself as an exclusive center, a requisite of systemic creation of sacred place.

But it is commonplace for shamanistic rites, like community prayer, to occur not only at propitious moments, and with the aid or agency of special persons, but also at special locations. Judaism of the Greco-Roman diaspora attempts to change synagogues into such sacred places.

A. T. Kraabel notes a tendency from the end of the first century on to build more elaborate niches in the synagogues for receiving or housing Torah (and Prophetic) scrolls.[12] This development not only includes synagogues first constructed in the second and subsequent centuries but also extends to the modification of older buildings where previously the synagogue had no such architectural feature. The design of these Torah niches often assumes the character of a portal.

And B. Goldman, in his study of the portal motif and ancient Jewish art and architecture,[13] presses home the observation that the portal constitutes a common feature of synagogue architecture, mosaics and frescoes, as well as of funerary art. One may find the portal-symbol, moreover, commonly used by other Greco-Roman cults—that of Isis and Osiris,[14] for example—but with one major difference; in these latter instances the deity stands within the portal, indicating that we face the gate to the realm of the god. The portal seems to bear the same significance in the Judaic context; the gate on tombs and in synagogues marks these locations as gateways to heaven, propitious (sacred) places for mediation between the divine and earthly realms. Indeed the framing of these portals by cultic objects, such as incense shovels, candelabra, shofar, and palm branches (*lulav*), lends further weight to such an interpretation of the portal motif.[15]

In the case of tombs, the presence of the dead makes the tomb a gateway, as we have argued earlier. But synagogues in themselves are not holy places. They can become *loci sancti* only by bringing within them some sacred object that itself is a portable locus of the sacred and link between the realms. The Scrolls themselves came to constitute for Greco-Roman Jews just such a holy object, a relic. In other words, as the word of God, the Torah was not only canonical and authoritative, but it also shared in the sacred power of the word (*debar* or *logos*) of the deity (as, to be sure, did the prophets in their performance of "miracles"). The presence of the Torah Scrolls makes the portal of the Torah niche a gate to heaven, as do the martyrs' remains in the tomb.

These in general terms are the conclusions, laid out in chapters 7 and 8, to which the analysis builds. But beyond the description and analysis of the particular, Judaism in the Greco-Roman diaspora, there remains the general, theoretical approach, vindicated, I hope, by the results of the study. Knowledge about the world and evaluation of objects in that world, I have maintained, have their basis at the mundane level in a gut feeling of self-evident truth, a gut feeling socially inculcated and reinforced. But the ground of that self-evident appropriateness of claims or values rests in the homologous relationship entailing among the various taxonomies of culture *and*, with regard to the anomalous, like the dead or Divine Men, in whether the culture welcomes (or requires) mediation across classificatory boundaries. A comparison of the taxonomic structures of social organization, cultic configuration, religious authority, theology, and cosmology—evidenced by

Introduction

Late Antique diaspora Yahwehists, on the one hand, in contrast to the "Restoration" community in fifth-century BCE Jerusalem, on the other, bears out the cogency of these theoretical claims. The latter drag in their wake both general and more specific methodological desiderata in the study of religion as culture; and they help one recognize and control for the culture of the study of cultures.

Magicians and Divine Men

The evidence about Jews in the Greco-Roman world offers much data about Jewish "magicians." But the very use of the term magician for this class of virtuosi bespeaks a taxonomic muddle. To cite a common adage: one man's religion is another's superstition. So too, one man's Holy Man is another's magician (or madman). And the scholarly treatment of these data gives more evidence of the truth of the adage than it shows that scholarship has become sensitive to the issues highlighted by the saying. Our discussion relocates these specialists within another category, the Late Antique Holy Man. Later, in chapters 7 and 8, we examine such classes of religious authorities in terms of a larger range of Judaic institutions and virtuosi, including the early rabbis; for one will want to explain the presence of one or another type within its respective context. Here again one enters the social anthropology of knowledge[1] in addressing the question, Why does a group find it self-evidently appropriate to posit the existence of "Divine Men," while for another such figures remain equally inappropriate, if not unthinkable?

Almost fifty years ago E. E. Evans-Pritchard declared a moratorium among cultural anthropologists on the term magic, at least insofar as one may neatly unravel magical from religious phenomena in a culture.[2] But to declare such a moratorium on "magic" because its use by scholars entails prejudicial (in the literal sense) assumptions of what counts as religion[3] itself begs the question of how within communities persons can use the label with consistency. J. Z. Smith has taken up this problem with regard to the Late Roman World. Smith points to the locative function of terms like "magic" and "magician"; they banish certain practices and certain practitioners to a "location" at or beyond the legitimate social boundary.[4]

Locative terms like "magician," however, partly map out that boundary along with still other negative labels, such as "heretic," "fool," "possessed," and "madman." Rules for use define the appropriateness of one or another locative. And to understand the specific characteristics of a "magician" will, therefore, flesh out equally specific classifications defining the (legitimate) social map beyond simply identifying the periphery of its boundary. To observe that Jews and other Late Antique Yahwehists were known among early Christians as adept magicians[5] not only shows us that Jews and others were beyond the pale of Christian society but also points to a corresponding (and licit) figure within Late Antique Yahwehistic communities, the Judaic Holy or Divine Man.

The New Testament evidence provides an apt point of departure for sorting out the issues pertaining to these nonrabbinic Holy Men.

I. THE NEW TESTAMENT EVIDENCE

A classic (Judaic) rival of the apostolic Holy Men remains the person of Simon (Magus) of Samaria. Acts, Justin Martyr, Irenaeus, and Eusebius all deem him worthy of comment.[6] And the tradition about Simon in Acts 8:9ff serves as an introduction to these Judaic personages.

> Now there was a certain man named Simon who formerly was practising magic in the city, and astonishing the people of Samaria, claiming to be someone great; and they all, from smallest to greatest, were giving attention to him, saying, "This man is what is called the Great Power of God." And they were giving him attention because for a long time he had astonished them with his magic arts.

The context of this passage is the success of Philip's mission in Samaria, a success based on his capacity to exorcise unclean spirits and heal the paralyzed and lame. The story about Simon now ensues. One cannot escape the conclusion that Simon did much the same thing as Philip before the latter's arrival. And just as Philip's talents won recognition of Jesus as a divine being, so Simon's exploits had earned for himself divine status. Acts, however, quite clearly qualifies Simon's success. Philip's accomplishments were real, that is, divine power acted through him; Simon's, in spite of the recognition he had achieved, were illusion and trickery. The former, then, was a Holy Man, the latter a *goes*, a magician (of the sleight-of-hand variety). But when

13

one cuts through the obvious layer of polemic in these passages, one invites the conclusion that Philip and Jesus, on the one hand, and Simon, on the other, cut much the same figure as religious virtuosi, and therefore, "Divine Men" like Simon, seem more the protagonists from the Yahwehistic side of Christian apostles than any traditional priesthood of the Jerusalem cult.

These hypotheses are further borne out by the curious story in Acts 19:11ff.

> And God was performing extraordinary miracles by the hands of Paul, so that handkerchiefs or aprons were even carried from his body to the sick, and the diseases left them and the evil spirits went out. But also some of the Jewish exorcists, who went from place to place, attempted to name over those who had evil spirits the name of the Lord Jesus, saying, "I adjure you by Jesus whom Paul preaches." And seven sons of one Sceva, a Jewish chief priest [sic], were doing this. And the evil spirit answered and said to them, "I recognize Jesus, and I know about Paul, but who are you?" And the man, in whom was the evil spirit, leaped on them and overpowered them, so that they fled out of that house naked and wounded. And this became known to all, both Jews and Greeks, who lived in Ephesus; and fear fell upon them all and the name of the Lord Jesus was being magnified. Many of those who believed kept coming, confessing and disclosing their practices. And many of those who had practised magic brought their books together and began burning them in the sight of all; and they counted up the price of them and found it fifty thousand pieces of silver.

As with the story of Simon, when the polemical and apologetic aspects of the tradition are accounted for, the general picture remaining paints a vivid scene of competition between Paul and other itinerant (Jewish) Holy Men.[7] Both "work the same side of the street," and in much the same way. Acts knows of no other type of Jewish religious virtuoso in the Hellenistic diaspora.

The story of Paul at Ephesus shows too some of the basic characteristics of this Jewish theurgy, more so than the Simon-narrative, in which we find more polemic and less substantive description. The Jewish exorcists travel from place to place offering their services. Still this does not place them on the fringes of organized Judaic society. Acts gives no indication that diaspora Jews or even diaspora leadership branded these itinerants as pariahs or marginal. No less so would be the case for Paul in the Church; for Paul as well was within the legitimate (Christian) order. In this regard note the ancestry of the seven exorcists. They are of the priestly caste; indeed they enjoy high status even within that elitist Judaic order. For whatever the title chief priest might have meant, for Acts it attests to the legitimacy of the exorcists within Judaic circles, their place at its center.

To some degree, the use by the sons of Sceva of the names of Paul and Jesus in their incantations "sets up" their denouement and serves the passage's polemical ends. But here too one confronts a common trait of "proper" Judaic incantation-formulae, as we lay them out from other bodies of evidence.[8] Acts suggests that the presence of foreign potentates, divine and semi-divine, in a charm need not disqualify it as Jewish and acceptable to even the most loyal diaspora Jew, commoner or elite.

II. JEWISH EVIDENCE FROM MANUSCRIPTS AND INSCRIPTIONS

The evidence of theurgy among Hellenistic Jews in the West, outside that is of rabbinic sources, comes primarily from two bodies of data, *Sefer HaRazim* and a "grab-bag" of materials, the majority of which were collected by Praezendanz under the title *Papyri Graecae Magicae* (hereafter, PGM). Neither document has been taken seriously as sources for the religion of Jewry. Scholars ignored the collection of materials in *Sefer HaRazim*, because it was (merely) magic; this issue we have put to bed. The Greek Magical Papyri suffered a double fate. On top of having won the designation of "magic," they were not deemed to have preserved Jewish data. But when one removes the foundation for rejecting nonrabbinic magicians as *ipso facto* non-Judaic, for that means to have accepted rabbinic labels of propriety, then PGM too deserves review for Judaic evidence.

In large measure E. R. Goodenough has done just that for PGM. How, then, following Goodenough, may one isolate Jewish from pagan evidence, especially in a milieu where pagans and Jews draw heavily from one another? As Goodenough points out,[9] what distinguishes Jewish incantations from pagan ones is, not that pagan divine names do not appear, but rather that they are used as epithets for YHWH and that the principal object of the charm remains YHWH. In pagan incantations, by contrast, various divine names retain their differentiation of referent; one deity is not homogenized to all others.[10] To be sure, Jewish incantations will sometimes use, for example, "Apollo" without intending the name as a synonym for Iao. But in these cases, if our incantation comes from Yahwehistic circles, such supernatural beings assume subordinate status to Yahweh; they remain his messengers (angels).

More recently we have been in a position to test Goodenough's criteria for distinguishing Judaic evidence among the Greek (and other) charms. With Margolioth's editing of *Sefer HaRazim* the scholar has a large batch of incantations undoubtedly used within a Jewish provenance. These Hebrew charms aptly serve as a control of sorts. And Goodenough's Jewish charms appear entirely commensurate with the traits of *Sefer HaRazim*. In fact it seems possible now to build up a vocabulary of "pagan" divine epithets that Jews consistently use as names for YHWH. One might also compile a list of preferred "pagan" subordinates. Helios and Ablanatanalba (a magical invention?), for example, remain a common choice for the former, Kriphoros-Hermes, for the latter.

a. Sefer HaRazim

The "magical" documents left to us by Hellenistic Judaism evince roughly two distinct categories of Holy Man, the priestly-magus and the Divine Man.[11] *Sefer HaRazim*, for example, sees as its practitioner the former figure, the priestly-magus. Such a Jewish magus knows intimately the hierarchy of divine beings and their functions. He, therefore, may enlist their aid through incantations, symbolic rites, prayer, and sacrifice. By means of his expertise the priestly magician mediated the powers of heaven and directed them to highly specific ends. But sacred power continues ultimately to reside in heaven, even while being called by the skill and knowledge of the Holy Man to bear below for appointed tasks. Typical, then, of *Sefer HaRazim*'s praxis is:

> If you should wish to inquire of the spirit of the dead stand before the grave and recount the names of the angels of the fifth camp [in the first heaven]. And in your possession [let there be] oil and honey mixed together in a new bowl (*py'ly*) of glass. And speak thusly: I adjure you [O] Spirit Kriphoros [Hermes] who dwells among the tombs above the bones of the dead, that you might accept from me this offering (*mnhh*) and [that] you may do my bidding and bring me x the son of y who has died and stand him before me without fear [of him], so that he might

tell me truths, withholding nothing (*bly khd*), and I will not fear him. And he will answer my query, which I require of him.

(Sefer HaRazim, ed. Margolioth, 1: 176–82)

Characteristic of this brand of praxis seems the admixture of theurgic with more liturgical and cultic aspects. On the one hand Kriphoros-Hermes is bound by an oath imposed upon him; indeed the invocation of the angels of the fifth heavenly camp, listed (incidentally) at the beginning of this "chapter" of the document, seems intended precisely to make the vow inescapable. One highly specialized group of divine subordinates may then be enlisted to secure the aid of some other divine potentate. (And as we might add, *Sefer HaRazim* admits pagan deities both among the invoked and the adjured.) On the other hand, the priestly magus entreats the spirit Kriphoros and bears an offering to please the supernatural being. The cultic character of the gift seems an inescapable conclusion. For the editor of the document in using the term *mnhh* echoes standard sacrificial terminology of the Hebrew Bible. That a *mnhh* should be offered firstly to a supernatural power (other than YHWH) and in a graveyard filled with what for the Pentateuch would be uncleanness of the most virulent kind seems at first glance astounding. But such issues we may put aside for the time being until we have discussed the dead in the conception of Late Roman Jewry.[12]

Our exemplary charm from *Sefer HaRazim* evinces most of the typical elements of the priestly-magus' stock and trade. We find the imposition of vows, here upon the power over whom control is sought, coupled, as mentioned, with enlisting the support of various benevolent, or at least cooperating, supernatural entities. The Babylonian Talmud in this regard offers a not atypical charm at b. Yoma 83b. I cite it because of its unquestionably Jewish (here rabbinic) provenance. We deal with an amulet against the bite of a dog.

"I, x the son of y, write upon the skin of a male hyena: Kanti, Kanti, Kloros, Ya, Ya, Yahweh, Sabaoth, Amen, Amen, Selah."

Again we have the invocation of divine names, but with seemingly two additions. I can make no sense of "kanti, kanti, kloros." Assuming they are not deities or divine beings of some sort unknown to me, they represent magical (non-sense) formula—much as "abracadabra" functions in the modern version of magic.[13] This type of gibberish remains typical of both Jewish and non-Jewish incantations. Finally, the semi-liturgical "Amen, Amen, Selah" of the Psalms appears pressed into service as an effecting agent of considerable potency.

Like the shaman of the Amerindians, the priestly magus remains much more than a peddler-of-potions. The charms themselves leave the impression that the "magician" is (merely) a technician. Nothing could be further from the truth in my view; we simply have been caught in the parallax of the greater part of the primary data. Where narrative evidence is at hand, the necessary corrective seems apparent. The theurgy works not because of the acquisition of the necessary technique only; rather, the technique can be efficacious in the hands of the theurgist because of his personal charisma. The priestly magus is a true Holy Man, not an engineer.

On this point, let us commence again with some evidence of unquestionably Jewish pedigree, the tradition preserved in Mishnah concerning Honi the Circle Maker, a Palestinian Holy Man.

A. They sound [the shofar] on account of any calamity which may befall the community, except for too much rain.

B. Once (*m'šh š*) they said to Honi the Circle-maker: Pray so that rains will fall.

C. He said to them: Go out and bring in the Passover ovens so that they will not melt.

D. And he prayed, but (*w*) the rains did not fall.

E. He made a circle and stood inside it.

F. And he said: Master [of the Universe] (Kaufmann, Parma: *rbwnw*; Loewe: *rbwny*), your children have turned their faces to me, because I am like a son of the house (*bn byt*) before you.

G. I swear by your Great Name (*nsb' 'ny bšmk hgdwl*) that I am not moving from here until you have mercy on your children.

H. The rains began to drip.

I. He said: I did not ask for this, but for rains of [sufficient amount to fill] cisterns, ditches, and caves.

J. They fell with vehemence.

K. He said: I did not ask for this, but for rains of benevolence, blessing and graciousness.

L. They fell as he ordered them (*yrdw ktqnn*),

M. until Israel went up from Jerusalem to the Temple Mount because of the rains.

N. They said to him: Just as you prayed for them to fall, so pray for them to cease (lit. go away).

O. He said to them: Go out and see if the Stone of the Strayers has been washed away.

P. Simeon b. Shetah sent [a message] to him.

Q. He said to him: You deserve to be excommunicated (*ṣryk 'th lndwt*), but what shall I do? For (*w*) you act petulantly before the Omnipresent like a son who acts petulantly before his father, yet (*w*) he does his will.

R. And concerning you scripture says: Let your father and mother be glad, and let her who bore you rejoice (Proverbs 23:25).
(Mishnah Ta'anit 3:8, trans. W.S. Green in W.S. Green, "Palestinian Holy Men and Rabbinic Tradition," *ANRW* II.19.2: 626–27)

The Mishnaic passage, even the narrative from B onward, is hardly unitary. We may follow W. S. Green's literary analysis.

We can identify four stages or components to the narrative. B-D contains the request for rain and Honi's initial response; E-L describes Honi's successful action; M-O treats the implications of the action and the response of the petitioners; and Q-R presents a saying of Simeon b. Shetah.[14]

Green goes on to point out the inner ambivalence of the narrative as we have it. Honi expects prayer to work: it does not (B-D). He tries other means, which we will discuss below, and the desired effects ensue (E-L). Finally, his nonliturgical methods are (curiously) described as prayer (in M) and his success looked upon with suspicion. The whole, then, seems entirely inelegant, as C appears out of place, and M's reference to prayer stands without an appropriate referent. With Green, I see E-L as the (or an) antecedent tradition (with perhaps C as well). Over this other, more pro-liturgical and anti-theurgic sections have been superimposed; some of the latter seem borrowed from yet another narrative. Our own interests, then, lie primarily with E-L.

At the heart of the narrative we find now familiar elements: some initial rite or praxis, here the drawing of the circle; the invocation of the name of the divine potentate, in our case rabbinized; and finally an interesting, although not uncommon, variation of the adjuration. Here the practitioner binds himself with an oath, forcing the deity to obey, lest he cause the profanation of his own name. S. Lieberman,[15] as Green mentions, sees this as a common feature of Judaic incantations. From the elements of the praxis it appears that we find in the narrative the counterpart to such charms as we have seen above. This being the case, the portrayal of the person of the theurgist, as opposed to his technique, appears an important piece of supplementary evidence. F implies that Honi's status assures the efficacy of his expertise, not vice versa, "Your children have turned their face to me, because I am like a son of the house before you." Even the antitheurgic saying in Q reflects the same view of the success of such practitioners: "You act petulantly before the Omnipresent like a son who acts petulantly before his father, yet he does his will." Theurgists then were charismatic figures, Holy Men, not mere mechanics with their own guild wisdom.

The notion that the "magician" must be of a different order of sanctity appears commonplace in the Late Roman world, even among its philosophical elite. Iamblichus provides an unambiguous statement.

> The theurgist commands mundane natures [which includes demons] through the power of the secret formulae, and does so no longer as a human being or as one who is using a human soul; but as existing superior to these in the rank of the gods, he makes use of compulsions beyond those proper to his personal nature. He does this not as though he could do any violence he had a mind to, but to demonstrate by such use of formulae just what power it is, how great and of what quality it is, that he possesses through his being one with the gods, a state into which knowledge of the secret symbols puts him.
>
> (Iamblichus, *De mysteriis*, VI, vi (Parthy ed, pp. 246f); cited with interpolations from E.R. Goodenough, *Symbols*, 2:158)

Given, therefore, his intimacy, indeed his personal participation, within the realm of the divine and heavenly beings, the priestly magus may aspire to a communality with the divine world unavailable to ordinary men. That is, a certain prowess as mystic accrues to his knowledge and charismatic status. It should not surprise us, then, that *Sefer HaRazim* has been cast, in part, as a journey of ascent through the seven heavens with incantations and theurgic rites merely interpolated into the account of the heavenly worlds.[16] The mystical (quasi-gnostic) vision of the seventh heaven and a pious doxology of the enthroned deity seem an entirely appropriate framing of the collection of theurgic materials.

> The Seventh Heaven is entirely of light—sevenfold [in brilliance]—and its light illumines all of the dwelling places. And in it is the throne of glory set upon the four beasts of glory [see Ezek. 1]. And there are the

treasuries of life and the treasuries of the souls. And there is no limit or end to the great light which is there, and the plethora of light (*'wr hmmwlh*) will light all the world. And angels hold pillars of light. And their light is like that of Noga and will not be put out, for their eyes are like sparks of lightning; and they are supported upon wings of light, and [they] praise in awe Him who sits upon the throne of glory. For He alone sits in His heavenly abode, demanding justice and searching (*mpls*) [out] righteousness, judging in truth and speaking in righteousness. And before him are open books of fire, and rivers of fire flow.

(*Sefer HaRazim*, ed. Margolioth, 7:1ff)

At the conclusion of the ecstatic vision, replicating in part the hierophantic traditions of Ezekiel 1 and Isaiah 6, the magus-visionary breaks into a song of praise.

Blessed is His name in His seat of Glory, and to be blessed in the splendor of His might.
Blessed is His name in the treasury of snow, and to be blessed in the rivers of flame.
Blessed is His name in the mists of magnificence, and to be blessed in the clouds of glory.
Blessed is His name among the tens of thousands of chariots, and to be blessed among the thousands of Shin'an (Ps. 68:18). . . .
Blessed is His name alone on his throne, and to be blessed in the resting place of His might.
Blessed is His name in the mouth of every soul, and to be blessed in the song of every creature.
Blessed is YHWH for ever and ever,
Amen, Amen,
Hallelujah.

(*Sefer HaRazim*, ed. Margolioth, 7:32ff)

Had "chapter" seven alone of *Sefer HaRazim* survived, one would hardly have surmised that we possessed a fragment of a theurgic document. The religion of these pericopae, indeed the praxis implied therein, seem more akin to the Hekalot literature of Late Antique and early Medieval rabbinism. The visions of the seventh heaven—in the Hekalot, of the seventh palace—and of the enthroned deity surrounded by the angels all find parallels in Hekalot Rabbati. So too the ecstatic-like hymn with which the document concludes, while not known to me from the Hekaloth tradition, shares the literary style of the psalms preserved in the Throne-texts.[17] The repetition of formulae, here *bruwk . . . wmbwrk . . . ,* exhibits the same mantra-like quality, which in the mystical traditions appears intended either to aid the entry into ecstasy or give expression to it.

This gnostic-mystic aspect of *Sefer HaRazim,* finally, cannot be viewed as extrinsic to the main agenda of the document. Quite the contrary: if anything the individual incantations appear less integral to the overall structure.[18] For *Sefer HaRazim* is organized as an account of the supernatural inhabitants of each heaven and their functions; the vision of the deity in the highest heavenly abode forms a logical, even demanded, conclusion. The number or particular content of the incantations remains, by contrast, relatively undetermined by the document's structure.[19] For instance, while the first several chapters provide large amounts of theurgic material, the latter ones give very little. Copyists obviously have lost interest in the incantations, as their primary purpose appears the concomitant world-view and mystical piety that underpins theurgic efficacy in the first place.

For the tradents, then, of *Sefer HaRazim* the figures of theurgic practitioner, mystic-charismatic, and ecstatic liturgist all come together in a single Holy Man located among Late Antique Jewry. Whatever we feel to be the inner contradictions in this mélange, the combination represented no insurmountable obstacle, either for the tradents, or their intended readers (or their clientele). To be sure, *Sefer HaRazim* seems dependent upon various and varied sources, but the fact that persons thought them able to co-exist reflects, I think, a social context in which certain Jewish Holy Men did bring together within themselves these diverse concerns.

b. Greek Magical Papyri and Other Fragments

The papyri and other fragments preserve a plethora of Jewish evidence. Much reaches us from Christian provenance, at this point in our discussion hardly a surprising fact. On the whole these fragments only reinforce the impressions gained from *Sefer HaRazim,* rabbinic literature, and the New Testament. Conversely, the rather more literary evidence discussed above places the fragmentary materials of the papyri in an intelligible context, something about which the fragments themselves necessarily remain mute.

Typical of the incantations transmitted by, and adapted to, Christian circles is a lengthy Coptic text, published by DeRossi and again by Kropp. Goodenough has identified it as Jewish in origin. I cite Goodenough's text;[20] he has highlighted Christian interpolations with use of capital letters.

Sketch the four angels before the curtain (*katapetasma*) of the Father, while you wear a crown of roses, have a twig of myrtle in your hand, and rock salt (*ammoniakon*) in your mouth.

[Offering:] Frankincense. Storax. Stacte. [Dove] nest (?). Kill six doves. Cinnamon. Oil of roses. A censer(?). Coals of white wood, of olivewood.

[The incantation:] I summon thee today, Thou who ru [lest] from heaven to earth, from [earth] up to heaven, Thou great Unique One (*monogenes*), Hear me today, for I call upon thee, Father, Holy One, Pantokrator, Thou Mind (*nous*) concealed in the Father, First-born-of all creatures and of all aeons, Ablanathanaphla.

Hear me today, for I call upon thee, who art above all aeons, First-born. . . of all angels.

May there hearken unto me all angels and archangels; may there be subject to me all spiritual natures (*phuseis*) which are in this place, in haste. For that is the will of Sabaoth. Help me ye holy angels. May all my enemies flee before me. [Four lines missing] May they flee before my countenance in silence. Michael, presiding over all strong powers, Raphael, presiding over health, Gabriel presiding over the powers, Arnael, presiding over the hearing [of prayers], Uriel, presiding over the crowns, Nephael, presiding over assistance, Akentael, presiding over the stars, Asentael, presiding over the sun, Eraphael, presiding over the day, Jeremiel, presiding over mixing bowls(?), Eriel, presiding over the waters, Phanuel, presiding over the fruits, Aphael, presiding over the snow, [Ak]rael, presiding over the sea, [. . .]ilael, presiding over the rain waters, [. . .]abuel, presiding over the bowls of . . . , [. . .]athiel, presiding over . . . , . . . presiding over . . . , Thauriel, presiding over the clouds, Abrasaxael, presiding over the lightening, Iaoel, presiding over every place, Sabael, presiding over what is good, Adonael, presiding over the entrance and exit of the Father.

(magical syllables).

That you come to me and stand beside me, and drive from before my face all impure spirits. May they all depart from before my face, so that they may not say: Where is thy God (Ps. 62:3)? May they all tremble before me and flee away.

IN THE NAME OF THE FATHER AND OF THE SON AND OF THE HOLY GHOST, AMEN, Twelve times.

Holy, holy, holy, Lord Sabaoth; heaven and earth are [fu]ll of thy (sic) glory (see Is. 6:3).

We praise thee. We praise all thy Holy Ones, Iao. We praise thee, Holy One of Sabaoth, First of heaven and earth. We praise thee, Adonai, Eloi, Pantokrator, first among the cherubim and seraphim. We praise thee, Marmaraoth, who art above the angels and archangels. We praise thee, Chamarmariao, who art before the fourteen firmaments. We praise thee, Thrakai, who has stretched out the earth as a cover over the abyss, who has hung [the heaven] on high like a vault. We praise thee, Manachoth, who has laid the foundations of the heaven and the earth, who hast established the fourteen firmaments upon the four columns. We praise thee, An . . . baom, who has come to gird this sword in the middle between the two hips. We praise thee, Thrakaim, who has assumed the role (*prosopon*) of Gabriel. We praise thee Lauriel, the administrator (*oikonomos*) of Raphael. We praise thee, Heavens. We praise thee, Earth. We praise thee, Sun. We praise thee, Moon. We praise thee, Sabaoth and all Stars. We praise thee, Araktos. We praise thee, Iao. We praise thee, Adonai, Eloi, Pantokrator.

Hear me. Come to me, good Gabriel, so that thou hearken unto me today, by virtue of this seal (*sphagis*) of Adonai, the Father, and of the fourteen amulets (*phulakteria*) which are in my right hand. That thou come to me at this place. That thou become an advocate for me, administrator and help, all the days of my life. . . .

Drive away all evil and impure spirits, be they male or be they female, be they from the heavenly region, be they from the earth, be they from the air. They must not be able to stand before me, Nor before thy great power, O God. Amen, three times.

. . . .

By virtue of the [power] of thy holy name, Iao, Sabaoth, Adonai, Eloi, the Pantokrator, today, as I call upon thee, Iao, Sabaoth, Adonai, Eloi, great and only God, who art within the seven curtains, who sittest upon the lordly, holy throne, do thou send Gabriel to me, the angel of righteousness, whose sword is drawn in his hand, while it rests in his right hand, that he may drive away before me all impure spirits. May they not be able to stand before me, but may they all flee before my face.

(magical syllables)

. . . .

Draw thy bow against the First-formed and all his powers. Gird thy sword against the First-formed and all his powers. Purify this place for me for 600,000 ells. Purify the abyss for me for 600,000 ells. Purify the east for me for 600,000 ells. Purify the north [for me] for 600,000 ells. Purify the south for me for 600,000 ells. Purify the west for me for 600,000 ells. Purify the air for me for 600,000 ells. So that they cannot come to me.

(magical syllables)

. . . .

Yea come. For I summon thee, good Gabriel, by the majesty of the great throne of the Father. For flames of fire are its [wheels]. Flames of fire are they which flare out. Streams of fire are they which surround it, which draw hither before him, that thou come to me, quickly.

Come, Gabriel [for I] summon thee, by the four living creatures that draw it—the face of a lion, the face of a bull, the face of an eagle, the face of a man—that thou come to me this day.[21]

(magical syllables)

I summon thee this day, Gabriel, by these amulets which are under the feet of the Father, before which thousands upon thousands of heaven and earth tremble, that thou come to me.

(magical syllables)

I summon thee, Gabriel, by the two great seraphim, each of whom has six wings, with two of which they cover the face, with two of which they cover the feet, while with two they fly, one after the other, while they call out and say: Holy, holy, holy, Lord of Hosts, heaven and earth are full [of thy glory] . . . the earth. . . in thy holy majesty that thou come to me.[22]

(magical syllables)

. . . .

I summon thee, Gabriel, by the holy names of the Father, Marinab, Marmaru, Balam, Phiou, Bathuriel, Iao, Sabaoth, Adonai, Pantokrator, Manuel, Sabaoth, Abathu, Jachaoi, Ichaoph, Sabaoth, in whom Daniel was concealed, that thou come to me at this place, where I am, for the sake of all the tasks on account of which I summon thee. Mayest thou strengthen me in all these all the days of my life. Amen. Twelve times. May my body be purified from every impure spirit, whether it be the spirit of a male demon, whether it be the spirit of a female demon, whether it be the spirit of . . . angelic, whether it be the spirit of the

First-formed. They must not be able to stand before me. Rather shall they all flee before [my face]. Amen. Twelve times. . . .

Goodenough seems entirely correct in asserting that this lengthy incantation stems from Jewish circles. The obviously Christian elements are few and quite extrinsic to both the content and literary style of the pericopae in which they appear. The repetitiousness of the text, not here reproduced in full for just that reason, happily allows us a sense of the incantation's literary conventions. These form the several invocations of the Trinity break, a reliable shibboleth of later accretions. The remainder of the text gives us nothing unexpected in the aftermath of *Sefer HaRazim*. To be sure, our incantation does not read like *Sefer HaRazim*. The repetitiousness, for one, contrasts the concise (indeed perfunctory) charms preserved in Margolioth's text. These differences, however, are apparently because *Sefer HaRazim* remains a highly "literate" collection, while the incantation before us is not intended as a literary endeavor, but a working text. In world view, allusions, imagery, theurgic formulae, however, the consonance of what appears in our charm and the more circumscribed incantations of *Sefer HaRazim* seems clear. The use of theurgic materials and amulets, especially of the preparatory offering, appears typical of our other evidence. We have here the standard admixture of a liturgical posture with the more commanding tone. On the one hand Gabriel and other angelic powers, including the heavenly bodies personified, are the object of praise. On the other, Gabriel, the principal target of the charm, appears commanded to do the magicians' bidding due to the invocation of his superior, YHWH. All this seems by now quite standard.

Less expected, seem elements more akin to non-theurgic materials of *Sefer HaRazim*. The latter we characterized as a mystic ascent through the seven heavens, with an account of the angelic inhabitants of each, the whole culminating with a vision of the enthroned deity and of ministering seraphim. In the "working charm" before us we find many of these mystic images. The principal verse of the hierophany of Isaiah 6 appears several times. Several stanzas of the charm recall the vision of Ezekiel 1, in all remarkably parallel to the "literary" text of "chapter" seven of Margolioth's document. In this Jewish charm, then, both the theurgic and charismatic-mystic motifs have been integrated, an integration outstripping evidence cited earlier. Indeed the theosophic and quasi-gnostic elements of the charm seem so pronounced that Rossi, the first to publish the text, mistook the fragment for a gnostic treatise, rather than an incantation.

The desired end of the charm appears rather general, complete immunity from every and all kind of evil and impure spirit. The First-born receives special attention. The figure appears to be the arch-power of evil; its title would seem to indicate some notion of a primeval catastrophe (or falling out) in which YHWH and his primary supernatural aid become adversaries. This concern for the exorcism of, or freedom from, demons remains a principal trait of Jewish (and Christian) charms, seemingly among diaspora Yahwehists in particular. To be sure, other ends are attested—the beneficence of the government,[23] the love of a woman, beauty,[24] etc. *Sefer HaRazim*'s incantations, for example, deal almost entirely with matters other than exorcising malevolent spirits. So too the tradition about Honi the Circle-maker, cited earlier, has the Holy Man cast as a rain-maker. Other magicians known to Palestinian rabbis, and sometimes frequented by them, cure illness[25] (not necessarily viewed as the work of demons), interpret dreams, and the like. I cannot deny that rabbis and other Palestinian Jews believed in the existence of demons. But still evil spirits appear less an obsesssion in Palestine than in the diaspora.[26]

If, moreover, the concern with demonic spirits splits along geographic lines, so too might it along temporal ones. Virtually all our evidence for exorcists, when they are not from the diaspora, seems at least post-70 (or 200). For example, Palestinian Amoraim talk much more about demons than do Tannaitic traditions. And the Palestinian theurgists and Holy Men before 70, like John the Baptist, seemingly do not claim they deliver from demonic forces.[27] John's baptism, according to the synoptic tradition, remained one of repentance. For Paul, immersion amounted to a mystical union with Jesus.[28] This contrasts sharply with the later and virtually universal notion among early Christians that the baptism was in the main the exorcism par excellence.[29] What sense may accrue to these geographical and temporal divisions, we shall reconsider below, but in the context of the larger picture.

Just as Jewish charms seem easily identified lurking beneath Christian copies and adaptations, Judaic incantations may be found among lists of obviously pagan papyri. At times the Yahwehistic texts remain "unblemished," on other occasions with minor (and quickly identifiable) pagan interpolations. For example:

I call upon thee who didst create the earth and bones and all flesh and every spirit, and who hast stationed the sea, shaken the heaven, separated the light from the darkness; the great Mind, who administereth the universe within a frame of law; eternal Eye, Demon of demons, God of gods, Lord of the spirits, the Aeon that wandereth not, Iao, Ouei; hear my cry. I call upon thee, ruler of the gods, high thundering Zeus, Zeus the ruler, Adonai, Lord Iao, Ouee. I am he who calleth upon thee, thou Syrian God, great Zaalaeriphphou. And thou wilt not disregard my cry. In Aramaic, Ablanathanalba Abrasiloa. For I am Silthachoouch Lailam Blasaloth Iao Ieo Nebouth Sabioth arboth Arbathiao, Iaoth, Sabaoth, Patoure, Zagoure, Barouch Adonai Eloai Abraam [Hebrew for "Blessed art the Lord, God of Abraham"], Barbarauo Nausiph; High-minded, Eternally Living, thou who wearest the diadem of the whole universe, siepe, saktiete, of life, of life, sphe, sphe, nousi, nousi, sietho, sietho, chthethoni, rinch, oea e eoa Iao, asial, Sarapi, olso, ethmouresini sem lau lou lourinch. Loose the shackles, make invisible, send dreams.

A spell for winning favour. So much is common, whatever you are asking for.[30]

YHWH in this charm remains the sole object of invocation, indeed the only appropriate object, given the epithets ascribed to him. The biblical creation story appears among the various allusions; the presence of some Hebrew and Aramaic remains unmistakable. Such terms as God of gods and Demon of demons need not trouble one. Despite their henotheistic overtones such designations of YHWH have been commonplace among Jewish circles from ancient times on. Even the use of "Zeus" may well stem from the Jewish circles in which the charm originated. After all, Helios became a standard name for YHWH among the charms of impeccable Jewish parentage.[31] The Samaritans, moreover, had long before renamed their temple after Zeus, according to Josephus;[32] their assimilation of YHWH and Zeus notwithstanding, they continued to enjoy a reputation as devout Yahwehists and monotheists, even among the Palestinian rabbis of the late first and the second centuries. Still the hand of the pagan borrower is, happily, obvious. The appositional, "thou Syrian God," will likely have come from the non-Jewish hand, perhaps with some expansion of the references to Zeus. From whom the nonsense words stem, if they are nonsense, remains next to impossible to determine.

The charm remains of special interest not only because of its pedigree and subsequent adoption but also because of its substance. Again we have a rather general incantation, aimed at no specific end. Its purpose seems acquisition of broadly encompassing power for the theurgist. That is to say, such an incantation appears intended to provide the basis for the theurgist's other dealings with his clientele. In this it resembles the lengthy charm (cited above) preserved in Christian circles. The second important aspect of its substance is the ground for expecting divine cooperation. The theurgist cannot, of course, adjure God himself, with reference to some more powerful being. But our "magician" could, as we have seen, bind himself by an oath in God's name. This would force the deity to cooperate lest he cause the practitioner to take the divine name in vain. In light of this possible and well attested tactic,[33] it seems significant that the practitioner prefers to appeal to his privileged status before the deity instead. Come to me YHWH, because it is I who call. "I am he who calleth upon thee." Here then is a parallel from a "working charm" to the more literary account in the story of Honi. There the tradition implies that the Holy Man's appeal to the deity will evoke response because, "I am Honi," a "son" of the divine household. Again, then, we confront the charismatic side of the theurgist; he assumes a status above normal men, and therefore his techniques work, not vice versa.

III. THE AUTHORITY OF THE HOLY MAN AND THE HIERARCHY OF DIVINE MEN

The Jewish theurgists encountered thus far entreat and compel the powers above to make manifest redemptive effects below; this they achieve through a variety of techniques—offerings and other ritual actions, magical syllables, adjuration of one power in the name of its superior, prayer, and praise. But these "magicians" remain more than mere skilled experts. Scholarship too often portrays Late Antique theurgists as (mere) technicians of sacred power. But the evidence suggests that so to view matters still blurs (more subtly perhaps) the locative category, magician, and the analytic characterization, Holy or Divine Man. Remembering that Paul and the Sons of Sceva, as well as Philip and Simon, cut similar figures, one may expect of our Judaic mediators more than technical skill and theurgic knowledge. Again mapping out the characteristics of a magician will help further flesh out the personage of the Divine Man. Acts 19:11ff admits that the sons of Sceva had won renown as exorcists. Their failure in the case at hand demands further consideration. As the demonic himself indicates, their appeal to Jesus and Paul in the incantation should under other circumstances have had the desired effect. What requisite conditions, for Luke-Acts, did not obtain? Sceva's sons lacked not technique but the authority to invoke such a powerful divine being as Jesus. What distinguishes the magician from the (true) Holy Man seems an issue of authority.[34] Without the requisite authority the magician has recourse only to lower beings or to the power of demons in overcoming yet other demonic powers. In exceeding his authority the magician courts disaster; he stands in danger of becoming subject to the very forces he strives to control.[35] Hence the accusation of Jesus' detractors as portrayed in the Synoptic Gospels; Jesus casts out demons by the power of Beelzebub, with whom Jesus is in league. Jesus exorcises, and the effects are real enough; but he remains a magician to his detractors because his authority does not extend to divine beings.

It follows that total freedom from demons characterizes the Holy or Divine Man. That state of being remains both a requisite, and a corollary, of his exercise of divine authority on earth, to have divine beings as his constant companions. Accordingly the Synoptic Gospels respond to would-be detractors of Jesus' "divinity" by stressing his imperviousness to demonic temptation and attack, on the one hand, and his authority, on the other. Matthew's version of the healing of the paralytic seems the most explicit in this regard.

> And behold, they brought to him a paralytic, lying on his bed; and when Jesus saw their faith he said to the paralytic, "Take heart, my son, your sins are forgiven." And behold some of the scribes said to themselves, "This man is blaspheming." And Jesus, knowing their thoughts, said, "Why do you think evil in your hearts? For which is easier, to say, 'Your sins are forgiven,' or to say, 'Rise and walk?' But that you may know that the Son of Man has authority on earth to forgive sins." He then said to the paralytic, "Rise, take up your bed, and go home." And he rose and went home. When the crowds saw it, they were afraid, and they glorified God, who had given such authority to men.
>
> (Matt. 9:2ff cf. Mark 2:1ff; Luke 5:17ff)

Matthew's principal purpose in the pericope seems the issue of forgiveness of sins; but the objective evidence of that authority in the editor's mind remains the healing of the paralytic. Successful theurgy and freedom from demonic attack attests to the virtuoso's divine authority because the latter seems a requisite for the former.[36]

Inscriptional evidence bears out the impression gained from narrative data. The "working charms" portray the virtuoso as an intimate of the divine realm. His prowess in ascending to heaven, there to view or hear divine secrets, his appeal to have divine beings as constant companions—these concerns appear with marked consistency among the "magical" materials. So to seek "mystical" experiences grounds the authority of the theurgist and provides the measure of the extent of that authority. The corollary, freedom from demonic powers (conceived as a permanent state of purity), also appears as a frequent preoccupation.

In this regard note that an account of the Seven Heavens provides the basic framework of *Sefer HaRazim*; to that skeletal structure incantation-material may accrue as copyists see fit. Without that cosmological-theosophical skeleton one could not account for even a most fluid text-tradition. That tradition ends with a vision of the deity on his throne-chariot borne by heavenly beasts and surrounded by an angelic chorus—all reminiscent of Ezekiel 1 and Isaiah 6. And at the conclusion of the ecstatic vision the theurgist-visionary breaks into a song of praise.

Had only "Chapter" Seven of *Sefer HaRazim* survived, scholars might have supposed it to be a Hekalot-like fragment, not part of a thaumaturgic document. Just this parallax affected the assessment of the lengthy Jewish incantation (cited above) first published by both Kropp and DeRossi and rendered by Goodenough (*Jewish Symbols* 2:174ff). Theosophic and quasi-gnostic elements so pervade the materials that DeRossi deemed the fragment a gnostic treatise. In this he erred and highlights our point. Intimacy with divine beings remains integral to claiming the status of Holy or Divine Man. While the latter and the "magician" may (at times) produce the same theurgic results, that intimacy sets them apart and guarantees the Holy Man unqualified success, particularly against demons (the partners of the magician).

The Kropp-DeRossi text aptly draws together these characteristics of the Holy Man-theurgist. The fragment commences with instructions for the ritual offering to accompany the incantation. But the remainder of the text invokes various angelic and divine powers for two specific ends. First, the virtuoso requests the (permanent) services of Gabriel. Second, the Holy Man wishes immunity (understood as purity) from demons and their banishment beyond a specified perimeter surrounding the theurgist's person. In sum, we have a charm for acquiring the essential requisites of a Holy Man, intimacy with (and authority from) divine beings and immunity from other (demonic) powers. As with the last segment of *Sefer HaRazim,* reminiscences of Ezekiel 1 and Isaiah 6 prominently figure in the text. Understandably those prophetic visions provided the theurgic virtuoso with a canonical tradition in terms of which he might express his relationship with the divine realm. That both theophanies marked the inauguration of the prophets to their prophetic office makes Isaiah 6 and Ezekiel 1 singularly appropriate to charms asserting the authority of the Holy Man.

Not only the Greek Magical Papyri of Jewish provenance and *Sefer HaRazim* but also early rabbinic traditions like that concerning Honi the Circle-maker depict such virtuosi as intimates of the divine world and its inhabitants. Honi in the mishnaic narrative binds the deity by a vow-incantation—"I swear by your Great Name that I will not move from this place" (M. Ta'anit 3:8).[37] He may, however, efficaciously invoke and adjure the deity because he enjoys a special status before the deity. Paul boasts authority, borne out by the power to heal; and he explains that authority in his appeal to mystical accomplishment. "In Christ" he was "caught up into the Third Heaven" (II Corinthians 12:1ff). In uniting in themselves these elements of thaumaturgy, mystical visions, "divine" authority and immunity from demonic assault these Jewish theurgists evince a pattern of religious virtuosity akin to the shaman in other cultures.

The evidence suggests, however, that neither all magicians nor all Holy Men enjoyed equal status. There remained a hierarchy in both the "licit" and "locative" categories. That differentiation within either category varied in accordance with two factors: the locus of authority and the nature of the virtuoso's tie with that source. Magician and Holy Man appear, then, less static, exclusive categories than labels mapping out territory along a continuum whose centre coincides with a legitimate social boundary.[38] The following diagram will help sort out matters.

Magicians lie above the horizontal axis and left of center; Holy Men occupy mirroring locations right of the vertical line. Indeed the correspondence of positions on either side of the center point allows one cogently to apply negative "locatives" to one's thaumaturgic opponents and (thereby) map out with specificity the subcategories of Holy Man. The reflecting, central axis marks the group boundary. We may further unpack the diagram with reference to data already cited.

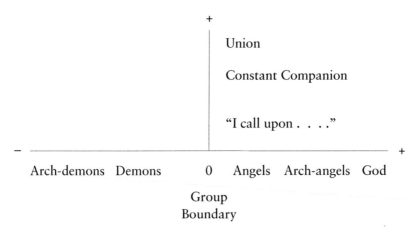

```
                        +

                    │  Union

                    │  Constant Companion

                    │  "I call upon . . . ."

─────────────────────┼──────────────────────  +
                    │
Arch-demons  Demons    0   Angels  Arch-angels  God

                    Group
                    Boundary
```

Our virtuoso of *Sefer HaRazim* stands close to and to the right of the center point.

His authority extends to adjuration of various angelic beings (perhaps even the deity) in the control of lesser forces. While this Holy Man boasts visions of the Seventh Heaven, the virtuoso enjoys no permanent relationship with any divine power; hence the reliance upon incantations.

The DeRossi/Kropp-incantation gives evidence of a specialist aspiring to a more lasting state of affairs, the permanent companionship of Gabriel "for all the days of my life" and concommitant freedom from demonic invasion. Such a practitioner henceforth need only call upon his angelic alter-ego in his praxis, a higher state of authority than our theurgist of *Sefer HaRazim*. As to beings of equal or higher stature than Gabriel, the Holy Man in question must revert back to invocation and adjuration. These figures, then, move upward and to the right of zero on the scale.

Other Jewish shamans did not content themselves with having an indwelling angelic spirit; some aspire to total union with Yahweh or with one or another of his principal hypostases.[39] We locate them in the upper right-hand corner of the diagram. To cite Morton Smith's characterization,

> the friends of a higher class practitioner would be apt to claim that he was not a magus, but rather, a "Divine Man." The "Divine Man" was a god or demon in disguise, moving about the world in an apparently human body. He could do all the beneficent things a magus could, and

he could also curse effectively—though of course he would curse only the wicked. He did his miracles by his indwelling divine power and therefore did not need rituals or spells. This was the critical test by which a Divine Man could be distinguished from a magician—so at least his adherents would argue. The magical papyri describe a number of rites by which one can obtain a spirit as a constant companion. A magician who has such a spirit at his service can also dispense with rites and spells, he need only give his orders and they will be obeyed. Moreover, there were some magical rites which were supposed to deify the magician, either by joining him with a god in a permanent and perfect union (as Paul claimed to be joined with Jesus), or by changing the form, nature or power of his soul so as to make it divine. A magician who had been so deified would thereafter be a Divine Man and would perform miracles by his own power, not by a spirit.[40]

Paul claimed perfect union with Christ; what precise status Paul claimed for the object of his mystical union one cannot say with certainty. But the early Church, particularly the Fourth Gospel, views Jesus as a divine being of the first order incarnate on earth, just as Simon the Samaritan's followers claimed for their master. The insistence on Jesus' ultimate authority on earth reflects this highest status of Divine Man. And the accusations of Jesus' detractors, in the Synoptics' conception, namely, that Jesus cast out demons in the name of the Prince of Demons himself, sets off Jesus' lofty position by providing the mirrored figure of negative valence in the upper left area of the chart.

The papyri also preserve rites from Judaic circles aimed at full-fledged self-divinization. Thus the following incantation:

But Thou, Lord of life, King of the heavens and the earth and all those that dwell therein (III Macc. 2:2), whose righteousness is not turned aside, . . . who has irrefutable truth, whose name and spirit [rest] upon good men, come into my vitals for all the time of my life and accomplish for me all the desires of my soul. For you are I and I am you. Whatever I say must happen. . . . For I have taken to myself the power of Abraham, Isaac and Jacob and of the great demon-god Iao Ablanathanalba.[41]

The liturgical elegance of this "incantation" is striking. What the user beseeches, at least by rabbinic standards, appears anathema. The text first asks to be possessed by YHWH so that he may share directly in God's immediate creative power. Here we find the perfect mystical union, which Paul claimed he enjoyed with the resurrected Christ. But our "prayer" in the end goes much further, for the text sees this particular union as either complete effacement of his identity or as the perfect "assimilation" of the human and divine persons. He becomes YHWH on earth.

No doubt for some Jews, even nonrabbinic ones, claiming to be YHWH himself remained overly pretentious or theologically unsound. For otherwise, why should the Holy Man-magician be content only with having Gabriel as a permanent companion? Thus other rites aimed solely at making oneself "an angel upon earth," an "immortal" among the throng of YHWH's supernatural aids.[42]

These data, we noted, usually have been deemed non-Judaic on purely a priori (i.e., rabbinic) grounds. And yet the "prayer" for self-divinization, and others like it, remains consistently devoid of pagan elements, which might disqualify them as Jewish. Indeed, the opposite appears the case, for as Smith notes,

> It is remarkable that no names of historical persons from Greek, Egyptian, or Persian traditions are used in the papyri as names of deities in spells, although such persons are named as authors of spells or magical books.

On the other hand,

> Jesus' name was used in spells as the name of a god. So were the names of Adam (PGM III: 146), Abraham, Isaac and Jacob, and of Moses and Solomon who were famous as magicians.[43]

For Smith this suggests "that magical deification may have been unusually prominent in Jewish tradition (as exorcism seems to have been)."[44]

IV. THE DEMOGRAPHY OF THE DEMONIC

Whether by priestly magus or by Divine Man, the Jewish communities of the Hellenistic world had recourse to sacred creative power from the heavenly angelic realms. In these men heaven and earth met, the one drawing sustenance from the other in a world seemingly under constant attack by demonic and harmful forces. Some discussion, then, of the nature and locus of those forces against which they fought will be in order; one may map out the demography of the demonic on the terrain of society.

The Jewish world of Late Antiquity may be divided into those who concerned themselves with demons and spirits and others who did not. One finds as well an in-between category, persons who believe in the existence and power of demons and spirits, but do little about them.

As Morton Smith has intimated, Jews in the ancient world were prominent in the field of exorcism. Acts' account of Paul at Ephesus makes power over the demons the *expertimentum crucum* of the truth of his Gospel over the teachings and life of Judaism, there represented by the seven exorcising sons of Sceva, the "chief priest." Several centuries later John Chrysostom seems unable still to dissuade his Antiochene (Gentile) Christians from going to the synagogue to be exorcised (and so healed).[45] Chrysostom insists, by contrast, that the synagogue is the locus of demons, rather than a refuge from them, an important point to which we return later. Finally, we possess a fair amount of texts and papyri (some cited above), the primary preoccupation of which is overcoming demonic forces. Our lengthy Gabriel charm, again preserved in Christian circles, seeks permanent freedom from demons for the shaman-magus (a freedom that is a requisite and indicator of the latter's authority). In the Greco-Roman diaspora, at the very least, belief in demons seems everywhere, and in all periods. No evidence attests to a major hole in this fabric, with Philo being odd man out. As is the ubiquity of belief, so too the attempts to be rid of the menace.

The data for Palestinian Jewry for the first several centuries of the common era seem less monolithic, but that diversity makes, as well, perfect sense, as we shall see. According to Josephus' account, the Sadducees believed neither in angels nor spirits, while the Pharisees did.[46] Curiously, however, neither Josephus nor the Tannaitic tradition about the pre-70 Pharisees depicts them as much concerned with exorcising those demonic powers in which they supposedly believed. Even in the New Testament the Pharisees are never cited for any attempts, successful or unsuccessful, at exorcism. But they exhibit an abiding interest in exorcism by others. The Pharisees of Matthew 12:22ff claim that Jesus casts out demons, because he himself is possessed by the prince of the demons. Jesus' retort makes reference to their own enterprises in this regard. Neither Mark (3:22ff) nor Luke (11:14ff), however, speaks of Pharisees in this pericope. Matthew clearly has tampered with the Markan tradition that he (along with Luke) inherited.

Earliest rabbinic tradition (i.e., before 200) also displays a remarkable lack of concern with demons and their exorcism. But this immediately finds sharp contrast in Amoraic literature, both Palestinian and Babylonian. Demons emerge from the rabbinic woodwork in veritable battalions.[47] They lurk in water bottles by the bedside at night, to be ingested by the unwary drinker. Others in human form seduce unsuspecting men and women and bear demonic offspring by them. Rabbis, who in Palestine before 200 or so (seemingly) did no business in casting out evil spirits, after that date portray themselves as experts in demon avoidance and exorcism. They direct people away from ruins (a favorite habitation of demons)[48] and see in some earlier (Mishnaic) law preventative measures against encounters with this ubiquitous foe. Babylonian Jewry turn Joshua ben Perahia into the arch-exorcist and invoke his name in their charms and amulets.[49] This seems ironic indeed since this pre-70 Pharisee is depicted in Mishnah (edited c. 200) as objecting to the theurgic practices of Honi the Circle-maker.

Diaspora Jews, then, remain demon believers and exorcists throughout. Second, Sadducees, Pharisees, and their early Rabbinic heirs show little concern with evil spirits until about 200 (although the Pharisees may occupy the middle ground). Third, the same rabbinic movement, inside Palestine and without, assumes soon after 200 the diasporic level of demon-phobia with a vengeance.

What all non-exorcists appear to have in common is an orientation to the Temple, its system of cleanness and rites of purification. The Sadducees were primarily Temple based by all accounts. Pharisees extended that Temple system to their daily lives, and in particular to their table fellowship. They likened themselves to priests, their table to the altar, their food to sacrifices. Hence Pharisees demanded maintenance of purity with regard to meals normally incumbent upon priests and Israelites in the Sanctuary. These rites of purification, and avoidance of uncleanness, normally a concern only for persons about to visit the Temple, the Pharisees performed regularly as part of their daily regimen.

The early rabbis, although they lived when the Temple no longer functioned, are not odd men out. As Neusner has shown,[50] the reaction of early rabbinism as depicted in Mishnah to the destruction of the Temple was to insist that nothing had changed. Mishnaic religion depicts a system in which the Temple still stands along with all Temple-centered rites, authority, and government. At the same time the Mishnah lays out as well the Pharisaic system in which that now-defunct cult is extended to the pots, pans, and foodstuffs in the home. Why the Mishnaic masters should have so dealt in utopia (in the literal sense) I cannot say. Perhaps they expected the imminent restoration of the cult, and meant to systematize and preserve its ritual for that not-very-distant day. By the latter decades of the second century, as Neusner has shown, that hope appears largely abandoned, no doubt in aftermath of the Bar Kochba disaster. The very editing of Mishnah, and with it the bringing to closure of Mishnaic law, may well reflect this loss of faith. And it is after that abandonment, it would appear, that rabbis, among other things, enter the world of the demons.

Direct access to the Temple cult and its system of purification, or in the rabbinic case expectation of that access restored,[51] correlates with relative lack of concern with demons and exorcism. On the other hand, those who seem most worried about evil spirits and who institutionalize methods and social roles for dealing with the problem appear at the same time more remote from the Sanctuary and purificatory rites. It would seem that these two systems, that of exorcism and of purification, fulfill parallel functions within their respective systemic contexts.

Many now see in the Temple system of cleanness and uncleanness an attempt on the part of Ancient Israel to locate, define, and ultimately to reintegrate those experiences, events, and objects that challenge their cultural definitions of "world" and "order."[52] Sources of uncleanness, like the leper, appear anomalies that defy classification in a cultural setting which little tolerates the mediation across such taxonomic boundaries. The identification of these moments and phenomena as sources of uncleanness, a type of chaotic "goo," and specification of the rites of purification help preserve that universe of categories; they reintegrate into the society those persons who have overreached the limits of classification. The point of designating uncleanness is that one may be, first, identified as beyond the pale of social order and, second, purified.

Diaspora Jews venerated the Torah of the Temple yet remained outside its concentric circles of order, consigned to the regions of uncontrolled confusion of social categories. There by other means they would reconstruct a "world." But in the absence of rites of purification, here at the Temple, the identification of uncleanness serves only to highlight (and ultimately to call into question) social definitions of that world. And the condition in which diaspora Jewry found itself even before 70, Palestinian Yahwehists too confronted after the Temple's destruction.

In the diaspora context, however, excessive boundary situations still had in some manner to be identified in order to be neutralized. A system of uncleanness (under Torah) required the Temple and its rites of purification; the identification of the demonic and rites of exorcism did not. The demography not only of demon belief but also of demons themselves bears out this view of matters. In identifying where demons are said to lurk (just as in identifying sources of uncleanness) we discern the social function of Holy Men and of their exorcisms.

The remarks of Jonathan Z. Smith here prove instructive.[53] Of Late Antique Christian literature he states:

> In these materials, "Devil Worship" functions primarily as a locative term which establishes outer limits or distance much as wild men or monsters are depicted as inhabiting the borders of antique maps. In the same way as in archaic traditions, the dwelling place of demons is in wild, uninhabited places or ruined cities—that is to say, beyond city walls or where walls have been broken or allowed to fall into disrepair—so "Devil Worship" lives either in the realm of the pagan (bearing in mind the etymology of the word) for whom the civilizing walls have not yet been erected, or in the realm of the heretic who, to employ one standard Talmudic metaphor, has "broken the fence" [b. Hag. 15a]. In the former, "Devil Worship" reflects incivility as ignorance; in the latter, incivility as perversity.

In consonance with Smith's remarks, Amoraic Rabbinism locates demons among ruins and cemeteries.[54] Babylonian Jewry, furthermore, attribute perverse sexual practices, among other things, to lilis and liliths, demons who assume the shape of a spouse for purposes of illicit sexual intercourse with a human. Where in Ancient Israel and early Rabbinism sexual perversity was a source of uncleanness, now it appears as the machinations of demons; and where cemeteries spewed impurity, now they harbor evil spirits.

The labeling, then, of someone a "magician" and something as "demonic" seems akin. In identifying magicians one safeguards the definitions of the social map by locating persons who blur and therefore challenge its reality and truth. Demons or those possessed by them appear similarly located. That perhaps is why Jesus' detractors in the Gospels may either label him a magician or, alternatively, one possessed by the Devil. So too we may better understand John Chrysostom when he tells his Gentile Christians that the synagogue is the dwelling place of demons. His flock, or many among them, saw nothing wrong with at once being Christian and at the same time participating in the synagogue liturgy. This violated Chrysostom's sense of where the boundaries of the Christian world lay and denied his basic taxonomy of Christian and Jew. But to see his wayward congregants as coming under the influence of demons meant as well to offer the promise of reconciliation, exorcism.

The exploration of theurgists (magicians to their detractors) and theurgy (magic for some), of demons and exorcism, in itself reveals much of the various and competing universes of Yahwehistic groups in the Late Roman World. The boundaries and the "territorial" divisions of that world of Yahwehists corresponds to a set of paired labels and phenomena. First, Judaic, charismatic Holy Men (whether priestly magi or Divine Men) constitute Christianity's magicians (or worse *goetes*), as no doubt do men like Paul for Jewish authorities. In so labeling the "other's" Holy Man the boundaries of legitimate religious authority seem drawn. Second, within the confines of the "Judaic" world, one party's sources of uncleanness stand in apposition (although not opposition) to another's demons, priests with exorcists, purificatory rites with exorcisms, incantations, and amulets, and finally, Temple with living Holy Men. The boundaries drawn by these binary pairs define not problems of self-definition among competing groups as much as the frontiers of meaningful accessibility to the Temple's structured world. Where the cult operates to purify the unclean, demons rarely appear bothersome. When for any number of reasons the Sanctuary remains remote, demons and Holy Men thrive, as in the Greco-Roman diaspora.[55] Thus Judaic "magicians" do not constitute a fringe element removed from the institutional center of the diaspora community. Quite the contrary, they often set up shop in the synagogue itself, along with the community's courts and senate. To this we return in our discussion of the synagogue in the diaspora.[56] We first consider another category of Jewish Holy Men, the dead. For not all the human beings who mediated between heaven and earth walked the earth. Many could serve in death more effectively than they had in life.

3

The Dead and Their Tombs

The dead came in the Greco-Roman Judaic world to exercise a mediating function in the commerce of the sacred between heaven and earth. For those familiar with Christianity in the Late Roman period, such a view of the post-mortem careers of certain individuals, and the correlative positive attitude to the dead and their remains, might appear commonplace and self-evident. The reader conversant with the Hebrew Bible and its thought tends to find a comparable role for Jewish dead an unlikely—if not impossible—state of affairs. But what was self-evidently abhorrent to some became for others the object of mediatory cults, the aim of which was to effect the downflow of God's sacred, life-giving power on earth. The transformation from one Israelite "universe of perceptions" to another, from Ancient to Late Antique Judaism, elucidates the latter's funerary and post-funerary rites and the concomitant role of the dead and of their tombs.

I. THE EXCLUSION OF THE DEAD FROM "WORLD" IN THE HEBREW BIBLE

Not all who mediated between the divine and earthly realms in Late Antique Judaism still walked the earth in flesh and blood. And so too, not all cultic activity on earth aimed at improving the lot of the living. By the second century and in all probability perhaps as early as the first century BCE, the dead of Israel had in various ways been enlisted in the struggle to maintain open lines of communication between heaven and earth. Concomitantly the living lavished considerable attention upon the dead in order that the latter might maintain their privileged status in heaven. This symbiotic relationship between Jewish dead and the living, as we discuss below, found expression in cultic activity about the deceased and later at his or her tomb, activity seemingly at odds with biblical and rabbinic norms.

For the Pentateuch, the dead remained excluded from God's presence, either in heaven or in his earthly dwelling at the Sanctuary. Indeed the dead and their tombs exuded forces bent apparently upon attacking the deity and his sacred order—the dead were aligned with the powers of chaos against those of holiness and life. Thus Numbers 19:11ff:

> He who touches the dead body of any person shall be unclean seven days;
> he shall cleanse himself . . . from Israel; because the water for impurity
> was not thrown upon Whoever . . . does not cleanse himself defiles the
> tabernacle of the Lord, and that person shall be cut off from Israel.

As a source of a destructive power that excludes the living affected by it from God's earthly abode, how much the more so must the dead themselves be excluded from God's heaven? Ancient Israel had no dualistic dichotomy of soul and body, allowing the former to fully escape the demise (and stigma) of the latter. Psalms and prophetic literature, for example, cite as reason for praising God, while alive, the inability to do so after death.

Thus in Isaiah:

> For She'ol cannot thank thee;
> death cannot praise thee;
> those who go down to the pit
> cannot hope for thy faithfulness.
> (Is. 39:18; cf. Ps.6:5; 155:14ff)

The Hebrew Bible, the Pentateuch in particular, remains reticent as regards talking about the dead and matters pertaining to them, corpse uncleanness being virtually the only exception to this conspiracy of silence. Almost no legislation is preserved in the Pentateuch concerning burial and mourning rites. This silence seems all the more deliberate, given that one must suppose that Ancient Israel, like all cultures, had some established practice in this regard. What little we know of these matters must be inferred from fragmentary evidence preserved in discrete narratives.

The conspiracy of silence, the dead as a source of chaotic power and their exclusion from God's presence, all present a mutually self-consistent negation of the role of the dead in God's sacred order. Life begins in the dust and ends there for Genesis 2, with no hint of post-mortem survival of any significant nature. For even if something of the deceased persists (in She'ol), he or she lies beyond the world of gods or humanity.

The gulf between such conceptions of the dead and death in biblical literature and that state of affairs which obtained in the Hellenistic diaspora seems vast. Whereas for the former the dead exuded materials bent upon destroying cultic efficacy, for the latter there appears every indication that the tomb was just such a locus of mediation between heaven and earth, with the dead acting as a particular type of mediator—a new priesthood. For one familiar with Numbers 19, and with the early rabbinic assimilation of that view of corpse-uncleannness, the exhortations of the author of Tobit must hardly appear of Jewish provenance. This first-century BCE document from the Hellenistic diaspora exhorts one to

> Pour out thy bread and thy wine
> on the tomb of the just,
> and give not
> to sinners.
>
> (Tobit 4:17)

This dissonance between what we shall see to be the practices and views of the Hellenistic diaspora, on the one hand, and of "biblical" (and, later, rabbinic) religion, on the other, largely dissipates when one considers other evidence for Antique and Late Antique Judaism. For other data both internal to the Hebrew Bible and among Apocryphal and Pseudepigraphal documents show a coherent development of views within the Palestinian milieu, a development of which diaspora practices seem a logical continuation. In these materials we find an emergent cult of the dead, which, it would seem, both the editors of the Hebrew Bible (in particular the Pentateuch) and the early rabbis attempt to suppress (or ignore). We begin, then, with a discussion of the antecedents, within the Palestinian scene, of the practices and beliefs of Late Antique Jewry.

II. THE DEAD IN ANCIENT ISRAEL: THE UNITY OF TOMBS, ALTAR AND CLAN

We have already identified the dominant stream of thought in the Hebrew Bible as regards the dead. They constitute a source of uncleanness, presenting a danger to YHWH's cult. For persons whose world revolves around the Sanctuary, as was the case for the Deuteronomic-priestly editors of the biblical text, the requisites of maintaining an efficacious sacrificial system, free from uncleanness, will remain paramount. For them, exclusion of the dead, and the suppression of views requiring close communion with corpses, appears at first glance understandable. But the views of the biblical editors hardly represent the normative religious practices of ancient Israel, either concerning the dead or concerning the requisites of an efficacious cult.

For some in ancient Israel the proper disposition of the "bones" of the dead, in particular of the elite dead, appears a matter of considerable importance both to the deceased and to the communal well-being. As L. Rothkrug has argued,[1] the importance of proper gathering and burial of the bones of such persons moves far beyond any concern for guarding the land against encroaching powers of uncleanness. Rather the proper burial of the elite dead, namely, in their family tombs, in corporate unity with the bones of their "fathers," in itself appears instrumental in maintaining YHWH's favor. II Samuel 21 preserves a remarkable narrative regarding the execution of the seven sons of Saul, and of the subsequent exposure and burial of their now excarnate remains. David had delivered these sons of Saul into the hands of the Gibeonites in recompense for a campaign Saul had unjustly carried out against this "protected" Canaanite clan. In response to Saul's transgression, so David's advisors thought, "there was a famine in the days of David for three years" (II Sam. 21:1). The conclusion of the extended narrative (at 21:9–14) follows.

> And he [David] gave them into the hands of the Gibeonites, and they hanged them on the mountain before the Lord, and the seven of them perished together. They were put to death in the first days of harvest, at the beginning of barley harvest. Then Rizpah the daughter of Aijah took sackcloth, and spread it for herself on the rock, from the beginning of the harvest until rain fell upon them from heavens; and she did not allow the birds of the air to come upon them by day, or the beasts of the field by night. When David was told what Rizpah the daughter of Aijah, the concubine of Saul, had done, David went and took the bones of Saul and the bones of his son Jonathan from the men of Jabesh-gil'ead, who had stolen them from the public square of Beth-shan, where the Philistines had hanged them, on the day the Philistines killed Saul on Gilboa; and he brought up from there the bones of Saul and the bones of his

son Jonathan; and they gathered the bones of those who were hanged. And they buried the bones of Saul and his son Jonathan in the land of Benjamin in Zela, in the tomb of Kish his father; and they did all that the king commanded. And after that God heeded supplication for the land.

At first glance the settling of the blood-guilt pertaining to the Gibeonites in particular propitiates the deity. But that need hardly be the case. Three distinct events in fact are candidates for means of atonement "for the land." First, the execution of the sons of Saul when hung "before the Lord"; second, the exposure of the remains on the mountain, while the flesh decomposed leaving the bones in full view; third, the gathering of all the bones of Saul and of his sons, both those at Jabesh-gil'ead and those resulting from the execution by the Gibeonites, to the family tomb in Zela.

As regards the second, the exposure, one may find such atonement-practices remarkable in light of that stance which identifies the dead as polluting, as opposed to redeeming, the land of the living. We have already seen Num. 19:1ff. (And for the case at hand Deut. 21:22ff provides a starker contrast.)

What now of the third propitiatory event, the gathering of the bones of Saul and his progeny to the family tomb of Kish, Saul's father, as (finally) restoring the deity's favor? The narrator (or subsequent redactor) appears to indicate that this act of David, perhaps more than the preceding ones, effectively atoned for the land. For why else should the state of affairs pertaining to Saul's and Jonathan's bones be introduced? The narrator or editor, thereby, indicates that a situation pursuant to the death of Saul and Jonathan (three years earlier), and not (or not only) the blood-guilt owed the Gibeonites have brought about the famine. Saul and Jonathan had died in battle against the Philistines. The victors subsequently hung their corpses on the city wall of Beth-shan (I Sam. 31). The men of Jabesh-gil'ead, in an act of daring and graciousness, stole the corpses, burned the semi-decomposed flesh, *and buried* their bones. But even though the excarnate bones had been interred, their proper deposition, for our narrative, had not been completed. For "God heeded supplication for the land" only after both the new set of bones and the *already buried* bones of Saul and Jonathan had been gathered together in their family tomb. In short, the corporate welfare of the living depended in some significant manner upon the corporate unity of the bones of the elite dead in their ancestral tomb.

45

There survives within the literature of Ancient Israel ample evidence attesting to the importance of "resting with one's fathers" and to a general fear, at least among the aristocracy, of burial elsewhere—even elsewhere in the holy land. Thus Jacob, before his death in Egypt, charges his progeny:

> I am to be gathered to my people; bury me with my fathers in the cave that is in the field of Ephron the Hittite, in the cave that is in the field of Machpelah to the east of Mamre, in the land of Canaan, which Abraham bought with the field from Ephron the Hittite to possess as a burial place.

> (Gen. 49:29ff)

Similarly, Joseph, now viceroy of Egypt, requests that his bones be carried from Egypt to Canaan, when the Israelites leave Egyptian territory. The redactor of the penultimate biblical narrative of Genesis through II Kings takes pains to have appropriate persons act upon Joseph's request. Moses "took the bones of Joseph with him" upon leaving Egypt with the people (Ex. 13:19); according to Josh. 24:32, Joseph's "bones" were duly "buried at Shechem."

The tradition in Joshua 24 especially highlights the integral relationship between the bones of the deceased, those of his ancestors, and the familial territory (*naḥalah*) as the only efficacious site for the family tomb.

> The bones of Joseph which the people of Israel brought up from the land of Egypt were buried at Shechem, in the portion of ground (*bḥlqt hśdh*) which Jacob bought from the Sons of Hamor the father of Shechem for a hundred pieces of silver; it became an inheritance (*nḥlh*) of the descendants of Joseph.

There seems no indication here, or in the narrative of Genesis 33:19, that the portion of ground was purchased expressly as a burial site. Quite the contrary. Jacob acquires the land so that he may have a place to pitch his tent, and there he "erected an altar and called it El-Elohe-Israel" (Gen. 33:20). In having Joseph buried on this familial "portion" of land, then, the narrator portrays a state of affairs in which the ancestral plot constitutes the location wherein the living (in their tents), the dead ancestors (in their tombs), and the tribal deity (via the familial altar) form an integral whole of considerable importance to the welfare of all. When the familial clan gives way to the more expansive tribal confederacy, Shechem becomes a principal cultic site. It seems likely that the narrative of Gen. 33:19 functioned to legitimate the locale as appropriate for sacrificial ritual and communication with the deity. The tradition that the same "portion (*nḥlḥ*) of the descendants of Joseph" served as the location to which ancestral bones were "gathered" appears not to disqualify the site as a cultic center. This assimilation of tombs to altars does not remain unique to the case of Joseph's bones. Gen. 33:6ff preserves an account of a similar instance.

> And Jacob came to Luz (that is, Bethel), which is in the Land of Canaan, he and all the people who were with him, and there he built an altar and called the place El-Bethel, because there God had revealed himself to him when he fled from his brother. And Deborah, Rebekah's nurse, died and she was buried below Bethel; so the name of it [the tree] was called "Allon-bacuth."

Taking, then, together the stories of Genesis and Joshua, along with the narrative about the gathering of Saul's bones and the consequent salutary affect on the land, one finds inviting the notion that the presence of the ancestral bones at Shechem may even have enhanced the efficacy of that major Israelite cult-center.

Whether God's favor depended upon the corporate unity of each and every "family of dead" appears difficult to surmise. To be sure, those examples provided by the biblical text concern the elite dead along with the elite among the living. The fate and life of the common folk remains of little importance to the Deuteronomic historiographer. This bias, which views Israelite history as an epiphenomenon of the relationships among priests, aristocracy, and the deity, finds its correlate in stressing the importance of gathering the bones of the princes to their ancestral lands.

Still a further corollary seems the exhumation of the (aristocrats') remains from their family tombs and their intermingling as both a sign and effect of God's wrath. Thus Jeremiah speaking of the impending destruction YHWH will visit upon Judah says:

> At that time says the Lord, the bones of the kings of Judah, the bones of its princes, the bones of the prophets, and the bones of the inhabitants of Jerusalem shall be brought out of their tombs . . . and they

shall not be gathered or buried, they shall be as dung on the surface of the ground.

(Jer. 8:1–8)

Jeremiah here completes the logical circle. Since the entombed dead and the living form, on their land, a salutary corporate order, then so too the dead, the living (and the land) share in whatever punishment the deity dispenses.

With such notions in view, the exile of the aristocratic and priestly clans to Babylonia will have presented for that group a serious problem as regards disposition of their dead. The bones of the deceased, now entombed outside the ancestral lands, will have highlighted, indeed contributed to, YHWH's punishment of his people. Consequently, redemption will have been conceived as the return both of the living and the dead to that territory where the corporate unity was again possible. Ezekiel, immediately subsequent to his "vision of the dry bones" (Ezek. 37), presents just such a view of matters. Verses 1–10 comprise the well-known "visual metaphor" of Israel's future redemption. The vision concludes with verse 11: "Then he said to me: Son of Man, these bones are the whole house of Israel." In verse 12, however, the metaphorical mode appears entirely abandoned, and one finds instead this curious description of how YHWH will in fact redeem the community.

> Behold they say, "Our bones are dried up, and our hope is lost; we are clean cut off." Therefore prophesy, and say to them, Thus says the Lord God: Behold I will open your graves, and raise you from your graves, O my people; and I will bring you home into the land of Israel. And you shall know that I am the Lord, when I open your graves, and raise you from your graves, O my people. And I will put my spirit within you, and you shall live, and I will place you in your own land; then you shall know that I, the Lord, have spoken, and I have done it, says the Lord (Ezek. 37:12–14).

The referent here seems no longer the living, depicted metaphorically as the exposed dry bones, but the dead buried outside the land—and thereby "cut off" from YHWH. They too require redemption, and the promise of returning the dead to the land of Israel becomes not a simile for Israel but an indication that the coming salutary acts will be all-inclusive and complete.

III. TEMPLE VS. TOMB:
PALESTINE IN THE SECOND COMMONWEALTH

The Pentateuch in its present formulation marks the final triumph of the Deuteronomic School and the successful assimilation of the priesthood to that movement. The Torah of Moses constitutes as well a systematic attempt to disassociate the tombs of the dead from the cult of YHWH. Those cultic sites, which rivaled Jerusalem, had seemingly evolved from local clan altars situated on family "portions." Here the living and the entombed dead formed, with YHWH at his altar, a corporate unity. Shechem, the principal rival of Jerusalem, was remembered as the tomb of Joseph and the inheritance of his progeny. Jerusalem, on the other hand, in attempting to co-opt to itself all worship, whatever the clan loyalties of the worshippers, in essence effected a revolutionary form of Israelite nationalism. The nation supplanted the clan, the Jerusalem Sanctuary, the clan altar, and, finally, Torah will have displaced local, tribal custom and regional tradition. The price, it seems, was paid by the dead; the Deuteronomic priests excluded them from the circle of sacred order and community centered upon the Temple. Indeed, without having so excluded the dead, the locus of clan unity and cohesion, such a national cult may well have proven impossible.

It should little surprise one, then, that Jerusalem had no burial site traditionally associated with it. In need of some mythic legitimation of the site as an efficacious one for cultic activity, the promoters of the Jerusalem Temple turned to the "binding of Isaac." Sometime in the Second Commonwealth those loyal to the cult of YHWH in Jerusalem begin to identify the Temple Mount with Mount Moriah of Gen. 18. Now not a burial, but a miraculous delivery from death, serves to legitimate a cultic locus.[2]

But the reestablished cult with its concomitant concern for purity from corpse uncleanness found its basis in an essentially utopian vision put forth in the Pentateuch. The Temple, as the sole means of constituting a sacred order on earth, could hardly meet the requisites of the majority of Yahwehists. Most lived too distant from the Temple site for the Sanctuary to play any significant role in effecting for them holy space. And this would hold true not only for those in the diaspora but also for many in the Judea and the Galilee (after the conversions of the latter to Judaism toward the latter part of the second century BCE).

The utopian vision of the Pentateuch and the implementation, or attempt to implement, the Torah's Temple-system will not have done away with the tombs of the dead as a locus of corporate solidarity. Ironically perhaps, the Deuteronomic-priestly reforms of the fifth century BCE, in separating the dead from the cult, made the tomb and the altar alternative modes of maintaining sacred, heavenly order in the earthly realm. And where that altar could not but be experienced as a remote reality, the tombs will have increased in importance, assimilating to themselves the functions of the old local altars (with which they had been associated). That tombs should come within the Yahwehist milieu to assume such functions should now appear more than credible—indeed expected—given the state of affairs in Ancient Israel. Certain developments circa the second century BCE regarding the fate of the dead, moreover, further enhanced the emerging cultic nature of burial places. Toward the latter part of the Second Commonwealth the dead assumed a new trajectory. The deceased abandoned Sheol, and their bodiless spirits ascended now to some resting place in the upper worlds, there (for many) to await resurrection at the eschaton.[3]

The dating of these developments remains, to be sure, problematic. The apocalyptic sections of the Book of Daniel and the more ancient parts of the Enochic literature provide clear attestations to the notion of resurrection. With Daniel one finds oneself in the former part of the second century BCE; as concerns Enoch, some scholars now believe a third century BCE date to be probable for parts of the document. But no evidence in these "visions" points to heavenly ascent of the deceased after death, only of select (living) Holy Men.[4] Still the literary characteristics themselves of Daniel and particularly of Enoch seem important. Enoch "in life" finds himself transported to heaven, where, with his angelic escort, he gains knowledge of hidden things and attains to a vision of the enthroned deity. If before death such ascents, whether in or out of the body, occur, then the ground appears prepared for such heavenly flights when the (righteous) soul or spirit has abandoned the body in death. By the first century CE, at the very latest, this new trajectory seems established (even without the attestation of Philo).[5] But the antiquity of the Enochic literature and its "gnostic"-like flight makes more likely an earlier date. By the end of the Second Commonwealth, then, and possibly several centuries before, the tombs became a gate to heaven, as were the altars of Ancient Israel, rather than a passage to the netherworld. One had only to decide that the gate may serve persons other than the deceased—a short step.

By Late Antiquity the dead, being in the neighborhood, as it were, become enlisted in the ongoing attempt to keep the upper and lower realms in communication and contact. While to some extent all dead could, and as we shall see did, perform this function in Late Antiquity, deceased Holy Men could do so more effectively. For the latter in life had already been closer to the deity and divinity. We shall, then, follow the careers of the dead on both planes, elite and "commoner," beginning with the former.

IV. THE DEAD IN LATE ANTIQUE JUDAISM

a. Patriarchs, Holy Men and Martyrs: Tombs of the Elite as loci sancti

In the Hellenistic period the earliest clear instance of pilgrimage to tombs of Israel's great revolves around the reign of Herod in the latter half of the first century BCE. Among the various building projects undertaken under his auspices remains the construction of a large-scale mausoleum in Hebron at the traditional site of the tombs of the Patriarchs, the cave of Machpela. Architects constructed a level platform over the area, enclosed the whole in a wall, and within the courtyard set six stone blocks in lieu of the tombs themselves. A typical Herodian water system collected rainwater for pools within the structure. The courtyard by all accounts was intended to accommodate in comfort large crowds of pilgrims.

In terms of architecture, most striking about the structure at Hebron is that the mausoleum replicates exactly Herod's Temple in Jerusalem as Josephus describes it.[6] The one is a scaled-down version of the other—with of course one major difference; in place of the Sanctuary, which occupied the center of the Temple compound, one has in Hebron the six raised tombs of the Mausoleum. These facts invite the conclusion that the Mausoleum, and in particular the tombs therein, were considered by its pilgrims analogous in character and function to the Temple cult itself. Here, as at the altar, heaven and earth met, and here, therefore, as at the altar, goods and services between the two realms might efficaciously be exchanged.

The "argument-from-architecture" remains admittedly suggestive only. But in the Byzantium period we have more direct evidence regarding the function of the Mausoleum of the Patriarchs.[7] Though banned from setting foot on the Temple Mount, Jews received permission to pray at the Mausoleum. On the basis of this act of conciliation, one may suppose that praying at the site had been a longstanding practice.

Indeed the tradition continued even after the rabbinization of the area—this in spite of the corpse-uncleanness that would have been contracted by anyone visiting the compound. That Jews, rabbinic or otherwise, would willfully contract corpse-uncleanness in order to offer prayers to the heavenly realm seems a stunning reversal of biblical notions (of the Deuteronomic-priestly type). For the Hebrew Bible, divine powers and forces of uncleanness could not coexist. The sacred altar must remain free from the encroachment of the unclean, lest the creation of sacred world centered upon the altar-site, should sustain irreparable damage. Having a tomb filled with uncleanness of the most virulent kind constitute the termination-point of a link between heaven and earth represents a revolution of conception, at least within a milieu defined by the Hebrew Bible.

Given, however, the tendency in Ancient Israel to seek salvific unity between the ancestors, the living and the deity by associating the ancestral tomb with the family altar and the clan's land, the cult of the mausoleum should little surprise one. The events of 720 BCE and of 586 BCE combined with the Deuteronomic-priestly reforms of the fifth century to sever the loyalties to the clan by banning the dead from the presence of YHWH and removing cultic activity to Jerusalem, a city that in essence belonged to no clan at all. Yet, it would seem, with loyalty to the clan (and the ancestral tomb) replaced by identification with the "nation" and the national cult, Israelites supplanted local tombs with a national Mausoleum of the Patriarchs, now removed from the sacrificial site. Ironically, then, the reforms of the fifth century BCE, which excluded the dead from the presence of God, paved the way for (indeed perhaps spurred on) the emergent (national) cult of the dead, centered on the graves of the ancestors of the *nation*. Hebron appears, in sum, the functional complement of Jerusalem; the Mausoleum is to ancestral tombs as the Temple is to the family or clan altar.

In the fifth century BCE the Deuteronomic and priestly "Alliance" attempted to forge a "national" identity and institutions; but cultural and political factors of the Greco-Roman world conspired to destroy that same construct. Hellenistic culture, with its cosmopolitan and international character, ultimately undermined national institutions, both political and religious. All over the Hellenistic world, cults became detached from their national anchorages and evolved into objects of private and individual loyalties across the Hellenistic map. One "voluntarily" joined cultic associations quite apart from ethnic origins.[8] Here one finds the cultic counterpart to the displacement of national priesthoods by individual (often itinerant) Holy Men. Both processes appear part of the whole cultural fabric.

The Yahwehists fit the general pattern, and even more so. They remain subject to the general cultural tendencies of denationalization and dispersion. But the complete destruction of their national institutions (in 70 CE), coupled with an already extensive dispersion of the people beyond reasonable access to the central cult, reinforced the Hellenistic pattern. We might expect, as part of the development of denationalized modes of mediation between heaven and earth, the emergence of a cult of the dead centered upon the local tombs of the diaspora (and Palestinian) communities—this in counterpoint to the (national) Mausoleum of the Patriarchs. Such, as we shall see later, appears precisely the case.

That tombs, local or national, may assume such a function has more to do with what has befallen the surviving spirit of the deceased and the possible services that the spirit may render, than (at least initially) with any integral holiness adhering to the entombed bones. The spirit of the Patriarch (or of other Holy Men) seems in some fashion both in his tomb and in heaven. He or she is privy to the requests of the supplicants and in turn has the ear of the deity. That the deceased constitutes an active intermediary, rather than a passive instrument of communication, seems evident. For prayer may be addressed to the deceased rather than to a divine being. More properly put, the deceased has become a "divine" being in some serious sense, and therefore, like God or an angel, may be efficaciously beseeched in prayer.

The Matriarch, Rachel, is a case in point, surviving even in rabbinic Judaism. It remains customary for barren women to visit the Tomb of Rachel to pray for progeny. The specific efficacy of this tomb for countering barrenness has to do with the particular person (and biography) of the entombed, who herself, according to the biblical narrative, long remained barren. In short, the specificity of function here alerts one to the active role played by the deceased; she above all ought to understand and sympathize with the problem. And supplicants usually address their prayers directly to her.

Pilgrimages to tombs of famous Holy Men were not limited to these few instances. The (alleged) tombs of David, Maimonides, and

Rabbi Simeon bar Yohai (to name but a few obvious examples) have all been objects over the centuries of such piety by rabbinic Jews, although the specific world-view that makes sense of these practices has been rigorously ignored (or suppressed) by the rabbis. Late Antique rabbinic sources relate that persons visited the gravesite of the rabbinic Holy Man Rav in order to procure its earth for theurgic purposes.[9] Rav functioned in life as an instrument of mediation (at least for those in third-century CE Babylonia who accorded such status to rabbinic figures). In death, therefore, his grave remained a gateway to heaven, not only for Rav but also for the downward flow of sacred power. But here even the material of the gravesite remains a locus of the sacred and of salutary efficacy. We have here a relic in the true sense.

Early Rabbinic literature views these developments with considerable ambivalence even when deceased rabbinic figures constitute the object of such cultic activity. To be sure, Rabbinism offered their (living) elite as more than equal to other Holy Men as regards theurgy.[10] Still the early rabbinic literature of Palestine and Babylonia refrained from delivering their deceased masters for the same ends. The sources do not view positively the veneration of Rav's grave. The Talmud enjoins that fences not be erected around graves, lest this aid in the identification (and use) of the sites as sacred territory.[11] Presumably they feared that the dead, even the rabbinic dead, might wrest authority from the living, ultimately undermining the rabbinic Holy Men. In any case, the survival of such rites in a hostile (or, minimally, ambivalent) rabbinic environment attests to their entrenchment among Late Antique Jews and among their rabbinized descendants.

With the denationalization of the cult of the dead, persons other than those who had accrued holy status in life might in death join the ranks of the elite. More precisely put, the manner of dying might win *post mortem* sacrality for the deceased and his or her tomb. By the beginning of the first century BCE evidence emerges pointing to the possible veneration of martyrs. II Maccabees 7 relates, with the requisite "detail" of Hellenistic historiography, the story of the torture and martyrdom of the "women and her seven sons" at the command of Antiochus IV. No doubt the narrative previously circulated on its own and enjoyed considerable popularity before either Jason of Cyrene or his (Alexandrian?) epitomist included the tale in their "histories." The story stands as a unit apart from its context, is entirely intelligible on its own and, indeed, interrupts the principal narrative of the book. Given, moreover, that the Palestinian editor of I Maccabees remained ignorant of the tradition in question, one may well locate its provenance in the Hellenistic diaspora. In sum, evidence for martyrology for Hellenistic Judaism dates to the beginning of the first and in all probability to the latter half of the second century BCE.

Still martyrology, although suggestive, does not in itself indicate the prevalence of a cult of martyrs. We have to wait several centuries for unambiguous evidence of the latter. Christian sources attest to the existence in third-century Antioch of the "Synagogue of the Maccabean Martyrs."[12] Here we find a "full-blown" martyr-cult housed in the synagogue. At some earlier period the Antiochene Jewish community had identified some local tombs as the graves of the "Maccabean Martyrs." They subsequently removed the remains to new tombs under the floor of a synagogue. By the third century the same community boasted not only martyrs' remains but also other "relics" such as dust from the Tablets of the Covenant and sundry other sacred artifacts. The assimilation of the tombs of the Maccabean Martyrs to the synagogue and its sacral function provides the clearest statement regarding the mediatory character of "graves of the saints." Just as prayer could be more efficacious at Ancient Israel's altars,[13] so now the effects of the synagogue liturgy are enhanced by the tombs under the synagogue floor. At both the altar and the tomb, heaven and earth meet; here the commerce between the earthly and divine realms may best take place.

It seems difficult to suppose that such martyr-cults among Hellenistic Jewry arose only in the third century. The relocation of the Maccabean Martyrs' remains to the synagogue presupposes a well-developed ritual in these regards at the original tombs. Given, moreover, the longstanding pilgrimages to the Tombs of the Patriarchs and popularity of martyrologies, the emergence of a cult of martyrs centered on the latter's graves might be expected any time from the middle of the first century BCE onwards. In any case, a date from the end of the first or early in the second century CE would constitute a conservative estimate. To suppose, as does Bickermann,[14] that the Cult of the Maccabean Martyrs emerged in the third century under Christian influence errs on several counts. First, to argue, as he does, that Judaism (normally) could not produce such a phenomenon begs the question of what, if anything, constitutes normative Judaism. Second, Bickermann simply ignores earlier, related evidence that makes such

Antiochene developments not only possible but also highly probable within a Late Antique Judaic milieu.

b. Common Dead: Ancestors as Mediators Between Heaven and Earth

With regard to the "common" dead, the evidence is at once more abundant, diverse, and hence somewhat more difficult to interpret. Here we face a variety of data, each with its own hermeneutical problematic. We begin with literary evidence (preserved in the main by a perturbed Late Antique rabbinate). The plethora of archaeological and artifactual evidence from Hellenistic Judaism concerning the dead and the necropolis may then more profitably be considered.

The Late Antique rabbinic document, Maseket Semahot,[15] preserves some suggestive information about the ongoing function the dead played among Late Hellenistic Jewry. Evidence attests to strewing food on the bier of deceased young adults ("brides" and "grooms") during the funeral procession. Food may also have been spread along the way of the cortege and perhaps at the burial itself. The tractate mentions as well the piping of wine and oil "before" these dead, a practice out of which the classical commentaries can make no sense. Of course, these practices replicate the wedding feast the "bride" or "groom" would have enjoyed had he or she survived to be betrothed and wed. But one cannot help but see here at least something reminiscent of *ex voto* offerings to the saints in early medieval Christianity.[16] The existence, moreover, of communal meals with the dead remained a familiar aspect of Hellenistic religions.[17] Even the apparent obtuse piping of wine and oil finds its parallel in the pagan catacombs of Rome, where pipes were driven down from the surface into the catacombs and libations thereby poured into the tombs.

None of these parallels need be significant; indeed they smack of parallelomania—that is, in and of themselves. Still we do know that the elite dead were the focus of a Judaic cult (at least of prayer). The use, furthermore, of foodstuff, wine, and oil as media of communion has antecedents both in Ancient Israel, in the context of the sacrificial cult, and in such Judaic sects as the Pharisees and Qumranians.[18] Cultic meals, finally, exist everywhere among non-Jewish Hellenistic religions apart from cults of the dead[19] and may constitute the basis for the early Christian Eucharist. Hence one finds a cultural milieu, among Judaic as well as non-Judaic circles of the Hellenistic world, in which communing with the dead via offerings of food, wine, and oil makes considerable sense.

In light of the above several pieces of evidence emerge as rather cogent. Semahot 8:1 is a case in point.

> One may go out to the cemetery for thirty days to inspect the dead for a sign of life without fear that this smacks of heathen practice.
>
> (Semahot 8:1, ed. D. Zlotnick, p. 57)

Evidently the "heathen practices" so disturbing to the rabbis entailed regular ongoing visits to the tomb within and beyond the thirty-day period.[20] One may presume as well that such trips to the cemetery sought ends other than inspection of the dead for signs of life. The interdiction hardly strikes at non-Jews: rather the passage implies that Jews engaged in these ongoing pilgrimages to commoners' graves and did so, no doubt, as Jews, not as participants in some expressly pagan ritual. To the rabbis any activity not sanctioned by Rabbinism and bearing resemblance to pagan ritual would be worthy of the title "heathen practice." Rabbinic behavior, notwithstanding its own resemblance to "heathen practice," will hardly prove problematic; nor do rabbis tend to legislate against particular pagan rites, when Jews do not involve themselves therein *qua* Jews. The language, then, of 8:1 evinces a rabbinic polemic against nonrabbinic ritual. In all, one is left with the impression that (nonrabbinic) Jews regularly engaged in religious rites of some sort at the tombs of their deceased. The tomb was a cultic locus. In terms of additional evidence, would that Semahot had given us further, specific interdictions about what *not* to do at the gravesite.

In this regard, however, one may resurrect Tobit 4:17 (cited earlier). Tobit's provenance is generally believed to be Antioch or Alexandria of the first century BCE, some three to five centuries prior to the redaction of Semahot. By our tractate's redaction, then, some form of ritual at the tomb involving offerings of food and wine will have enjoyed longstanding popularity, at least among Jews of the Hellenistic diaspora.

Semahot's injunctions regarding the use of foodstuffs at the funerals of "brides" and "grooms" may now be interpreted more persuasively in terms of some cult of the dead.

> (8:2) A canopy should be made for the "bride" and the "groom" from which both that which is fit and that which is unfit for food may be suspended. So Rabbi Meir. Rabbi Judah says: "Only that which is unfit for food may be suspended from it."

What things may be suspended from it?

Nuts unsuited for food; pomegranates unsuited for food; loaves unsuited for food; strips of purple; lagenae or flasks of myrrh oil.

And what are the things that may not be suspended from it?

Nuts fit for food; pomegranates fit for food; loaves fit for food; lagenae and flasks of sweet oil.

The general rule is: It is forbidden to benefit from whatever is hung on the canopy.

(8:3) Strings of fish and pieces of meat may be scattered before brides and grooms in the dry season, not in the rainy season; in no case, however, pieces of cooked fish, mushrooms, and truffles, or sesame, although a spoonful may be taken and cast.

The general rule is: Whatever spoils may not be strewn before them.

(Semahot 8:2–3, ed. and trans. D. Zlotnick, pp. 57–58)

The passages from Semahot present the exegete with some internal anomalies, as the "contortions" of the classical commentators (cited by Zlotnick) indicate. The confusion among Semahot's interpreters seems compounded by the (a priori) assumption that a Judaic "cult of the dead" remains unthinkable.[21]

Without the various monkeys riding on a variety of exegetes' backs, the upshot of the passage seems clear. Just as food strewn on the ground during the dry season will not quickly spoil, so unripened food will not quickly decompose. 8:2 (Judah and the lists) and 8:3 may be seen as one in intention. The (relative) "permanence" of the foodstuffs used in this respect seems appropriate to the deceased. For even while their bodies will shortly decompose, they themselves, in excarnate form, have taken on the "garb" of eternity in heaven. As are they, so is their food, offered by the living in communion with the dead.

Again what Late Antique Rabbinism attempted to suppress (or minimally reinterpret in other terms), medieval Rabbinism clearly evinces. Regular visits to the tombs of the family remain commonplace among traditional, rabbinic Jews. There one customarily addresses the deceased, asking that he or she intercede with the divine powers on behalf of surviving relatives.

The artifactual and archaeological evidence for Hellenistic Jewry indicates as well that the common tomb functioned as a portal to the realm of the divine[22]—initially, at least, for the deceased and, therefore, perhaps for the prayers of the living. Parallel to the new conception among Jews of Hellenistic and Roman times that the dead ascend to heaven, rather than descend to the nether world, one finds the development of new modes of burial and of a remarkably consistent vocabulary of funerary art. Here we may hope to review only the more important data.

Typically,[23] the deceased Jew of Late Antiquity would have been anointed with oils and spices, taken to a rock-hewn burial chamber, and left in a *koch*, a coffin-like excavation usually cut perpendicular to the wall of the chamber. A chamber might have from half-a-dozen to a dozen such *kochim*. Here the corpse was left to decay until at some later period (eleven months in some traditions) the relatives collected the bones, anointed them with wine, oil, and herbs, and deposited the remains in a miniature sarcophagus (an ossuary). The bone-boxes were left in one corner of the chamber; the *koch* could be reused. Again, given the taboo against contracting corpse-uncleanness, one finds curious a ritual that entails multiple contractions of corpse-contamination. Whatever was believed to have been accomplished by this "secondary burial" obviously outweighed the interdictions about uncleanness (even for Jews living in close proximity to the Temple).

One finds inviting the notion that each of the two burials represents a distinct rite of passage for the dead on their journey from earth to heaven, with the secondary burial effecting the final ascent to the divine realm. For the most blatant distinction between the first and the second entombments seems the presence of flesh at the former and its absence at the latter. In the Jewish conceptions of the period, whether rabbinic[24] or nonrabbinic, flesh, more than bones, represented that part of the individual most susceptible to the powers of chaos. Early rabbinic law, saddled with the biblical notion that both flesh and bones of a deceased contaminate, nevertheless clearly distinguishes, where it can, the virulence of one source of uncleanness from the other. Flesh, for example, in any amount contaminates by overshadowing; only the greater part of the skeleton, however, effects the same. In early rabbinic homiletic texts,[25] moreover, flesh seems the medium of susceptibility to the forces of the corruptible and the corrupting. Here, then, even rabbinic thought mirrors a negative assessment of the flesh so often found in early Christianity (gnostic, Pauline, and ascetic) and in Hellenistic religions.[26]

That Philo, from the nonrabbinic side of the street, will have shared as well this general evaluation of the corporeal hardly requires further argument.[27] Perhaps, at secondary burial, the deceased, now free from his flesh, the last anchor to this realm, may ascend to the divine world as a transformed being. His clean bones attest to his freedom from this lower abode and the demonic powers that rule it.[28]

The funerary art commonly associated with ossilegium lends further support to our interpretation of secondary burial. Representations on the ossuaries evince a remarkably consistent and limited artistic vocabulary. Bone-boxes exhibit a double portal or circular devices, and more frequently both.[29] Neither representation appears solely on bone-boxes. They are commonplace themes in funerary art, along with such other devices as palm branches, grapevines, grape clusters, wreaths (really another circular device), candelabra, *shofar*, and incense shovels.[30] Symbols borrowed from the Temple cult are immediately recognizable among the representations, an observation not to be taken for granted. A host of traditional themes and ritual objects will have offered themselves to Palestinian and diaspora Jews as candidates for religious art. Among others, one might have expected some Torah-scrolls. The Temple, moreover, played no active role in the life of Jewry after 70 CE; for diaspora Jews that situation had prevailed already for several centuries prior to the cult's demise. (And, in any case, the Pentateuch's Temple-centrism, if not entirely utopian, could find its counterpart in reality only for those living in the immediate environs of Jerusalem.) The choice, then, of sacrificial objects as funerary art seems deliberate and significant inasmuch as it appears curious.

Such Temple symbols may be apocalyptic in nature; in many Late Antique eschatological notions the rededication of the Temple figures as part of the end of time. The dead who will rise at the eschaton will participate in the renewed cult. Still without ruling out this view of matters altogether, it fails entirely to satisfy. First, one cannot say how widespread was the assent to these particular eschatological and apocalyptic views, in Palestine or beyond. Second, such symbolism appears (in Palestine) on tombs dating both before and after the Temple's destruction; eschatological hopes centered particularly on a reestablished cult at the end of time could hardly have been a cogent notion. Third, and more important, Yahwehism in the Hellenistic age and especially in the Late Antique world displays a hearty interest in the immediate post-mortem careers of the dead. Persons survive death as bodiless spirits ascending as "transfigured" beings to heaven.[31] That Hellenistic Jews would have had as their immediate concern some future descent from heaven and near-divine status to resume life on earth in the flesh seems out of phase with such post-mortem expectations. One may, then, with difficulty associate the use of cultic objects in the funerary art of Hellenistic Jewry with such apocalyptic notions.

The antecedent discussion establishes a longstanding association of tomb and cult, both in Ancient Israel and in Greco-Roman Palestine. The Tomb of the Patriarchs constitutes a supplementary Temple, although quite different in kind. And the synagogue of the Maccabean Martyrs assimilated the communal prayer of the synagogue, itself a cultic substitute, to devotion at the graves of the martyrs. At both Temple and tomb sacred space is made available. Cultic symbols on tombs express this association. The art is salvific in meaning, but not (necessarily primarily) in eschatological terms. Rather the tomb is the counterpart to an altar, and the dead mediate at a sacred locus that joins the realms. The ascension of the dead from the tomb to heaven creates that locus, first for the transformation of the deceased themselves and subsequently for the living.

This interpretation of cultic themes in funerary art dovetails with other (so-called non-Jewish) representations found in Hellenistic Jewish tombs; grape clusters, vines, portals, and the like all find their parallel in the symbols of Hellenistic salvation-religions and mystery-cults. Wreaths, branches, grapes, and vines have their provenance in the Dionysiac mysteries. The double-arched portal again is commonplace, particularly in the art from the cult of Isis and Osiris. But in the "pagan" context the portals are not empty, as they appear on Jewish funerary artifacts. Under the arches stand the deity and her consort ready to welcome the now liberated initiate. On the Jewish tombs and ossuaries the portal represents the gate to heaven and to YHWH. Symbols both of the Jerusalem cult and of other Hellenistic religions on Jewish tombs communicate a self-consistent message; the tomb constitutes an opening to heaven and to the divine.

The archaeological and artifactual evidence in and of itself cannot indicate with specificity the functions of tombs and of the dead in Late Antique Judaism. That tombs were links between heaven and earth says nothing about whom they served or how. To be sure, we must surmise that the common dead constituted the principal traffic along the artery. That the common tomb had utility for others appears likely, especially so in light of later "rabbinic" practice and the ritual and art associated with the Late Antique gravesites. In sum, the literary evidence at hand strongly suggests that commoner's tombs served the living. Funerary art is wholly consistent with such a conclusion, in that the burial place appears associated with the cult. The tomb is a new altar; the dead, a new sacerdotal functionary; and some dead at least, for example, the martyrs, a new and perhaps more efficacious sacrifice. The "holy and pure" dead join the living Holy Men in the commerce of the sacred.

4

The Life of Torah in the Diaspora

Moments of intense sacrality, of linkage between heaven and earth, appear mediated for Hellenistic Jewry by a variety of intermediaries, living and dead. But what of the more mundane, hour-to-hour life of the Hellenistic Yawehist? At this level too an ordered, that is to say, sacred, world must exist with requisite divine legitimation. The island of order endures between moments of extraordinary mediation. For the Judean Jew before 70 (at least in theory) the regularity of the Temple ritual assimilated to itself both ordinary and extraordinary means of world-maintenance. To a certain extent the Jews of the Mediterranean world outside the Holy Land could share in the reality created and maintained by the Temple cult. Funds flowed from the diaspora to maintain the Sanctuary in Jerusalem. Through such support one might participate vicariously in the sacrificial service and its benefits, even if the intensity of the experience was considerably lessened by distance. (Ritual, after all, ought to be acted out or minimally witnessed.) So adamant was the diaspora Jew in forwarding monies to Jerusalem that here as in other cases Rome felt compelled to legally exempt Jews from standard policy.[1] Rome forbade the export of large sums of money from one province to another, for obvious and sound economic reasons. Rome, nevertheless, looked the other way as regards payment of the half-shekel by diaspora Jewry to the Jerusalem Temple. When in the middle of the first century BCE Flaccus, a Roman official in Asia Minor, confiscated monies destined for Jerusalem, the Jewish communities in question brought him to trial after his tenure in office. Obviously the community felt that its right of custom would outweigh strictly legal considerations in the Senate, before whom the case was heard.

Still the link with the Temple of such a vicarious kind could hardly have sufficed, and what little world-maintaining function the cult could play for the Greco-Roman Jews of the diaspora ceased after 70 in any case. Torah provided the only medium of sacrality sanctioned by revelation, at least for Yahwehists of the post-Deutero-priestly stream; much of Torah, however, could hardly have applied to life in the diaspora.

In standard handbooks the argument at this point often reverts to the deductive, drawing on hindsight. Namely, those injunctions in Torah which could apply outside the immediate vicinity of the Temple became of primary importance, while other institutions, such as the synagogue and prayer quickly developed to fill lacunae. What in fact remains of direct evidence of the ritual life of Hellenistic diasporic Jewry is sparse and nonspecific. The largest and most extensive bodies of Greco-Judaic literature, the writings of Josephus and Philo, talk almost exclusively of the (cultic) ritual life as depicted in the Pentateuch, not about contemporary practice. The same obtains for evidence from early church writers, who everywhere concern themselves with defining Christianity against Judaism and, more frequently, Judaizing, but nevertheless rail primarily against practice as depicted in the Old Testament. The challenge is the neighboring synagogue and Jewish Holy Men; the argument defines the Christian cult against a distant or (after 70) nonexistent sacrificial service.[2] This represents, perhaps, an effective mode of polemic and apologetic, but does little to help us piece together the life of Torah of Late Antique Yawehism.

Evidence, such as it is, does allow some claims about Judaic ritual and practice for the period and areas in question, and, if only for the sake of greater comprehensiveness, this chapter aims to lay out those data. In general our information comes from circles outside Yahweh ism, with the exception of the Church. By far the most common themes for non-Jewish comments on the life of Torah seem to be Sabbath observance, circumcision, and abstention from eating pork. Rites of passage (other than circumcision), festivals, liturgy, synagogue functions, for example, receive little attention. Why, I cannot say. One could with difficulty conclude that the data of interest to non-Judaic authors reflects priorities within the Judaic world. Most of what was written about Jews in the Late Roman world, and outside the Church, comes from "Hellenistic historical geographies."[3]These late Roman writings were meant to entertain as much as inform. Consequently they favored the bizarre and the distinctive over the mundane and familiar. Hence the painted faces of the natives of Gaul might receive more attention than their marriage patterns, and, perhaps, Sabbath, circumcision and abstinence from pork constituted equal curiosities for the Greco-Roman reader of historical geographies. Still we may consider in turn those aspects of the life of Torah for which evidence exists.

I. THE SABBATH

Roman literati as early as the second half of the first century BCE evince knowledge of the Sabbath and related practices. Hence Ovid:

> Nor let Adonis bewailed of Venus escape you, nor the seventh day that the Syrian [sic] Jew holds sacred. Avoid not the Memphian shrine of the linen-clothed heifer; many a maid does she make what she was herself to Jove. Even the law courts (who could believe it?) are suitable to love; often has its flame been found in the shrill-tongued court.
>
> (*Ars Amatoria* I, 75–80, Kenny 134aR, trans. J. H. Mozley, LCL,
> M. Stern, *Greek and Latin Authors*, 1:348)

For Ovid, it would seem, the Sabbath is at once a barbaric rite of some distant Syrians as well as a cult ceremony common in Rome itself. There seems already here some indication that "Romans" participate in selected Judaic rituals as part of a developing syncretism in the capital. More direct evidence of widespread participation in selected Sabbath rites comes from Seneca in the first half of the first century (*via* Augustine).

> Along with other institutions of the civil theology Seneca also censures the sacred institutions of the Jews, especially the Sabbath. He declares that their practice is inexpedient, because by introducing one day of rest in every seven they lose in idleness almost a seventh of their life, and by failing to act in times of urgency they often suffer loss. . . . But when speaking of the Jews he says: "Meanwhile the customs of this accursed race have gained such influence that they are now received throughout the world. The vanquished have given laws to their victors."
>
> (*De Superstitione*, apud; Augustinus, *De Civitate Dei*, VI, 11, Dombart and Kalb F145R–F593, H. Hagendahl, *Augustine and the Latin Classics*, 1, Goetenberg 1967; trans. W. M. Green, LCL;
> see M. Stern, *Greek and Latin Authors*, 1:431)

Still Greek and Latin authors appear to know little of Sabbath ritual, and even less that is accurate. Three themes reoccur. First, the Sabbath enjoins refraining from work, as we have already seen from Seneca. Second, "lamps" are lit, for Seneca, among other "neo-orthodox" Romans, would have the authorities "forbid lamps to be lighted on the Sabbath, since the gods do not need light, neither do men take pleasure in soot."[4] Finally, and on the surface quite erroneously, one finds the recurrent theme that fasting occupies a central place in Sabbath ritual.[5] Of the reading of the law and prophets on the Sabbath, to which Acts gives evidence, we find no mention outside Christian sources. Setting aside fasting for the moment, it appears at least inviting that "pagan" authors depict the Sabbath as the extended community of Sabbath-keepers among the Roman populace practiced the ritual.

II. CIRCUMCISION

References in Hellenistic Jewish literature,[6] especially among the Apocrypha and Pseudepigrapha, the earliest Christian documents,[7] and among Greek and Latin authors[8] make any lengthy discussion of the evidence for circumcision among nonrabbinic Jews as unnecessary as it would be time-consuming. For most persons neither Jewish nor Christian the custom was at best bizarre and for many barbaric. So characteristic of Jewish piety is circumcision in the minds of Greco-Romans that suppression of Jews "naturally" attains expression in injunctions against the rite, whether out of anti-Judaism or out of some desire to civilize the barbarian seems less clear. Thus the anti-Jewish measures of circa 135—whether accurately recounted or not is of no consequence in this context—remain strongly associated with banning circumcision, and even after the ban was lifted proselyte circumcision was (officially) forbidden.[9]

Jewish writers of the Hellenistic Period, at least those associated with the Hasmonean cause, make the issue of circumcision the outward sign of differences between the "Torah-loyalists" (i.e., the pro-Hasmoneans) and the "assimilationists" (i.e., the anti-Hasmoneans). The latter, according to I Maccabees, underwent surgical procedures to efface evidence of circumcision, a practice incidentally taken by other Jews at other times throughout the Greco-Roman world.[10]

The evidence from early Christianity attesting to circumcision among Greco-Roman Jews needs little attention from us. For Paul the sign of the old covenant was precisely circumcision.[11] His struggle to allow Gentiles into the new covenant made possible by Jesus without undergoing circumcision—formal conversion to Judaism—makes no sense if the rite had not been characteristic of diaspora practice.

Although it seems self-evident that diaspora Jewry practiced circumcision and initiated others into their community in part by means of this rite, it remains its blatant nonobservance, indeed militant effacement, among some Jews that demands some consideration. The evidence attests to Jews and other Yahwehists who, while not circumcised, nevertheless claimed either still to be Jews or at least to be in some significant sense practitioners of Judaism. Here, of course, Christianity provides an obvious point of departure. I have no intention of attempting to sort out the Pauline-Jerusalem controversy over the relationship between the Church and Judaism and the place of circumcision in that controversy. After Paul had already won his case, however, the problem of the Judaizers continued for centuries, but in different terms. In the Judaizer controversies of the second, third, and even fourth centuries the leadership of the Church, much to its consternation, continued to witness the selected practice of Judaic rites by uncircumcised Gentile Christians. Such rites included observing Jewish Fasts (to which we will return later), some type of Sabbath and festival observance, and at times actual visits to the synagogue.

What self-understanding allowed Gentile Christians so to ally themselves with Judaic forms and institutions, I shall not say (as of yet). But at least as interesting seems the issue of what self-definition of Judaism (or of Jews) in the Greco-Roman world allowed, perhaps encouraged, such limited practice of Judaism and affiliation with Jewish institutions by those who had no intention of undergoing circumcision.[12] Certainly to specify that unless these parties had undergone circumcision they lie outside the formal bounds of the study of Judaism seems injudicious. That would amount to setting normative standards culled from one group of professed Yahwehists to judge what seems another group of professed Yahwehists. The issue cannot here constitute the object of systematic treatment. The evidence remains still too thin for these uncircumcised Yahwehists. But they were allowed in the synagogues, whether baptized Christians or not, participated in the liturgy on an ongoing basis, and practiced with the Jewish community many of its more distinctive rites. That is to say, they seem to be more socially integrated into the organized synagogue community of the circumcised than one might expect of some "pagan" cult which "borrowed" from Judaism. Synagogue authorities, then, recognized, or were forced by general popular consent to recognize, the significant Judaic status of these Yahwist parties.[13]

III. DIETARY RESTRICTIONS

As with circumcision there survives a plethora of evidence from the first half of the first century CE onwards of dietary restrictions among the Jews of the Greco-Roman diaspora. Greek and Latin authors, excluding the early Christian writers, seem to have known of dietary laws among the Jews as restricting pork only. Thus in Josephus's report of Apion:

> The remaining counts in his indictment had better perhaps have remained unanswered, so that Apion might be left to act as his own and his countrymen's accuser. He denounces us for sacrificing domestic animals and for not eating pork, and he derides the practice of circumcision.
> (*Aegyptiaca*, apud: Josephus, *Contra Apionem*, II, 137, trans. H. St. J. Thackery, LCL; M. Stern, *Greek and Latin Authors*, 1:415)

So too, for example, Erotianus in the second half of the first century:

> Some say that the "sacred disease" is of divine origin, because this disease is god-sent, and being of divine origin it is said to be sacred. Others suppose that superstition is implied. They say that one should inquire to which type the sick man belongs, in order that if he is a Jew we should refrain from giving him pig's flesh, and if he is an Egyptian we should refrain from giving him the flesh of sheep or goats.
> (*Vocum Hippocraticarum Colrectyo cum Fragmentis*. F33: *De Morbo Sacro*, p. 108, Nachmason, 1918; trans. M. Stern, *Greek and Latin Authors*, 1:446)

Greeks and Romans seemed generally at a loss in accounting for abstinence from pork among Jews. By the end of the first century it appears to have been generally accepted that swine were particularly revered by Jews. Petronius remarks[14] that "the Jew worship[s] his pig-god." More speculative in tone is Plutarch.

> Callistratus headed them off by saying, "What do you think of the assertion that it is precisely the most proper type of meat that the Jews avoid eating?" "I heartily agree with it," replied Polycrates, "but I have

another question: do they abstain from eating pork by reason of some special respect for hogs or from abhorrence of the creature? Their own accounts sound like pure myth, but perhaps they have some serious reasons which they do not publish." . . . , said Callistratus, . . . "I think the Jews would kill pigs if they hated them, as the Magi kill water mice; but in fact it is just as unlawful for Jews to destroy pigs as to eat them. Perhaps it is consistent that they should revere the pig who taught them sowing and plowing, in inasmuch as they honour the ass [*sic*] who first led them to a spring of water. Otherwise, so help me, someone will say that the Jews abstain from the hare because they cannot stomach anything so filthy and unclean."

"No indeed," countered Lamprias, " . . . the Jews apparently abominate pork because barbarians especially abhor skin diseases like lepra and white scale, and believe that human beings are ravaged by such maladies through contagion. Now we observe that every pig is covered on the underside by lepra and scaly eruptions. . . ."

(*Questiones Convivales*, IV, 4:4–6:2, pp.669C–672B, trans. H. B. Hoffleit, LCL; M. Stern, *Greek and Latin Authors*, 1:550ff)

Plutarch adds little in terms of concrete knowledge of Jewish dietary rites in the Hellenistic world, except for his passing mention of the injunction against eating the flesh of the hare. Greco-Roman Jewry, then, were not so selective in their observance of Leviticus' injunctions as the "pagan" evidence might otherwise seem to indicate. In sum, the Greek and Latin authors concentrate on the injunction against the hog, probably because it is more apparent (therefore known); in their more benign moments the restriction seemed to them a bizarre rite of a barbarian people. At less forgiving moments it was a superstitious reverence for a less than respectable species.

Evidence from Early Church writings contributes somewhat to our picture of dietary rites in the Hellenistic diaspora. Paul, in his struggle with the Jerusalem authorities, fought for, among other things, freedom of the Gentile Church from dietary restrictions.[15] Since his appeals resulted from Judaizing tendencies of his churches in Asia Minor and Syria, we may suppose that the impetus for dietary observance among his Christian communities had more to do with the attraction of Jewish practices visible across the street in the local Jewish populace than with the sensibilities of Peter and James in Jerusalem. The compromise of Paul and Peter on this issue for similar reasons no doubt reflects concerns of the Hellenistic diaspora community.

Flesh suspected of having been offered or dedicated to gods other than Yahweh remained forbidden for the Christian, as it already was in Jewish circles.

IV. FESTIVALS AND LITURGY

The evidence for the Jewish calendar of sacred feasts falls considerably short of what we have for Sabbath, circumcision, and dietary restrictions. Evidently the festivals hardly sparked Roman and Greek curiosity. (Or feasts were assimilated in their minds to the Sabbath.) Generally for the Roman or Greek historian only the unusual edified and entertained—the general aim of classical histories and enthnographies.[16] Philo and Josephus devote much time to exegesis of biblical injunctions regarding festival observance, but pay little attention to contemporary observance of Greco-Roman Jewry.

The Church writings too are oddly silent about Jewish festivals and liturgy in the diaspora. They level their polemics against a now-defunct Temple cult, an attempt, no doubt, to define their legitimacy with respect to Torah. Still John Chrysostom in the fourth century has left us sermons occasioned by the Jewish celebration in Antioch of New Years, the Day of Atonement, Tabernacles (and Assembly?).[17] He attests as well to the blowing of "trumpets" on the New Year and to fasting on the Day of Atonement. Beyond that he provides little information, with the exception of one important fact; he could not keep many of his Christians away from the synagogue on these occasions, a matter which we discuss below at length.[18]

Greek and Roman evidence from other than Christian sources for diaspora practice comes primarily from Plutarch, again in his *Questiones Convivales*.

> At this, all did urge him and beg him to go on. "First," he [Moeragenes] said, "the time and character of the greatest, most sacred holiday of the Jews clearly befits Dionysus. When they celebrate their so called Fast, at the height of the vintage, they set out tables of all sorts of fruit under tents and huts plaited for the most part with vines and ivy. They call the first of the days of the feast Tabernacles. A few days later they celebrate another festival, this time identified with Bacchus not through obscure hints but plainly called by his name, a festival that is a sort of 'Procession of Branches' or 'Thyrsus procession,' in which they enter the Temple [sic] each carrying a thyrsus. What they do after entering

we do not know, but it is probable that the rite is a Bacchic revelry, for in fact they use little trumpets to invoke their god as do the Argives at their Dionysia. Others of them advance playing harps; these players are called in their language Levites, either from Lysios (Releaser) or, better, from Evius (God of the Cry). I believe that not even the feast of the Sabbath is not completely unrelated to Dionysus. . . The Jews themselves testify to a connection with Dionysus when they keep the Sabbath by inviting each other to drink and enjoy wine. Now thus far one might call the argument only probable; but the opposition is quite demolished, in the First Place by the High Priest, who leads the procession at their Festival wearing a mitre and clad in gold-embroidered fawn skin, a robe reaching to the ankles, and buskins, with many bells attached to his clothes and ringing below him as he walks. All this corresponds to our custom. In the second place, they also have noise as an element in their nocturnal festivals, and call the nurses of the god 'bronze rattlers.' The carved thyrsus in the relief on the pediment of the Temple and the drums (provide other parallels). All this surely befits (they might say) no divinity but Dionysus."
(*Questiones Convivales*, IV, 4:4–6:2, pp. 669C-672B—Hubert = F69R; trans. H. B. Hoffleit, LCL; Stern, *Greek and Latin Authors,* 1:550ff.)

Plutarch clearly has conflated a number of festivals occurring in succession during the autumn, the Day of Atonement ("so-called Fast"), Tabernacles, and perhaps New Years ("trumpets"). The focus, however, seems Tabernacles, with references to the building of booths and the procession of palm branches. The whole, finally, becomes assimilated to the Dionysiac cult.

The source of Plutarch's description seems problematic. With the descriptions of the garb of the High Priest, a reminiscence, several parties removed, of the Temple service in Jerusalem might stand behind the passage. (The text cannot, at least, have its origins in the Septuagint, as much of what he "describes" may not be adduced from biblical sources alone.) Alternatively, Plutarch, writing in Egypt during the latter part of the first century CE, may reflect the practice at Onias' Temple, which is closer in time and place to the author. While these remain the strongest hypotheses, some idiosyncrasies of the passage suggest a third possibility. Curiously absent from the description, which in many ways seems startlingly detailed (even if assimilated to Dionysiac rites), appears any mention of sacrifice. That is to say, nothing described by Plutarch necessitates the cultic setting of Onias' or the Jerusalemite Sanctuary. The rites might be carried on in a synagogue.

Several considerations and data outside the present context make this third hypothesis less farfetched than it might otherwise appear. First, one would expect early synagogue ritual, in the face of the effective (or real) absence of the sacrificial cult, to adopt as much as possible of the Temple rites, legitimated in Scripture and by longstanding usage in the Sanctuary. This tendency may be well documented, for example, in Qumran. There the "cult of the sacred community" replicated the Temple in structure and in function, as far as the covenanters were concerned.[19] The Temple hierarchy of priests and Levites might be appropriated into a new form of liturgical life. If, moreover, the system of *ma'amadot*,[20] the local priestly "watches" as described in early rabbinic literature, may never have existed (or not in its Mishnaic mode), there remains the fact that for early Rabbinism such nonsacrificial, cultic gatherings might appropriate much of the Temple system, especially its sacred castes.

That in some fashion this appropriation may have taken place in the Hellenistic diaspora might find an echo in the story of Paul at Ephesus.[21] There, according to the tradition in Acts, Paul entered into competition with seven Jewish exorcists said to be sons of the "chief priest" Sceva. There seem few possibilities as to the sense in which Sceva may have been chief priest. Any relation with the Jerusalemite high priesthood appears unlikely. The title, no doubt, had significance within the local setting, the Jewish community at Ephesus. Communal or religious praxis necessitated, it would seem, the identification of members of the priestly caste for other than honorific or formal reasons (as in traditional Rabbinic Judaism). Otherwise it would be senseless to designate a "chief priest." A relationship might entail, then, between Sceva and Plutarch's "High Priest."

V. THE LAW AND THE PROPHETS

Whatever little we know of specifics of Jewish liturgical life in the synagogues,[22] evidence indicates that the reading of the Pentateuch and Prophets, and the enshrining of the sacred scrolls in the synagogue, constituted a major mode of mediation in the life of the community. Apart from rabbinic literature, Acts, even if inaccurate about Paul's itinerary (and about particulars of his preaching career), nevertheless assumes that on Sabbaths Jews read portions of the Law. Selected readings of the Prophets followed. And in some instances an exposition of the passages concluded this section of the service. Virtually every synagogue (from the second century CE on) excavated within and outside the Holy Land has as an architectural feature a niche front of the hall in which scrolls of the Law probably were deposited.

The pseudonymous letter of Aristeas to Philocrates, written sometime in the late second or early first century BCE, and Philo and Josephus, each in their own manner, attest to the centrality of the Torah to the Greco-Roman diaspora. The tradition of the miraculous translation of the Pentateuch into Greek at the request of Ptolemy II[23] demonstrates the need of Hellenistic Jewry to see its Bible (in Greek) as having been legitimated by the deity. In the Translation of the Seventy, according to the story, Yahweh in effect re-reveals his Torah in Greek for his Greek-speaking followers. This tradition, no doubt, antedates Aristeas, for that document, although based upon the translation story, shifts its focus elsewhere—namely, to the elaborate conversations between the sages and the king. In making the means of apologetic something other than the narrative that occasions the whole, the author attests to the fact that he has used what already was circulating as a stock story.

Philo, writing some one hundred or more years later, frames his entire apologetic for Judaism in terms of biblical allegory. To defend Jews and Judaism, for Philo, means to show the consonance of the biblical narratives and injunctions with the best of Hellenistic (that is, Stoic and Middle Platonic) thought. Of the contemporary practices of his Alexandrian Jewish community, Philo says little; they never in themselves merit their own apologetic in Philo's mind. So too Josephus, who as a prelude to his defense of the antiquity of the Jewish nation, must prove that the biblical literature outstrips other literatures in accuracy.[24]

Rabbinic documents are replete with evidence attesting to the importance of biblical texts in the liturgical life of the Jewish community, at least rabbinic ones. But, in addition, earliest rabbinic literature gives ample indication that regular readings of the Law on Sabbaths, festivals, and perhaps during midweek took place in the antecedent non-rabbinic synagogues of the middle and late first century CE.[25] Mishnah, at all junctures where Torah-readings are the object of concern, assumes as given the universal practice of scriptural readings in the synagogue. What rabbis would not think of debating in any fashion at the beginning of the second century probably predates them.

That the mere presence of the scrolls of Torah and Prophets made the synagogue a sacred locus,[26] a place where heaven and earth met, finds its most explicit expression in the fourth-century sermons of John Chrysostom, later to become Bishop of Antioch. Chrysostom preserves the excuses his Judaizing parishioners offer for their regular visits to Jewish Houses of Assembly.

> But since there are some who consider the synagogue to be a holy place, we must say a few things to them as well. Why do you reverence this place when you should disdain it, despise it and avoid it? "The Law and the books of the prophets can be found there," you say. What of it? You say, "Is it not the case that the books make the place holy?" Certainly not. This is the reason I especially hate the synagogue and avoid it, that they have the prophets but do not believe in them, that they read these books but do not accept their testimonies [concerning the coming of Jesus Christ].
>
> (Homily 10 Against the Jews, *Patrologia Graeca* 48.850, trans. W. Meeks and R. Wilken, *Jews and Christians in Antioch* [Missoula MT: Scholars Press, 1978], pp. 94f)

VI. FASTING

One final aspect of mundane Judaic praxis deserves treatment. While fasting within Israelite tradition has a longstanding history before the first to fourth centuries CE,[27] we might not have expected to find such a rite a principal characteristic of Hellenistic Judaic piety. For Greek, Latin, and Christian writers alike, Jews fast. Next to abstention from pork, Sabbath observance, and circumcision one finds fasting on the "short list" of Judaic rites most obvious to "outsiders." Indeed authors usually conflate other data, Sabbath for example, with abstention from food and drink. Thus Petronius, writing sometime in the first century CE, remarks,

> The Jew may worship his pig-god and clammer in the ears of high heaven, but unless he also cuts back his foreskin with the knife, he shall go forth from the people and emigrate to Greek cities, and shall not tremble at the fasts of the Sabbath imposed by the law.
>
> (*Fragmenta*, No. 37—Ernout = Baehrens, PLM, IV,97, p. 98, trans. M. Heseltine, LCL; Stern, *Greek and Latin Authors*, 1:444)

So too, Pompeius Trogus, reflecting, he believes, the practice of Syrio-Palestinian Jewry:

> Thus Moyses having reached Damascus his ancestral home took possession of Mount Sinai, on his arrival at which, after having suffered together with his followers, from a seven days' fast in the deserts of Arabia, he, for all time, consecrated the seventh day, which used to be called the Sabbath by custom of the nation, for a fast-day, because that day had ended for once their hunger and their wanderings.
>
> (apud: Iustinus, *Historiae Phillipicae*, Libri XXXVI, *Epitoma*, 2:14, trans. J.S. Watson, London, 1902; trans. revised by Stern, *Greek and Latin Authors*, 1:3)

Finally it is worth citing Martial of the latter half of the first century, who includes in his poetic list of foul odors "the breath of fasting Sabbatarian women."[28]

One might be inclined to take these references to fasting with a grain of salt. The abstention from food and drink on the Day of Atonement, among the more obvious festivals to the Greco-Roman eye, may have become detached from its moorings, become representative of Judaic practice, and assimilated in Greco-Roman literature to the Sabbath. Still, other factors mitigate against so easily explaining away matters. First, the reference to the fasting of Sabbatarian women does not seem to be the result of mere conflation of otherwise well known conceptions (or misconceptions) circulating among Greek and Latin authors. Rather we appear to have an allusion to practices known to the author or his source. It remains an open question whether he refers to Jews or some more "peripheral" group which has assimilated Judaic praxis.[29] Second, Palestinian and Early Rabbinic evidence supports the hypothesis that fasting occupied an important place in Jewish piety of Late Antiquity.[30] The late first century provides a document, Megilat Ta'anit, which lists days on which one may not fast. Mishnah alludes to its existence. And still later rabbinic literature glosses Megilat Ta'anit.[31] None of this makes sense outside of the context in which fasting occurred with great regularity. Third, *Sefer HaRazim* lists fasting among the means of purification commonly demanded of the Jewish priestly-magus before performing his theurgic rites. Fourth, John Chrysostom in his homilies *Against the Jews*[32] (occasioned admittedly by the Day of Atonement) gives the impression that Jewish piety entailed fasting on a regular basis. Certainly rabbinic literature would agree that fasting every Monday and Thursday evinced great piety.

VII. THE LIFE OF TORAH

The general picture emerging from the evidence at hand seems at once innocuous, in other respects surprising, and still, even at these latter junctures, entirely consonant with what we already know of Judaism in the Greco-Roman diaspora. That the Sabbath, festivals, the reading of the Holy Books and their very presence in the synagogue should occupy important places in the mundane mediation of the sacred may little surprise one.[33] So too with circumcision. Other aspects that emerge consistently from the data we would not have supposed from elsewhere. There appears to have emerged in the diaspora synagogues a liturgical structure based heavily upon the replication of a distant, or after 70 a nonexistent, Temple cult. Priests may have continued to act as principal intermediaries in this mundane cultus without sacrifice, Levites engaged in their traditional role of instrumentalists and singers. Here diaspora Judaism in the Greco-Roman world takes a rather different tack than Rabbinism, which supplants one figure of sacred authority, the priest, with another, the rabbi, rather than attempting to preserve traditional roles of sacred persons.[34] Also, whereas Hellenistic Jewry seems to have differentiated administrative power (in the *archontes*)[35] from mundane liturgical mediation (in the form of priests) and from extraordinary sacred virtuosi (in the person of the Divine Man), Rabbinism eventually merged all three in the person of the rabbi.

Still nothing of the Hellenistic alternative seems out of phase either with antecedent Judaic practice or with other evidence we have seen to this point for the contemporary Greco-Roman Yahwehistic community. The structure of the Life of Torah in the Greco-Roman world plays its part in decentralizing the locus of sacredness and denationalizing it. Holy stuff may be made available in the absence of Holy Men offering mediation of the extraordinary kind where the sacred scrolls of the Law and Prophets are located, where the members of the priestly cast dress in their traditional vestments and attempt to replicate as best they can ancient rites, where the sacred cycle of Sabbaths and festivals enjoined by Yahweh are celebrated. But the praxis of Torah, insofar as it becomes a decentralized, denationalized rite, remains distinct from the cult of Torah as expressed in the Herodian Temple.

For the latter produces not loci of sacred order, but a single, unique order, with respect to which the entire world is oriented. For Jewry in the Greco-Roman diaspora, the life of Torah defines not such a comprehensive "system" of cosmic order, but a source of feasts and taboos appropriating the past (as depicted in traditional stories), mediating the power of their deity and reinforcing the religio-ethnic identity in a highly varied Hellenistic society.[36]

Fasting, as a regular mode of ritual-behavior, seems a more novel aspect of our evidence. But in an age and milieu in which Philo begs to be liberated from the corporeal to attain apotheosis, and in which the dead freed from their flesh may rise to heaven and intercede for the living, the attainment of holiness through the periodic rejection of bodily needs makes perfect sense. Here again we find sacred stuff made available through the initiative of the individual, not through an institution, and by means that attempt to transcend the world in part by rejecting one's needs within this realm. This mode of sacredness is consonant too with an early Church where an Encratic ethos emerges, and with a "paganism" that sees among other things the rise of Neo-Pythagorism (and, later Neo-Platonism) and its asceticism. Indeed as Frederick Wisse[37] noted, Encratic piety was a dominant mode of religiosity in the second and third centuries, one in evidence across various religious boundaries. In part this explains for him the existence of the Nag Hammadi library, whose documents stem from both within and outside Christian circles; some evince the influence of Judaism, but without clearly coming from ethnic Jews. What "ties together" the Nag Hammadi texts remains their Encratic and ascetic concerns. To save oneself in this world entailed, for many (even for persons other than Gnostics), saving oneself from it—an individual pietistic quest, even if pursued within a community.

The Synagogue

In a study of mediation of the sacred in diaspora Judaism one would have expected a discussion of the synagogue (and its cult of prayer) earlier on. First, the synagogue and "service of the heart" usually is touted as the diaspora's chief, virtually only, contribution to the history of "authentic, normative Judaism" as it finds its ultimate expression in rabbinic religion. But more so, and second, scholars have taken quite seriously the rabbinic epithet for the synagogue, namely, "the small Sanctuary." They have read this rabbinic phrase as indication that the synagogue was considered by Jews of the Greco-Roman period to function, writ small, analogously to the Temple cult in Jerusalem, finally to replace the latter after 70. Third, students of Ancient Judaism often have deemed the synagogue to be both the principal and earliest institution of diaspora Judaism; not a few still locate its origins in the Babylonian Exile in the sixth century BCE; these scholars continue to see in Ezekiel's, "And I shall be unto them as a small Sanctuary," a clear reference to the synagogue. J. Gutmann has comprehensively documented the history of modern scholarship concerning the synagogue's origins and early function.[1] We have no need, then, to summarize that history, nor even extensively to appraise it. We note only these few observations.

First, there is no clear attestation to the existence of synagogues until the second century BCE at the earliest.[2] The use of the passage in Ezekiel in essence rests upon the rabbinic midrash on the verse;[3] the plain sense of the passage refers to Yahweh as their new Sanctuary, as opposed to some institution. Indeed the opposition of Yahweh and institutions seems precisely the point of the passage. Second, no evidence pertinent to the nature and function of the synagogue is evident until the middle of the first century CE.[4] Finally, much of what appears in scholarship regarding the development of the synagogue rests upon speculation quite unencumbered or constrained by data.

The synagogue of the later Hellenistic period, both literary,[5] inscriptional,[6] and archaeological for which materials[7] exist, appears a multifunctional affair. Briefly put the synagogue, at least in Asia Minor, Syria, Greece, and Italy, constituted the principal center and unit of Jewish communal organization, this in much the same manner as the parish-system in late medieval England or France. The synagogue leadership, then, remained essentially lay "rulers" of the Jewish *ethnos* in the empire, and the liaison between the people and the Roman authorities. Thus the largely politico-administrative character of the evidence concerning the synagogue, the "(place of) assembly," or simply "the commune." And herein lies the reason why the synagogues in some cases were afforded space by the Roman authorities within the latter's local "office-complexes." One could hardly imagine the authorities donating such space to Dionysiacs, for example or for a Judaic sanctuary (*miqdaš*), were the sacramental function the primary activity of the synagogue.

Such a view of the synagogue explains as well the close integration between its administrative structure and the larger Jewish communities,[9] such as that of Rome. Indeed, the titles borne by the functionaries at both levels are similar, and the institutions parallel. Synagogues were "ruled" by an *archesynagoges* ("ruler of the community") often in conjunction with a *gerousia* ("senate") of elders. So too in a city like Rome all such parish units themselves came under the authority of a senate and its ruler (*archon*), in some locales (as in Alexandria) bearing the title *ethnarch* ("ruler of the *ethnos*"). Since from Hellenistic times on *ethnos* denoted an official, legal political entity (*politeuma*) within the host empire,[10] the administrative structure of *archontes* and *gerousia* would have constituted the "legal" government and administration of the Jews within their larger political settings. How these government functionaries of the Jewish communities were "chosen" for office varied widely within the period and across the geographic area in question. No doubt in many locales positions remained hereditary privileges. In sum the major function played by the synagogue and its officers as purveyors of government and justice opens anew the synagogues as a locus and institution mediating between heaven and earth.

Again from the first century CE on we possess clear attestation to the synagogue as a place of community prayer and locus of the forms of divine mediation.[11] Indeed, in the Alexandrian milieu, at least as represented by Philo, one finds not a synagogue but a *proseuche*,[12] a place of prayer, a temple. Mishnaic law assumes that communal prayer and the reading of the Law and the Prophets as sacramental acts occurs in the synagogue, although not necessarily or exclusively so.[13] And Acts' mission in Syria,[14] Asia Minor and Greece and Macedonia, polemical and apologetic as that depiction may be, attests as well to a synagogue liturgy into which were integrated readings from the Law and the Prophets, followed by a "sermon" on the lecture. Finally, Chrysostom, in the late fourth century CE, attests to the same.[15] In all these data, covering the geographical and temporal span of the Late Antique diaspora, neither the *archesynagoges* nor the *gerousia* assume any liturgical, sacerdotal function. They are not officiants in the mediation of the sacred. We have, however, already seen some suggestive evidence that members of the priestly caste continued outside and after the sacrificial cult to play a priestly role within a liturgical setting.[16] As to the specific nature of that role we may not even speculate. But we suppose, based upon the existence of some priestly function within communal prayer, that communal prayer within the synagogue provided a locus of sacred power analogous to that of the Temple.

The Jerusalem cult was the systemic creation of the sacred on earth. The Sanctuary was the center of holiness defined by the systematic organization of people about that center in terms of successive levels of "status." The Sanctuary, access to which was limited to ministering priests, was surrounded by the inner court of the altar, that area in which both ministering priests and clean Israelite males might circulate. About the latter was the court of women, into which the officiating priests might not venture; and beyond the court of women lay the court of the Gentiles, that is, the world, presumed to be unclean but dependent upon the sacred power emanating from the Temple. While this sacred cosmos could be created by such human organization anywhere—"at *whatever* place I shall cause my name to dwell" (see Deut. 15:20; 16:2, 11, 16; 26:2)—at any one moment that place was exclusive, unique, and at the center of a systemic order defining all other space and assigning it its place.

This the synagogue, even at those moments when the community was at prayer, could never replicate, not while the Temple stood, to be sure, nor after its demise. No synagogue could effect the systematic ordering of people that was possible in the Temple courts; and archaeological evidence supports this claim, for no synagogue remains of the period evince such an arrangement of space.[17] To be sure, no synagogue could view itself as an exclusive center, a requisite of systemic creation of sacred place. What model, then, of mediation of the sacred does communal prayer in the synagogue (even with priestly officiants) reflect?

Communal prayer might legitimately be viewed as a type of group incantation, the repetition of established word-formulae and rites, which may be replicated anywhere and simultaneously in any number of locations, provided they occur at the propitious moments—near sunrise, after zenith passage, at the new moon, etc. The hereditary priesthood is equally well suited to such a shamanistic model of cultic activity. It is part and parcel of the shamanistic model that rites be carried out at opportune moments and by appropriate individuals. We have already discussed priestly-magi and Divine Men (in chapter 3). These persons are links between heaven and earth, they would maintain, because the deity fashioned them as such; in the nature of things they *are* of a different order, as their charismatic gifts would indicate. Israelite priests, too, might be conceived to be of a different order of human, chosen by deity, as indicated not by theurgic powers but by lineage *cum* etiological myth as to the origins and the "chosenness" of that lineage. Etiological myths remain everywhere common features of the shamanistic pattern of religion, particularly as regards propitious places for mediation of the sacred, but not uncommonly of mediators, or a hereditary caste of mediators. That the history of the priestly caste in Ancient Israel has its origins before and outside the ascendancy of the systemic model of Deuteronomic Reformation, that is in the decentralized, local cultic sites, seems in the current context particularly apt. The priesthood, the origins of which as a sacerdotal caste lie in the shamanistic type of cult among the Ancient Israelites, later came to play a comparable function in a cult of Yahweh outside of the Temple system and in another shamanistic cult of Yahweh in the Greco-Roman diaspora.

Viewing synagogue liturgy within the shamanistic pattern of religion finds further support in the extensive participation of Gentile Christians and pagans in that cult. Gentile Christians, as we shall discuss more fully in the next chapter, not only attended synagogue services, participated in the liturgy, and selectively observed Jewish rites and taboos, but were also welcomed by the ethnic Jews who permitted this participation, harboring no illusions that these Yahwehists would formally join the Jewish *ethnos* through conversion. The

Temple system could never tolerate such blurring of ethnic boundaries, because the systemic model largely functioned though the maintenance of clear social frontiers. Nonsystemic, shamanistic patterns could afford to remain less xenophobic in this regard, as seems to be the case both with diaspora Judaism and with non-Deuteronomic cults in Ancient Israel.

It is commonplace for shamanistic rites to occur not only at propitious moments and by the agency of special persons but also at special locations. The synagogues, at least in the earlier centuries of the Hellenistic period, seem not to have been such places. As institutions of the community they must be able to be located "wherever" the community might "set up shop." Holy places, that is, places believed to be links between heaven and earth, created as such in the nature of things, may never be "wherever" by definition, at least not phenomenologically speaking. If we are correct in our interpretation of synagogue liturgy in the Judaism of the Greco-Roman diaspora, then attempts to change synagogues into sacred places by some means should little surprise one. Just such a development may be documented.

A. T. Kraabel has noted a tendency from the end of the first century on to build more elaborate niches in the synagogues for receiving or housing Torah (and Prophetic) scrolls.[18] This development includes not only synagogues first constructed in the second and subsequent centuries but also extends to the modification of older buildings where previously the synagogue had no such architectural feature. The design of these Torah-niches often assumes the character of a portal. And B. Goldman in his study of the portal motif and Ancient Jewish art and architecture[19] presses home the observation that the portal constitutes a common feature of synagogue architecture, mosaics, and frescos, as well as of funerary art.[20] In the context of tombs the stylized character in many instances of the portal indicates that it functioned as a symbol within Late Antique Judaism and cannot be dismissed as a decorative device.

One may find the portal-symbol, moreover, commonly used by other Greco-Roman cults—that of Isis and Osiris,[21] for example—but with one major difference; in these latter instances the deity stands within the portal, indicating that we face the gate to the realm of the god.

Given its widespread symbolic use in the Hellenistic world, the portal probably assumed the same, or minimally similar, significance in the Judaic context, namely, that the gate on tombs and in synagogues marks these locations as gateways to heaven, propitious (sacred) places for mediation between the divine and earthly realms. Indeed the framing of these portals by cultic objects, such as incense shovels, candelabra, *shofar,* and palm branches (*lulav*) lends weight to such an interpretation of the portal motif.[22]

In the case of tombs, the presence of the dead makes the tomb a gateway, as we have argued earlier. But synagogues in themselves are not holy places; I know no etiological myths for synagogues, and I cannot conceive how there could be. They can become holy places only by bringing within them some sacred object which itself is a portable locus of the sacred and link between the realms. Assuming that the portals built into the interior walls of the synagogues housed Torah scrolls,[23] it appears that the Scrolls themselves came to constitute for Greco-Roman Jews just such a holy object, a relic. In other words, as the word of God, the Torah was not only canonical and authoritative, but also shared in the sacred power of the word (*debar* or *logos*) of the deity (as, to be sure, did the prophets in their performance of "miracles"). If one understands the Torah scroll as a relic, as well as Yahweh's authoritative teaching, then the taboos that apply to its preparation and handling (but not to codices of the text for study) make eminent sense. Both the Scroll and the codex contain the same text; only the Scroll functions as a relic in the formal synagogue liturgy, is paraded, like a relic, through the congregation, and is venerated, like a relic, during that procession. The presence of the Torah scrolls makes the portal of the Torah-niche a gate to heaven, as do the martyrs' remains in the tomb.

Such a view of matters finds corroboration in the late fourth century in Chrysostom's homilies against the Jews. As we shall discuss more fully in the next chapter, Chrysostom, at the time still a parish presbyter, could not keep many of his Gentile Christians out of the synagogues. In attempting to rehabilitate these Judaizers, Chrysostom offers us the reasons they adduce for their attraction to the synagogue. First, the oaths administered during judicial proceedings in the synagogue are more "awesome."[24] Second, his Christians go to the synagogue to use the services of Jewish Holy Men, who exorcise demons and provide incantations and amulets.[25] Third, "the scrolls of the Law and the Prophets are there," making the synagogue a "holy place."[26] As they would at the tombs of the saints, Chrysostom's Christians go to the holy place to pray, in this case to participate in the public liturgy of the formal Jewish community Sabbaths and on Holy Days. The Jews with whom these Christians prayed, in all probability, similarly viewed the significance of the scroll of the Law and the Prophets.

Perhaps the clearest example of the importation of relics into the synagogue, so as to render it not simply communal space but sacred place, remains the Synagogue of the Maccabean Martyrs in Syrian Antioch. As mentioned in chapter 4, at some time prior to the late third or early fourth century CE the parishioners of the synagogue in question exhumed the bones of the "Maccabean Martyrs" from their tombs on a mountain near Antioch and reinterred the remains under their synagogue. But the community's appetite for relics did not stop with martyrs' bones (nor, as we might assume, with Torah scrolls either). Again by the late third or early fourth centuries CE, the same synagogue boasted possession of Aaron's flowering staff, dust from the Tablets of the Covenant, and some wood splinters from the Ark of the Covenant.[27] (All of the latter rested in the Torah receptacle with the Scrolls.) I know of no other synagogue in the ancient world that so excelled at the collection of relics. The synagogue of the Maccabean Martyrs points *grosso modo* to a conception of the synagogue according to which its function as the location for public worship (at least) is greatly enhanced by turning the space into sacred place. This transformation occurs by means of assimilating portable "links" between heaven and earth (relics) to the House of Assembly.

Of the actual content and structure of the liturgy we have only the barest notions. We may, nevertheless, lay out the evidence such as it is. Acts, as I have had occasion to mention, knows of readings from the Torah and Prophets,[28] and this is followed by a sermonette expounding on the readings. From the evidence from Acts, one may surmise that this "sermon" was not the prerogative of any single functionary of the synagogue, for Paul as a visitor often appears honored with the function. But in this regard, I hesitate to give assured credence to Acts, as such a portrayal of Paul's *modus operandi* furthers one of Luke-Acts' central *Tendenzen*; the Gospel was everywhere first offered to the Jews. One may glean some evidence from Mishnah, but with extreme caution only. For recent research concerning that document makes it ever more difficult to expect Mishnah to reflect, in most instances, anything other than its utopian view of sacred reality, without necessary regard to antecedent or contemporary practice.[29] Still if one asks, What does Mishnah take for granted about liturgy in its own earliest stratum of discussion?—here, I believe, the student treads on firmer ground, because that which stands (logically) prior to Mishnah cannot, in this instance, have been provided by yet another "utopian" document, the Pentateuch. The latter has little if anything to say relevant to liturgy. With respect to prayer, then, Mishnah's point of departure likely is the actual state of affairs in the synagogues of the late first century.[30]

Further along this line of inquiry, the synagogue liturgy already in this era probably included the following "building blocks":[31] call to prayer (*bareku*); the "Hear O Israel" (*shema'*) with some manner of introductory and concluding benedictions; the "supplication" (*tefilah*); scriptural readings, likely with vernacular translations.[32] One may further surmise that a morning and afternoon liturgy were practiced; whether on a daily basis I cannot say. The existence of an evening public prayer appears more difficult to establish.[33]

Without knowing the text of the liturgy in that era, one may offer interpretations of its meaning and logic with the utmost temerity only. If, however, one supposes for the sake of argument that the *shema'* included anything like those biblical passages used in the later rabbinic liturgy (a reasonable hypothesis), then the basic structure and "logic" of public liturgy seems clear enough. One first reminds the deity of his own contractual agreement with the petitioners, as set forth in the god's own words (that is, in the *shema'*); subsequently, in the *tefilah*, the supplicants request (demand?) benefits under the agreement. In this the "logic" of the liturgy bears close resemblance to that of an incantation (or vice versa). For the *shema'* reminds parties that they are bound by a longstanding oath; indeed the deity may be conceived to be even more effectively bound by reading (to him) his own sacred "oath" *ipsissima verba*. Then requisite goods and services may more effectively be vouchsafed (in the *tefilah*) from the "bound" god. That the people too appear bound by the contractual oath should in no way mitigate this interpretation of matters. Even in the incantation, as we have seen,[34] the practitioner-petitioner must meet the necessary standards of purity, through fasts, abstinence from sex, moral "pollution," and the like, before approaching the deity. Incantations too appear "two way streets."

In sum, the synagogue in itself is no gateway to heaven, of the shamanistic type. Nor does it constitute the locus of sacred order on the systemic model of the Temple. To be sure, it appropriated symbols and forms from the Temple—the *shofar* and *lulav* on murals and reliefs, perhaps a specialized role for priests. But in the main, synagogues could not (or, minimally, did not) create order through systemic cultic activity. Primarily a multifunctional organ of communal life of the Jewish *ethnos*, the synagogue might play the role of *locus sanctus* for public celebration and prayer by assimilating to itself other sacred objects, relics, such as martyr's bones and Torah Scrolls. Or the synagogue in another context might welcome within its walls the Holy Man.

The "fit" between the demographics of the diaspora synagogues and the early Gentile churches invites inquiry into the relations between them. And the presence of relics in the synagogue further drives home such issues. It seems plausible, for example, to see in the division of labor in the synagogues (that is, lay administrators, priests and Holy Men) the model for an early church organization, which appears to replicate just such a structure of authority. Evidence, however, is not equal to sorting out such matters of borrowings and historical dependence. (Indeed, I am not sure what would such constitute adequate evidence or appropriate criteria in regard to these matters.) But consideration of the relationships existing between churches and synagogues, in light of their similar institutional structures and views concerning the mediation of the sacred—to that we may turn with some expectation of concrete results.

The Synagogue and the Church
Remarks on the Sociology of Jewish-Christian Interaction

Parallels evinced across various religious groups may often remain just that, lines of tradition that never converge historically. The not-so-hidden agenda of much of this work includes a claim that real parallels of structure and content existed between early Gentile Christianity and the Hellenistic Judaism with which it shared the Mediterranean basin of the Late Roman period. One might, therefore, expect a more "powerful" hypothesis to emerge from this discussion: that Early Christianity borrowed extensively from contemporary Judaism. Odd as it may seem, I intend entirely to sidestep any such claim. What one would need in terms of evidence for such a thesis seems prodigious indeed and rarely attained. This of course has not stopped many in similar situations from making comparable statements. For myself at least, I am prepared to concede a complexity to cultural exchange and fusion that refuses to reduce itself to simple borrowings. Before these issues, therefore, let me retreat in discretion.[1]

Having made these disclaimers, I shall make a rather more forthright assertion. The evidence pertaining to Judaism in the Hellenistic diaspora indicates that the sociologies of the Early Gentile Church and the Synagogue were closely intertwined for the first three or four centuries of the common era. Put simply, uncircumcised Gentile Christians (probably among other uncircumcised parties) not only practiced Judaic rituals but also attended synagogues and celebrated with the formal Jewish community, attended at times Jewish law courts, went to Jewish charismatic Holy Men to be healed and exorcised, and did all this *qua* good Gentile Christians. On the other hand, there seems every indication that the Synagogue remained aware of this participation, did nothing to stop it, on the one hand, and made little or no attempt to lure these Christians into the formal

Jewish community via proselyte circumcision, on the other. To be sure, just as Christians patronized Jewish priestly magi, Jews patronized Christian ones, and, even more perplexing yet, Jewish Holy Men referred (*qua* Jews) to Christian Holy Men in their incantations for their Jewish clients.

Again, Chrysostom in late-fourth-century Antioch provides the most unambiguous evidence. First, his homilies against the Jews not only provide evidence for the observance of various feasts and fasts among the Jews of his area, but also the sermons were occasioned by the participation of a significant number of his congregants in those Judaic rituals. Thus in the fall of 386, Chrysostom interrupts a series of sermons on the Arian heresy to tackle the more immediate and pressing problem of "Judaizing."

> And many who belong to us and say that they believe in our teaching, attend their [the Jew's] festivals, and even share in their celebrations and join in their fasts. It is this evil practice I now wish to drive from the church. Sermons against the Anomoeans [Ariansl can be delivered at another time and the delay would not work any harm. But if those who are sick with Judaism are not healed now when the Jewish festivals are "near at the very door" (Matt. 24:33), I am afraid that some, out of misguided habit and gross ignorance, will share in their transgressions, and sermons about such matters would be pointless. If the offenders are not present to hear what we say today, afterward medicine would be applied in vain, because they would have already committed the sin. This is the reason I am in a hurry to take up this matter before the festivals. That is the way doctors do things. They deal with the most urgent and acute sickness first.
>
> (*Homily 1 Against the Jews, Patrologia Graeca,* 48:844–845, trans: W. Meeks and R. Wilken, *Jews and Christians in Antioch in the First Four Centuries of the Common Era,* p. 86)

Chrysostom's problem of Judaizing is not new to the early church. Ignatius rails against the practice of Judaism by Gentile Christians. While the problem begins with Paul, what Ignatius and Chrysostom term Judaizing seems of a different order. For Paul, Judaizing appears to have been, essentially, the denial that a Gentile Church was possible. For Paul's opponents, to be Christian implied becoming (formally) a convert to Judaism.[2] Some evidence from Acts[3] (and perhaps the Pauline Epistles), however, does suggest a graduation in the first century to a new Judaizing, the selected practice of Judaic ritual by Gentile Christians never intending formally to convert.

Chrysostom's homilies give us some indication as well of how the members of the synagogue viewed participation by Christians in their formal, communal rituals. For he must account for the positive reaction of Jews to these additional co-celebrants by claiming that the Jews are insincere; behind the backs of these Judaized Christians, says Chrysostom, the Jews mock you and gloat over their success seducing the followers of Jesus into transgression.[4]

We have already seen that Jewish Holy Men were known to be particularly adept at healing and exorcising. In this, Christian charismatics and Jewish priestly magi were in direct competition. Thus the story in Acts about Simon the Samaritan and Philip, and later about Paul and the seven sons of the chief priest, Sceva.[5] No doubt the sense of competition was made more acute for these virtuosi, when the putative adherents went to the competition for such divine worldly salvation. While early rabbinic literature knows of persons within the rabbinic movement hiring the services of Christian charismatics or Jewish holy men healing in Jesus' name[6] (like Sceva's sons), early Christian documents treat us to a picture from the opposite side of the street. Again Chrysostom appears most explicit in his portrayal of matters.

> If some healing remedies are shown to you, and someone says that they are able to heal, and for this reason he goes to the Jews, expose their magical tricks, their spells, their amulets, their potions. The Jews appear to be incapable of healing in any other way, for they do not truly heal. Far from it. I'll go even further and say this: if they truly heal, it is better to die than to run to the enemies of God and be healed in this way.
>
> (Homily 8 Against the Jews, Patrologia Graeca, 48. 934, trans. W. Meeks and R. Wilken, Jews and Christians in Antioch, p. 116)

Chrysostom's argument provides an apt example of what appears the typical way of dealing with the putative "miracles" of one's opponents. First, he implies that they are mere illusion, just like Acts contra Simon. That is, Jewish Holy Men are mere goetes, carnival magicians. Second, if they do heal, a concession he must make in face of the belief of those Christians who attend Jewish healers, Chrysostom maintains that it must be through incantations and amulets. That is to say, Chrysostom, when he allows for Jewish charismatics to be more than *goetes*, pegs them at the level of priestly magi, leaving the class of Divine Man for Jesus and his charismatics. Thus the healings of the Jews he later contrasts with the methods of Jesus.

> Likewise, the man who had been sick for thirty-eight years, and who went each year to bathe in the pool, was rebuffed each year and was not healed (John 5). But each year he saw others delivered from their infirmities because they had friends who could look out for them. He who was destitute of friends went unnoticed and was constantly passed over. But he did not run to diviners, nor did he go to charmers or wear amulets. He relied solely on the help of God, and for this reason he was finally healed in a marvelous and extraordinary way.
> (*Homily 8 Against the Jews, Patrologia Graeca*, 48. 936 trans. Meeks and Wilken, *Jews and Christians in Antioch*, p. 117)

Chrysostom, then, cites the "fact" that Jesus had no need of charms, incantations, or the help of various divine potentates in order to effect his healings. We have already seen that this constitutes the "objective" difference between the magi and true Divine Men.

That *Homily 8 Against the Jews* responded to a real issue rather than rhetorical issues in the early Church seems further borne out by the evidence for Christian amulets and incantations. Just as the sons of Sceva borrow the names of Paul and Jesus in their incantations, Christian Holy Men obviously borrowed heavily from Jewish charms. E. R. Goodenough alerts us to this state of affairs.[7]

> In other . . . [charms] the Christian elements are slight and quite easily recognizable intrusions in what appear to be very old Jewish forms. . . . . a charm in Syriac [for example] . . . opens with an invocation of the Trinity, goes on to quote the first verses of the prologue of the Fourth Gospel, and then suddenly changes to what seems to me a purely Jewish invocation:
>
> By the power of those ten holy words of the Lord God, by the Name, I am that I am, God Almighty, Adonai, Lord of Hosts, I bind, excommunicate, and destroy, I ward off, cause to vanish, all evil, accursed and maddening (lit., misleading) pains and sicknesses, adversaries, demons, rebellious devils, also the spirits of lunacy, the spirit of the stomach, the spirits of the heart, the spirits of the head and the spirits of the eyes, the ills of the stomach, the spirit of the teeth, also the evil and the envious eye, the eye that smiteth and pitieth not, the green coloured eye, the

eye of every kind, the eye of all spirits of pain in the head, sweet and soft (doleful) pulsations, seventy-two such sweet and mournful noises, also the fever, cold and hot, visions fearful and false dreams, as are by night and by day; also Lilith, Malvita, and Zarduch, the dissembling (or compelling) demon, and all evil pains, sicknesses, and devils, bound by the spell, from off the body and soul, the house, the sons and daughters of him who beareth these writs, Amen, Amen."

The body of the charm as cited certainly comes from a Jewish provenance. Here we have then not merely the product of a Christian Holy Man whose worldview and cultural patterns depend upon some antecedent Judaic tradition, as for example is the case with the Gospels. There seems here virtually no integration and assimilation of the Jewish elements to the Christian. Rather the Jewish incantation has had appended to it a Christian prologue. It would seem then that not only did Christians visit Jewish priestly-magi, but also Christian healers made free use of charms of their Jewish contemporaries—just as the sons of Sceva seem to have done with Christian formulae. In short, the sociology of the Jewish and Christian communities appear to be intertwined both at the level of common believer (to Chrysostom's consternation) and at the level of shaman-healer (as shown by the free trading of incantation texts with little attempt at integration).

That most of the unambiguous evidence for the "confused" sociologies of the Church and synagogue survive only in Chrysostom's sermons appears both frustrating and instructive. With Chrysostom we find ourselves in late-fourth-century (Syrian) Antioch. Some half century and more has elapsed since Constantine's "conversion" to Christianity and his edict of toleration. Some three-quarters of the city's inhabitants profess the "true faith." The opportunities for martyrdom and confessorship appear, for good or for ill, long passed. The Jews unknowingly stand on the edge of their own dark ages under late Roman or early Byzantine rule; they could not have been perceived by their Christian neighbors as a powerful force in comparison with the glories of Church expansion in the fourth century. And still Chrysostom could neither halt the praxis of Judaism among his Gentile Christians, nor impede their actual participation in ritual along with the formal, Jewish community. So stunning are these facts that one might confidently rely upon an argument *a fortiori* for an earlier age. If in the period of the Church's triumph Judaizing flourished, how much the more so in years of persecution of the Church, when

Judaism enjoyed licit status under Roman law and the prestige of antiquity, while Christianity did not?

As much as I would be prepared to rest my case on such an argument, it seems neither prudent nor necessary. While no earlier evidence offers the specificity of Chrysostom's, some corroborating data does survive for the post-Pauline Church. We may, for the sake of argument, even if not for edification, review those data here.

The lion's share of the relevant evidence comes to us from the letters of Ignatius, the *Didache* and the *Didaschalia Apostolorum*. In both cases we find ourselves in the early second century in the Syrio-Asian world. In neither instance does one find that form of Judaizing which characterized the early Pauline-Jerusalem disputes. Jewish Christianity seems long gone. Here, as in Chrysostom's sermons, Gentile Christians, harboring no intentions formally to join the Jewish community by undergoing circumcision, engage in selected Judaic rites.

In Ignatius' Epistle to the Magnesians, the Sabbath appears prominently.

> Do not be led astray by wrong views or outmoded tales that count for nothing. For if we still go on observing Judaism, we admit we never received grace. The divine prophets themselves lived Jesus Christ's way. That is why they were persecuted, for they were inspired by his grace to convince unbelievers that God is one, and that he revealed himself in his Son Jesus Christ, who is his Word issuing from the silence and who won complete approval of him who sent him.
>
> Those, then, who lived by ancient practices arrived at a new hope. They ceased to keep the Sabbath and lived by the Lord's Day, on which our life as well as theirs shone forth, thanks to him and his death, though some deny this. Through this mystery we got our faith, and because of it we stand our ground so as to become disciples of Jesus Christ, our sole teacher. How, then, can we live without him when even the prophets who were his disciples by the Spirit awaited him as their teacher? He, then, whom they were rightly expecting, raised them from the dead when he came.
>
> We must not, then, be impervious to his kindness. Indeed, were he to act as we do, we should at once be done for. Hence, now that we are his disciples, we must learn to live as Christians—to be sure, whoever bears any other name does not belong to God. Get rid, then, of the bad yeast—it has grown stale and sour—and be changed into new yeast,

that is, into Jesus Christ. Be salted in him, so that none of you go bad, for your smell will give you away. It is monstrous to talk Jesus Christ and live like a Jew. For Christianity did not believe in Judaism, but Judaism in Christianity. People of every tongue have come to believe it, and so been united together in God.

> (*Ignatius to the Magnesians*, 8–9, trans. from C. Richardson, ed.
> *Early Christian Fathers*, pp. 96–97)

Ignatius argues his point by turning the prophets of Ancient Israel into proto-Christians. Not only did they foretell the coming of Christ, but they also had already begun to live the Christian life and abandon Judaic ritual. For this they won the hatred of Israel and persecution. The theme that the Jews spurned their prophets is commonplace in the earliest Christian literature. That they evoked such a response because of their rejection of Jewish rites appears a new twist. The Sabbath provides the paramount example, perhaps because its observance was particularly characteristic of the Judaizers.

In *Ignatius to the Philadelphians*, the author makes the provenance of Judaizing influence clear. The "error" stems from Gentile Christians, not Jews or Jewish-Christians.

> Now if anyone preaches Judaism to you, pay no attention to him. For it is better to hear about Christianity from one of the circumcision than Judaism from a Gentile [Christian].
> (*Ignatius to the Phil.* 6, trans. from Richardson, ed.
> *Early Christian Fathers*, p. 109)

We have with Chrysostom been alerted to Christian observance of Jewish Fasts. The *Didache* gives evidence of a similar situation. It cannot, indeed, does not wish to, discourage the praxis of fasting by Christians. Fasts, it would seem, constituted a major element of Christian piety from Pauline times on. The redactor of the *Didache*, however, entreats the faithful to fast on days not customarily used by Jews as fast-days.

> Your fasts must not be identical with those of the hypocrites (i.e., the Jews). They fast on Mondays and Thursdays; but you should fast on Wednesdays and Fridays.
> (*Didache* 8:1, trans. from Richardson, ed.
> *Early Christian Fathers*, p. 174)

Finally the *Didache* gives evidence of Christian use of Jewish liturgy.

> You must not pray like the hypocrites, but pray as follows as the Lord
> bid us in his Gospel: "Our Father in Heaven, hallowed be your name
> . . ."
>
> (*Didache* 8:2, trans. from Richardson, ed.
> *Early Christian Fathers*, p. 174)

It would be inviting to speculate that such prayers occurred in the confines of the synagogue itself, as certainly occurred among Chrysostom's Christians. Unfortunately, the evidence in the *Didache* will not bear the weight of such an assertion.

Less cited either for its anti-Judaic texts or for the evidence it provides about "Judaizing" in the first several centuries of Christianity remains the *Didaschalia Apostolorum*.[8] The document seems more difficult to place than the *Didache*. The *Didaschalia*, however, probably postdates the *Didache*, but predates the Apostolic Constitutions, edited in the latter half of the fourth century. We find ourselves, then, somewhere between the mid-second and the mid-fourth century, and probably in Syrian Antioch, since the liturgy of the *Didaschalia* evinces Antiochene traits. In any case, the provenance will not have been Egypt—a point that in subsequent chapters will command our attention.

The *Didaschalia*, essentially a pastoral document like the *Didache* and the *Constitutions*, contains an extensive discussion of what it terms the "Second Legislation."[9] The latter seems to refer to either the Pentateuch as a whole, its legal portions (or some parts thereof), other "canonical" Judaic legal documents (of which we are unaware), or some combination of the above. Whatever combination or permutation one accepts, at issue remains Judaic law and ritual practice, and the upshot of the *Didaschalia*'s discussion is an exhortation to Christians to neither venerate nor observe the rites contained in this Second Legislation. Given the pastoral character of the document one seems justified in seeing, once again, (Gentile) Christian observance of Judaic ritual as the occasion for the *Didaschalia*'s polemic. Pauline argument, as we would expect, appears frequently, but I would insist that the problematic faced by the editors of the *Didaschalia* remains distant from that of Paul. Not whether Gentile Christianity is possible, but Gentile-Christian assimilation of, or outright participation in, Jewish observance concerns us here.

Some may rightly consider our discussion here an excursus to the monograph as a whole. Their point, in some respects, would be well taken. (For this reason our discussion declines any pretense of having exhausted sources relevant to interactions among Jews and Christians.)[10] Still I maintain that the (representative) evidence treated herein for the confused sociologies of the Gentile Church and the Greco-Roman Synagogue up to and including the fourth century of our era bears upon any understanding of that Judaism (as well as upon the question of the Judaic background and context of Late Antique Christianity). First, the data attest to a certain "fuzziness" in the definition of boundaries in both camps, the Church and the Synagogue. Or to put matters more accurately, their identity structures were not such as to exclude co-celebration and praxis. We deal, then, with a Judaism that apparently recognized in some serious sense a (legitimate) Yahwehism extending beyond the more limited circle of the circumcised, here to Gentile Christians, whom, according to Chrysostom, the Jews seemed to welcome at their formal observances in the synagogue. For anyone even remotely aware of Rabbinic Judaism this constitutes an astounding fact about diaspora Hellenistic Judaism. Second, the confusion of sociologies lends more credence to our claim, made earlier and more extensively stated below, that early Gentile Christianity and Greco-Roman Judaism shared common structures, and that the latter formed the background and context for much of the former up to and including the fourth century of our era. Or, perhaps more accurately put, each formed a significant part of the religio-cultural milieu of the other for an extended period of time. Third, and less obvious, the fact of frequent crossover, at least from Christianity to the Synagogue (and sometimes in the other direction as well), lends support to an interpretative tactic that pervades parts of our study. That is, we allow the data of one group to illuminate (although not actually supplement or supplant) the evidence from the other.

But there remains one question that ought to be raised here, even if addressed more fully only later (in chapter 8): why should the boundaries between Hellenistic Judaism and early Gentile Christianity, as represented in the documents cited, remain so vague for so long? After all, the Jerusalem Church under the policies of Peter and more importantly James has even no vestigial hold over the Christianity of Gentile Christians of the second, third, and fourth centuries. Even the communalities of structure and of content in themselves do little to explain the confused sociologies. Borrowings yes, but hardly the phenomena for which Chrysostom, Iganatius, the *Didache,* and the *Didaschalia* provide evidence.

In this regard, the provenance of our evidence deserves further comment. There seems good reason to suppose that virtually all of the sources cited in this chapter stem ultimately from Syrian and, more particularly, Antiochene traditions.[11] To be sure, evidence for Judaizing in the Church survives elsewhere. Ignatius addresses his exhortations to churches outside the Antiochene sphere; they obviously must understand and share the "problems" to which Ignatius refers. Earlier, moreover, we have seen evidence for a Judaization of pagans in Rome. So the extension of (quasi-) Yahwehistic status to noncircumcised parties may characterize Jewish communities farther west than Syria or Asia Minor. Still it may not be either insignificant or accidental that the lion's share of the more specific evidence comes from Syria. Wayne Meeks, among others, has convincingly argued that Christianity first emerged as something distinct from Judaism in Antioch during Paul's lifetime.[12] Indeed, for just this reason Gentile Christianity too finds its origins in Antioch, for the emergence of a distinctive group identity (allowing of course for shades of gray) provided the minimal requisite for the possibility of the Gentile mission. The evidence Meeks musters in support of this claim seems convincing. Acts tells us that the Antiochene followers of Jesus were the first to call themselves Christians and so explicitly distinguish themselves from Jews. Evidence from Acts and Galatians indicates that the mission to the Gentiles began as a scheme of the Antiochene church, to be sure carried out by Jewish "converts" to the Jesus-cult. These original Apostles to the Gentiles did not count Paul or Barnabas among themselves; the redactor of Luke-Acts makes use of his literary license as a typical Hellenistic historian to append the names of his heroes to the traditional Antiochene list of originators of the mission to the Greeks. In short, Antioch may be said to be the birthplace of Christianity proper and of Gentile Christianity in particular, not Jerusalem. So Meeks.

We face then a situation in which the birthplace of Gentile Christianity and indeed Christianity as something distinct from Judaism remains at the same time the locus at which for centuries the sociology of the two "distinct" groups remains most blurred, where "crossover" seems most frequent, and "Judaizing" an ongoing problem for Church officials—in all an understandable state of affairs. For that place where a distinct Christian identity first emerged might well remain less secure in that distinctive self-definition than places into which Gentile Christianity was imported ready made as it were.

These facts not only have the virtue of making sense of the Antiochene provenance of the most explicit documents concerning Judaizing, but also offer some not unimportant hints in the searching out of the Judaic background to early Gentile Christianity—hints for those who would reassess these issues in detail. It makes sense under the circumstances to look to Antiochene Judaism, rather than to either Judean religion or Rabbinic Judaism, for significant contributions to the structures of early Gentile Christian piety. (Unfortunately, one would like to know as much about the Jews of late first- and second-century Antioch as we know for Antiochene followers of Jesus.) In spite of the relative dearth of Jewish evidence from Antioch, the surviving data tend to confirm our suspicions.

Still, the appeal to the Antiochene provenance begs important questions. Precisely what self-understanding or world-view among early Gentile Christians allowed the blurring of the frontiers between Church and synagogue? That Antiochene followers of Jesus (indeed originally all former Jews) first called themselves Christians makes the question all the more cogent. As architects of a separate identity they will more consciously have had at the fore issues defining their relationship to Jews and Judaism. This question, among others, will occupy us in the subsequent chapters, in which the shape of the whole on both fronts will emerge with greater clarity.

Christians, Jews in the Greco-Roman
Diaspora, and Rabbis

The data for Jewish piety in the Greco-Roman diaspora, materials often preserved in Christian sources, gives evidence of close contacts as well as significant parallels across the (sometimes blurred) boundaries separating Christian and Jew. This stands in contrast to rabbinic documents. Attempts to find Christians and Christianity among the pages of early rabbinic literature exhibit strained and tortuous argumentation and little in the way of plausible results.[1]

Our own data raises anew issues pertaining to the relationships between early (Gentile) Christianity and Judaism (in the Greco-Roman diaspora), with particular attention focused on the Syrian-Antiochene communities and those of Asia Minor. One may overstate the case, to be sure. Palestinian Judaism in the Second Commonwealth does stand behind much of Christianity—the view of most "backgrounds of early Christianity." But early Christianity as we know it from its earliest literature seems already a "gentile" phenomenon. And ties with Palestinian Judaism remain indirect at best, mediated by the "followers-of-Jesus cult" in Jerusalem. That medium of contact moreover, will not have lasted very long. The Jerusalem group was virtually extinct after 70 CE, and it had in any case lost much of its influence and authority, thanks to Paul (and others), within the two or so decades after circa 50. Beyond that the Palestinian Judaic tradition was mediated, again indirectly, through Judaism in the diaspora in the formative years of the Church, through Antiochene Judaism in particular.

The upshot of this seems twofold. First, classical "backgrounds of early Christianity" in concentrating on Palestinian forms of piety before 70 remain at best less than half the story, and at worst skew that half in not seriously considering the lines of transmission of that tradition to the early Gentile Church. Second, works that compare early

Rabbinism with the early (Gentile) Church analyze what in essence are parallel historical phenomena, both of which arise independently from antecedent Judaic tradition and which, in large measure, independently develop. That the source of much of early Christianity may be found in early Rabbinism, then, seems true, if at all, only in the most remote sense. In reality, the actual contacts between Rabbinism and early Gentile Christianity in the first several centuries will have been infrequent and relatively unimportant for either group. (And, after all, Rabbinism was not active in those communities where early Gentile Christianity thrived.)

The other Judaic context of early Christianity lies in the Judaic piety and praxis of the Jews of Syrian Antioch, Asia Minor, and the like. What follows (in this and the subsequent chapter) pulls together from the data a description of that Judaism, attempts an analysis and interpretation of the whole, and finally tries to relocate the various "parties" in the scene.

The direct evidence for Antiochene Judaism (our modal case for much of the Greco-Roman diaspora) allows the following claims. Community organization centered on the Synagogue, and the "secular" functions of the community had their locus there in the hands of the standard lay leadership. Antiochene Jews probably had their *archesynagogoi* (rulers of the assembly/Synagogue), *gerousion* (senates) and its elders, in the general administrative pattern of most of the Hellenistic diaspora. Courts and other administrative, economic and legal functions no doubt came under the jurisdiction of this organizational structure, all within the physical confines and purveyance of the Synagogue.

But it distorts the picture to view this layer of Jewish life as devoid of sacrality. The very location of such mundane aspects of communal life in the confines of the Synagogue ensured in part the sacralization of the life of the *politeuma*, the Jewish political entity. This was certainly so in Antioch. As Chrysostom tells us, his own Christians believed that the Synagogue was a "holy place," if only because the scrolls of the Law and the Prophets abided within the Synagogue's walls. At the Synagogue, heaven and earth met in some significant sense, a link effected by the presence of God's only words—as if the deity's revelation, a projection of himself, continued to attract divine heavenly power to its earthly place. How appropriate, then, that the administration of sacred oaths as a principal mode of the courts was housed in the holy confines of the synagogues. Synagogues, again certainly in Antioch, might acquire holy status other than by means of housing the Torah scrolls. The bones of the "Maccabean Martyrs," supposedly executed and interred near the city of Antioch, had been exhumed from their mountain resting place and reinterred under the floor of one of Antioch's synagogues. E. Bickermann finds this fact so startling that he insists the practice, "foreign to Judaism," must be a later Christian influence upon Antioch's Jews.[2] But Bickermann's stance seems question begging. He assumes that because rabbis would not do such a thing, no Jew of Late Antiquity—all things being equal—could engage in a cult of martyrs. The hypothesis that Rabbinism in this age constituted normative Judaism provides his hidden (and indefensible) premise. Add to this the observation that Judaism in the Greco-Roman diaspora had since the first-century BCE martyrologies of the Maccabean supporters, and the cult of the martyrs in the Antiochene Synagogue, looks like substantially a Jewish, not Christian, affair. The lines of transmission may run in the reverse direction of what Bickermann supposed; any Antiochene Christian cult of the martyrs may have found legitimation in a Judaic cult.

In Antioch and elsewhere in the Hellenistic Jewish world one went to the Synagogue to contact those who dispensed amulets, incantations, exorcisms, and the like. Thus the priestly-magus remained not on the fringes of official Judaic society but at its heart and center. He assumes an institutionalized role within the structures of religio-communal authority. Our Divine Men too might be located in the Synagogue, although Chrysostom does not tell us so—perhaps because in principle Chrysostom may not admit of the existence of Jewish Divine Men at all. The Church reserved this status for Jesus alone. While Priestly Magi and Divine Men constituted living loci of sacredness, points of contact between the upper and lower realms, their location in the Synagogue with its Scrolls may have enhanced the efficacy of their cures. At the same time the presence of the Holy Men in the Synagogue may have reinforced the latter's status as a holy place, where prayers might most efficaciously be offered to heaven.

About the liturgy of the synagogues at Antioch or elsewhere in the Greco-Roman diaspora we know relatively little. Liturgy there was a fact well attested in Christian literature; rabbinic documents too assume that Jews in the Greco-Roman world pray, often or always, however, in Greek. The participation of Chrysostom's Christians in the Synagogue service makes sense only insofar as a great deal (or perhaps all) of the liturgy, and readings transpired in the vernacular. We have seen some evidence indicating a special role within the liturgy for members of the priestly caste, a role necessitating the differentiation of a priestly hierarchy. If Sceva was a chief priest, one would expect a "common" priesthood as well with its distinct privileges and responsibilities. In this, the Synagogue as a locus of sacredness acquired by various means replicates the Temple.

The life of Torah, such as was possible in the diaspora, the Synagogue as Holy Place, the administration of the community at the sacred locus, the offering of prayers in such a fashion as to recall on the one hand the Temple service and incantations on the other, the recompense to living Holy Men and the mediation of dead "saints" and martyrs—these constituted the principal modes of mediation of ordered (sacred) "world" for the Antiochene Jew. And one may generalize the picture to include much of the Greco-Roman Jewish diaspora.

One last item of Jewish piety, however, deserves reiteration. Jews fast—all Jews do so, and apparently do so frequently. In short, lay asceticism of a sort bears a large burden of the pietistic praxis of the Jewish community in the diaspora, and indeed of the wider circle of Hellenistic Yahwehists too. (And Leviticus' dietary restrictions accommodate themselves well to this pattern of piety.) In the religious world of Syria and Asia Minor in Late Antiquity, such lay asceticism should little surprise us. The flesh, that which fasting rejects, seems an obstacle to reception of sacred stuff and a haven for the demonic. Fasting, then, becomes the counterpart to purification in the Temple system, and self-indulgence (which courts demonic possession), the counterpart to uncleanness in the ancient sources. Saintliness of person replaces purity of person. One would, however, be mistaken to see in this the moralization of the Temple cult. Saintliness seems less a moral quality than a physical state of being, in which positive (divine) and negative (demonic) materials must be properly managed. Now, however, as with so much of diaspora Judaism, that management sees a de-nationalization and de-territorialization in the movement from priests in a central national sanctuary to the ascetic piety of the ordinary Jew and Yahwehist. Thus far our composite of Judaic piety in Syria and much of the Mediterranean world under Roman rule. What now of early Gentile Christianity of Syria and environs?

First, the religion of Antioch's Christians became in a sense paradigmatic for much of the Roman world. This initially was so because the mission to the Gentiles emerged from the initiative of the earliest Antiochene "Christians." That trend, however, repeated itself regularly over the first several centuries of the Christian Era, if the transmission of literary and liturgical traditions is any indication. It remains commonly accepted, for example, that the Eucharistic liturgies of Asia Minor, Greece, and ultimately Rome itself in the *Apostolic Canons of St. Hippolytus* all reflect and depend upon the Antiochene liturgy, as distinct from the competing Egyptian *agape* texts.[3] If Syria continued as the birthplace of dozens of heresies in the first three centuries of the Church, the region was also the exporter of "orthodoxy." So too the great pastoral documents other than the Canons attributed to Hippolytus—namely, the *Didache, Didaschalia Apostolorum,* and the *Apostolic Constitutions*—all evince a linear literary interrelationship that ties them in significant ways to the Antiochene tradition.[4] To talk of Antiochene Christianity, then, seems at once to make statements pertinent at least in general outlines to emergent Roman "orthodoxy" and "orthopraxy."

At the levels of piety and mediation of the sacred, the "fit" between the early Gentile Church and the Judaism of Syria and Asia Minor appears striking. In both cases there emerged a distinct hierarchy of authority and division of labor displaying much the same structures.[5] Among Christians, lay leaders such as deacons, deaconesses, and "the widows" assumed (like the *archontes* and elders) religious and public-service roles. Like the Syrian Synagogue (and those of Asia Minor and points west), the early Gentile Church provided the center for the organized communal life of its adherents. As in the Synagogue, the lay leadership arbitrated matters of day-to-day concern. To be sure, no formal court system will have been required, as no formal, Christian, legal structure was in force distinct from that of the Roman administration. (Christians did not possess, nor could they aspire to gain, the status of *politeuma*.) Yet the "secular" functions of the Synagogue probably were paralleled in the *ecclesia*.

Beside these "public servants" one finds the presbyters and the episcopate, roughly parallel roles in the Hellenistic Synagogue. Indeed the episcopate in function first resembled, it seems, the ethnarch among the Jews and increasingly assimilated to itself sacerdotal authority.

Less formally part of the hierarchy, but no less integral to its structure, seem the various types of charismatic figures we have mentioned in antecedent chapters. For the Church these included prophets, exorcists, apostles, and, still later, saintly figures wielding theurgic power such as the Stylite Saints. Somewhere within this hierarchy of semi-divine mediators one may locate the dead saints and martyrs whose relics link them to the surviving community, so that they may be called upon in heaven to serve the needs of the living. Finally, at the apex remains the single "Divine Man" for the Church, Christ, in contrast to the many, Jewish Divine Men. All this existed in Judaism of Syria and Asia Minor.

For lay piety, the points of contact appear equally cogent. Lay asceticism and an ethic of saintliness characterized the common piety of Jewry in Syria and in the Greco-Roman diaspora. So too in the Churches of Syria and Asia Minor. Fasting was a major aspect of Christian, lay piety, as were other ascetic practices.[6] Young widowed women, for example, would often vow not to remarry, dedicating their lives instead to the needs of the Christian community. This prefigures later phenomena in the church to be sure. But one must distinguish these phenomena from one another as well. We do not talk here of either anchoritism or monasticism, since in this case the essential aspect remains serving the community from within its regular social confines, but to the exclusion of seeking the pleasure and security of the life of the householder. Syrian widowhood, then, stands in contrast to Egyptian elitist asceticism, as the latter emerged in the first four centuries of the Christian era.

Even the cults of the dead and of the saints, with their pilgrimages to local shrines and tombs, find parallels among the Jews of Late Antique Syria and Asia Minor. Jews prayed at the tombs of the dead, especially the elite dead. Christians, according to the *Didaschalia Apostolorum*,[7] celebrated eucharists at the cemetery. At some point, both communities moved the bones of some of their dead into the church or synagogue, as the case may be, to enhance the mediatory efficacy of the place of prayer.[8] The parallels, then, not only of detail but, more important, of structure and pattern seem everywhere indicated. This stands in contrast to the usual point of comparison, "pharisaic-rabbinic" Judaism of the late first and subsequent several centuries. In what ways rabbis remain distant from these phenomena may properly put into perspective in the case we have attempted to make for Judaism in Syria, Asia Minor, and points further west. But that distance in itself must be viewed in its proper framework, lest we weaken our case by overstatement.

Until recently, modern scholarship has not tended to view early Rabbinism as an instance of the larger Hellenistic pattern of religion. The rational-legal and bureaucratic aspects of Rabbinism assumed considerable importance for the *Wissenschaft des Judentums*, whose historiography oftentimes served apologetic purposes.[9] The lawyer-homileticist-rabbi who emerged from nineteenth-century histories constituted the perfect embodiment of the "religion of reason." In an age in which Jews sought respectability according to "Enlightened" standards, the *Wissenschaftliche* historians offered the classical rabbi as a prototype of the nineteenth-century enlightened believer.

But such a view of the character and function of the early rabbis can stand only by systematically ignoring a host of data preserved in rabbinic literature. Rabbis were not mere interpreters of the Law; they professed to constitute the very embodiment of Torah. That Torah, moreover, comprised not only the Pentateuch, the Written Torah, but an Oral Torah as well, vouchsafed to Moses ("Our Rabbi") on Sinai, and incarnated, as it were, in the rabbis of Late Antiquity.[10] Torah, for the rabbis, seems to have been much like the *logos* in certain respects for Philo and like the Holy Spirit for the early Church. The Law expressed God's sacred order of "world" on this plane of existence, but Torah was also the first creation, the firstborn of YHWH, and through Torah the world was created. Torah, for the rabbis, linked, therefore, heaven and earth, constituting that power or principle which created order out of chaos and which in the life of the rabbinic Jew maintains that order against the onslaught of the demonic powers of chaos. The rabbi, not a set of documents, mediates the Heavenly Torah on earth; as a walking living Torah, he constitutes the locus of the sacred power of the deity.

Understood in these terms, rabbis, among other things, ought to be able to perform many of the same functions and feats as our nonrabbinic Priestly Magi and Divine Men in Hellenistic Judaism and as the charismatics of the early Church. Indeed, according to rabbinic literature, rabbis could bless and curse efficaciously, resurrect the dead, exorcise demons, heal the sick, interpret dreams, make those dreams come true (or forestall their coming to pass), and kill, if need be, with a look.[11] The rabbinate, of course, opposed magic and decried its practice by (other) Jews: yet they did much the same thing, designating their own behavior as acts of Torah—much as the Christian Holy Man performed acts through the Spirit. Surely this seems a case of Philip and Simon revisited; what my Holy Man does is the power of heaven: what yours effects is mere magic, or illusion and trickery and still worse, perhaps, as Chrysostom says, the work of demons.

As an embodiment of Torah the rabbi did not remain earthbound. Thanks largely to G. G. Scholem, we now have detailed knowledge of early rabbinic, esoteric traditions, the goal of which was to ascend through the heavens, past the angelic guards, to attain a vision of the demiurge upon his throne of glory.[12] Concomitant with these mystical ascents described in the Hekalot texts, we possess Sefer Yesirah, an early medieval rabbinic compilation that professes to reveal those configurations of letters and numbers which comprise the substratum of creation. Scholem has convincingly argued that many of the Hekalot traditions date to the second or third century of our era, that is, to nascent Rabbinism itself. Thus while the author of *Sefer HaRazim* described his vision of the Seventh Heaven, and not too long after Paul who "in Christ was caught up to the Third Heaven,"[13] rabbis too had their praxis of ascent to the palace of the Throne of Glory. Even in death the rabbi seems to have remained a locus of sacred power. We have mentioned above the pilgrimages of early medieval times to the tombs of great rabbinic personages. Witness the tradition preserved in the Babylonian Talmud[14] that when Rav (the early-third-century Amora) died, the "common" folk would come to his gravesite for handfuls of dirt. The earth from his tomb was believed to possess medicinal qualities. Early Rabbinism, Judaism in the Greco-Roman diaspora, and early Christianity each offered its own Holy Men as mediators between heaven and earth, having in all three cases, it would seem, similarly defined the religious problematic of their worlds. All three communities proposed their idiomatic transformations of the same mediatory pattern in lieu of the Temple cult in Jerusalem, which until the first century (or so) had provided that cosmic order on earth. In attempting to come to grips with life without the Temple, whether by necessity or by choice, Greco-Roman Jews, Rabbis, and early Christians turn primarily to individuals, not central national loci or (state) institutions as modes of mediating the sacred. "Map" is no longer maintained by recourse to sacred immovable "territory" in the Late Roman world. And in this our three groups appear typically Late Antique.[15]

Having, however, so clearly relocated Rabbinism in the larger Late Antique milieu, we must take with the left what has been given with the right. In spite of important commonalities across all three groups, Greco-Roman Jewry in the diaspora, Gentile Christianity, and Rabbis, both concourse and confusion characterize the relations between the former two, with Rabbinism remaining peripheral to both. Why should even Antiochene Jews, especially, not have adopted some of the rabbinic solution? It seems Rabbinism, at least from its inception toward the end of the first century until the latter part of the second, effectively withheld[16] its system from the larger part even of Palestinian, let alone diaspora, Judaism.

Rabbinism from its outset portrayed itself as the heir of the Pharisees. Yet there appears every indication that the heirs chose to depart radically from these pre-rabbinic figures. Where by all accounts pharisaic Judaism encouraged a (new) form of piety aimed at the transformation of lay praxis,[17] Early Rabbinism formulates a means to holiness applicable to the elitist-"philosopher"-holy-man alone. Where Pharisees, it would seem, preserved their traditions in Aramaic,[18] the *lingua franca* of most of Palestine, the rabbis early on adopted Hebrew almost exclusively for their literary endeavors, a language not spoken and barely (if at all) understood by the vast majority of their coreligionists. Whereas Pharisaism may have actively missionized Gentiles from the Greek-speaking world, Rabbinism (at least officially) discouraged the study of Greek—no doubt with little success—and evinces little enthusiasm for proselytism. Whereas Jews in general accepted a large collection of documents in Hebrew, Aramaic, and Greek as religiously edifying,[19] the rabbis of the late first or second centuries read out of the canon of holy books virtually all documents not preserved in Hebrew and written (as far as they believed) after the time of the Hellenistic conquest of the Orient. [20]

The evidence from Mishnah-Tosefta underscores this view of matters, both as concerns its literary and substantive traits.[21] Mishnah speaks a utopian language, in the strict sense of the word. That is, Mishnaic Hebrew reflects no living mode of discourse outside the circle of masters and disciples. First, in the first and second centuries, as mentioned, Hebrew had long ceased to constitute the language of everyday life. Palestinian Jews required Aramaic translations of their Torah. Elsewhere, Jews depended either on Aramaic or Greek versions of their sacred documents. Papyri and inscriptions reinforce the notion that Greek and Aramaic bore the burden of everyday commerce and social intercourse. But these facts notwithstanding, the Hebrew of Mishnah could hardly constitute the living language of any community, even of a Hebrew-speaking one. Mishnah has couched its content in forms and formulary patterns, assimilating all idiomatic and everyday traits of language to its limited and disciplined modes of speech. Mishnaic language seems intentionally divorced from the "real" world, creating its own plane of reality, at once more subtle and complex, at once more regular, delimited, and defined. That world exists only within the rabbinic circles, and even at that, still "three feet off the ground" of the daily, social world of that small elite group. Mishnaic Hebrew could not have served the mundane requirements of the rabbinic masters and disciples.

Mishnah's content only reinforces this view of matters. For all its substantive concreteness, its concern with pots and pans, it reflects no real life, and at many junctures it could not provide the blueprint for a community. Here too we find ourselves nowhere (utopia), except in the minds of the rabbis. Most of Mishnah's pericopae assume a context in which the Temple still stands, priests still minister, the old forms of Jewish self-government function, Jews still live primarily in close proximity to that central cult, and so forth. After 70, and most of Mishnah is post-70, none of these conditions exist. Indeed some of them may never have obtained. Ironically, early rabbinic discussions about government and authority cannot even imagine rabbis as significant functionaries in such a system, preferring utopian actors to a rabbinate.

What Mishnah does not talk about edifies as much as what the document treats. While Mishnah discusses liturgical matters, there remain blatant lacunae. For one, to reconstruct the Late Antique Synagogue, even a utopian, rabbinic one, would be difficult, if not impossible, on the basis of rabbinic evidence. The early rabbis expend more energy elaborating a cultic system, which remains inoperable, than a synagogue-structure, which exists everywhere around them. As J. Neusner has remarked in his treatment of the Mishnaic Law of Holy Things, Mishnah reacts to the loss of the Temple by asserting that nothing has changed.[22] The impression gained from Mishnah's legal lacunae may be augmented from (later) rabbinic stories. Those Amoraic sources which depict rabbis in active communal roles, perhaps mistakenly so, preserve a sense of reticence a propos rabbinic participation in the life of the Synagogue. Thus, for example, the story of a rabbi confronted by his student in the Synagogue: during the Synagogue liturgy the master had recited Mishnah, and when questioned by the disciple, the rabbi retorted, "They by theirs, and we by ours."[23] Study (of Mishnah), more than communal prayer, constituted the rabbinic mode of mediation and transcendence, a mode that by definition allowed the participation of only the elitist circle of masters and disciples, while excluding the vast majority of Jewry. Is it no wonder, then, that archaeology has discovered only synagogues that fly in the face of rabbinic law? More recent scholarship has stated partly on this basis that Rabbinism was not normative Judaism in second- (or third-) century

Palestine. Perhaps it is less the case that no one listened to the rabbis than that the rabbis as yet had little to say to Jewry as a whole.

This picture of Mishnaic Judaism stands in sharp contrast not only to pre-70 Pharisaic religion but also to post-Mishnaic (or perhaps post-Ushan) Rabbinism. The insularity of rabbinic circles from 70 to about 170 seems all the more blatant when viewed in the slightly more extended context of their ancestors and their immediate rabbinic heirs. Pharisees preserved, it would seem, their traditions in Aramaic, and they may have missionized in Greek and Aramaic. Rabbis devised their peculiar Hebrew and may have shunned the study of Greek. But third-century Amoraic Rabbinism returns to Aramaic for even in-house rabbinic business, and tells stories of Rabbi Judah the Prince teaching Greek to his sons in preparation for their careers as communal leaders and intermediaries between Jewry and the Roman government.[24] Whether this is true of Rabbi Judah, I cannot say. Representative of a different outlook among third- and fourth-century, Palestinian rabbis—that it certainly is.[25]

As with a transition in language, so too with literary form. Concurrent with this turnabout in Palestinian (and emergent Babylonian) Rabbinism, one sees a new (para-Mishnaic) rabbinic literature, the Halakic Midrashim. These exegetical documents seemingly reject the radical intellectual independence that Mishnah claims for its rabbis, and insist instead on grounding rabbinic law in scripture, understood to be both an organic whole and inclusive of all Torah-knowledge. In all a significant modulation, if not a complete rejection, not of Mishnaic halakah, but of Mishnaic method and processes.[26]

What in sum had Rabbinism in the 100 years after the destruction attempted? J. Z. Smith's terminology here serves.[27] As elsewhere in the Hellenistic World, we have moved away from territoriality, from national cults and their central sanctuaries. Where Rabbinism differed seems to be in the renationalization and reterritorialization of Judaism in the aftermath of 70. But the national and cult locus was in the mind of the rabbi, not on the Temple Mount. The Temple cult in Mishnah survives unscathed as the only proper constituent of sacred order, as do the "classical" national institutions of self-rule. Even the national language, Hebrew, is resurrected for the occasion. But the whole survives in a nonmaterial form, in the intellects of the circle of masters and disciples.

As to the ritual of being a rabbi, as opposed to the (utopian) religion of early rabbinic literature—here we stand more firmly within the Hellenistic processes of deterritorialization. To be a rabbi, one requires no recourse to Temple or the Temple Mount. Priestly status gained one nothing. Even the Synagogue, the decentralized, denationalized *locus sanctus*, might be done without. For the rabbi had a more effective means of transcendence—study. Even the presence of the holy scrolls seems extrinsic to the religion of being a rabbi. For sanctity came not in possessing or reading the written Torah, but rather in debating the oral one. When rabbis prayed, one has the impression they did so within the circle of masters and disciples (later in the House of Study), not with the community in the Synagogue. Rabbinism, then, in these matters appears radically Hellenistic. The ethos of mediation via the individual Holy Man, not the national cult and traditional priesthood, here seems carried to its logical conclusion. Here too we find a type of intellectual encratism of which Philo would have been envious. Still, this mode of rabbinic religion almost by definition will have affected few Jews let alone Christians.

Why the rabbis from 70 to 170 should have so structured matters, I cannot say. Early rabbinic literature remains notoriously opaque to questions of biography, even intellectual biography.[28] Perhaps, this early rabbinic movement might profitably be interpreted as an intellectual version of the Qumran community. The saving of the covenant people by the few in the small sectarian group, a *she'erit hapletah*, a remaining remnant, the aftermath of 70. Whatever the motivations, Rabbinism of this period disqualified itself as a pan-Judaic movement. Non-rabbinic Judaism (diasporic or Palestinian), then, not only exhibited a structure more consonant with "mass" requisites (or, more accurately, requisites of a "lay" religion) in the Hellenistic world, but also constituted the only realistic "game in town" down to the last decade or so of the second century. By that time Rabbinism had lost any opportunity in the Roman world for significant expansion.

Conclusions

*The Commerce of the Sacred
and the Social Anthropology of Knowledge*

The evidence examined points throughout to a distinction between Pentateuchal-cultic patterns of "world" and a decentralized "shamanistic" mediation of the sacred. Put simply, the hidden issue has been the Temple cult, in its Second Commonwealth version, and the Deuteronomic-priestly document, the Pentateuch, which provides its legitimation. For Rabbinism the essential question was, "Whence sacred order in the aftermath of 70?" For other Jews the problematic both after 70 and, as we have seen, for many centuries before, seems the source(s) of sacred (salvific) power outside or apart from the Deuteronomic Temple. And in its own way, Christianity, itself a post-Pentateuchal religion, faced the same situation, the definition of a sacred world apart from the Temple, but with the ghost of the Temple and of the cult of Torah everywhere present.

The rabbis, we have maintained, straddle the fence with regard to the issue at hand. In Mishnah, the Temple system remains intact but transmuted to the realm of utopia, along with its concomitant legislative and judicial structures, and its sacred language, Hebrew. Post-Mishnaic sources, by contrast, show rabbis to be Holy Men, akin to their counterparts among nonrabbinic Jews and within early Christianity. Mishnaic rabbis constitute a group apart from others; in post-Mishnaic Rabbinism that boundary melts, and Mishnaic utopianism to a large degree does with it.

For other Jews both in Late Antiquity (as in Ancient Israel), the mediatory, shamanistic-like pattern correlates with distance from, or outright rejection of, the sociopolitical entity associated with the Jerusalem cult. And in the early Church, we may add, the acceptance of, or distancing from, more charismatic forms of sacred mediation appears correlative with distinct forms of church organization and distinctive "drawings" of the "boundaries" of legitimate social interaction.[1] When "the church" is conceived as the body of Christ and the new Temple (and is so organized), the role of Holy Men flags (indeed is curtailed), and the participation of Christians in formal Jewish functions rends that sacred "catholic" order. The locus of sacredness then becomes unique, exclusive, and ever-present in the very order and definition of a unitary, Christian polity.

In sum, the distinction between Temple-like religion and mediation by various and varied holy intermediaries appears integral to the tensions and dynamics evinced in Late Biblical and Late Antique Yahwehism as a whole. Indeed a social and historical, not only phenomenological or analytic, division between these religious patterns of constituting the sacred on earth is apparent.

If in the range of materials in which we have worked the Temple seems a peculiarly Yahwehistic-Judaic "problem," the distinction between "Temple and Magician," to borrow once more J. Z. Smith's turn of phrase,[2] constitutes a more extensive phenomenon in the Late Antique world. Smith has noted within the Hellenistic milieu a general move from sacrality based on temples and priesthoods, to mediation of the sacred by Holy Men practicing theurgy. And he has maintained that "maps of sacred order" in the anthropological sense no longer overlay and fit national boundaries (in the geopolitical sense). In his words, in the Hellenistic world, "map is not territory." To a large degree, our data may be subsumed under these two categories: Temple vs. Holy Man; national-territorial cults vs. "de-territorialized" patterns of sacred order. But the very correlation between the Jerusalem cult and national territory, on the one hand, and between Holy Man and "decentralization" or "de-territorialization," which our materials evince, on the other, points beyond Smith's descriptive categorization to a more general problematic, namely, to the relationship between beliefs and patterns of ritual and our experience of the social world. To frame matters as a question: Why does what seems *self-evidently* false, unthinkable, or abhorrent to some, appear *obviously* true, appropriate, or venerable to others? With this question one broaches the realm of the social anthropology of knowledge, of shared perceptions. Israelite attitudes to the dead and their tombs, discussed earlier, provide an appropriate entree to these issues as they pertain to "explaining" our evidence.

Conclusions

I. SELF-EVIDENCE AND SCHOLARS OF JUDAISM

Bickermann supposed, as we have seen, the cult of relics in the Synagogue of the Maccabean Martyrs to be a Christian importation—this because such goings-on are "foreign to Judaism."[3] Bickermann's claims in this regard may prove instructive, even though they remain not only question begging but also false. For question-begging claims indicate the measure to which cultural knowledge possesses the ring of self-evident truth for those who would make such statements about how things "really are." Bickermann, a scholar steeped both academically and personally in post-biblical rabbinic Judaism, cannot come to grips with a Judaic system, viewed as equally plausible, in which tombs are the site of veneration of the dead, and in which the earthly remains of these saints constitute valued objects in the mediation of the divine. He rightly "feels" these phenomena to be entirely out of step with Judaism as he "knows" it. It is to this *affective* character of cultural knowledge that M. Douglas points,[4] and in this context I wish to review the facts at hand.

II. THEOLOGY AND SOCIETY: STRUCTURAL HOMOLOGIES AND THE SELF-EVIDENT CHARACTER OF SHARED PERCEPTIONS

Let us, for the moment, assume Bickermann's stance. Namely, Hellenistic Jews adopted an essentially non-Judaic (that is, nonbiblical) relation to the dead, and to their remains from their Christian (or pagan) neighbors. Yet what has allowed them so to adopt matters? The self-evidently inappropriate behavior and views for Torah-loyal Jews were, apparently, no longer self-evidently inappropriate for Jewry in the Greco-Roman diaspora, in spite of their own loyalty to Scripture. That is, the "gut feeling" of knowing the dead and their tombs to be unclean has faded before a comparably affectively grounded knowledge of the semi-divine character of the dead. In what does this affective ground to the apparent "rightness" of "knowledge" find its basis? Douglas in *Purity and Danger* had once supposed that all phenomena which defy a culture's classification of the world, thereby creating "world," would be met with abhorrence. Such beings, objects, states of affairs, and conditions presented a danger to culture, because they called into question the reality of that socially constructed "world."[5] And the dead proved the paradigmatic case of that which threatened the sense of order.

Ethnographic evidence has called into question this assumed negative reaction to all beings that defy classification. But Douglas, in *Purity and Danger,* had already shown that the "gut reaction" to objects deemed impure relates to their "fit" (or here their lack of "fit") with other socially defined taxonomic systems in the culture. So the sense of the propriety of cultural knowledge rests in the consistency across various taxonomic systems of meaning and order. Cultures consist of numerous classificatory structures, rendering ordered and meaningful various facets of their universe. The homologous relationship among these substructures of a culture makes each taxonomy a reflection, on the one hand, and a representation, on the other, of all other systems of classification operating in the society's "universe."[6] To entertain notions or to engage in behavior that threatens to weaken this homologous and emotionally satisfying arrangement will be met, not with reasoned argument to the contrary, but with an affectively nuanced rejection of such claims or behavior—that is, an entirely a priori denial. Objects, claims, and behavior that defy or challenge the systems of classification will no doubt immediately be recognized and dealt with at the level of "gut reaction."

Ethnographers, however (and since 1970, M. Douglas among them), now may document many cases in which such anomalies evoke a positive affective evaluation, rather than feelings of revulsion. An anthropology of knowledge would have us search for aspects of cultural systems that account for this equal but opposite reaction. Again homologies among taxonomic systems will (and do) obtain. Thus for some, tombs remain unclean; for others, sites of mediation between heaven and earth. For the former, moreover, we would expect animals that straddle taxonomic boundaries to be unclean, for the latter, they will be deemed sacred species. For the former, man-god would constitute an impossibility and claimants to such status, blasphemers; to the latter, such beings would prove saviors. For the former, persons who mediate across defined social boundaries will constitute a danger—so magicians, heretics, and demon-worshippers; for the latter they may be welcomed individuals.

Thus some societies define boundaries in order to allow, perhaps facilitate, the crossing of them under certain circumstances. And the positive response to such "crossings" will be reflected in all homologous systems of classification in the cultural system (especially the social). Other cultures, at the opposite end of the continuum, draw boundaries in order to defend their inviolate status; they will defend those ramparts throughout their social, cultic, and cosmological universe. Thus far, then, the results of the debate ensuing upon Douglas' *Purity and Danger* and finding a more acceptable resolution in her "Self-evidence."[7]

III. THE DEAD, AND OTHER DIVINE MEDIATORS, IN THE SOCIAL CONTEXT OF SHARED ISRAELITE PERCEPTIONS

Attitudes to the dead in Ancient and Late Antique Judaism, and the roles ascribed to them, their remains, and their tombs, may indeed be profitably viewed in terms of the social anthropology of knowledge. That is, evaluations of the anomalous deceased, elite, and commoner, within the Deuteronomic-priestly and Greco-Roman contexts respectively, find their homologies in other correlative taxonomies. The Deuteronomic-priestly Reform of the fifth century BCE forged a national cult in Jerusalem and the immediate environs, a cultic system in which the very creation and maintenance of a single, unique center of sacred place was effected *by means of* the careful drawing of social boundaries perceived as inviolate. The Temple of the Second Commonwealth constituted the center of ordered world, so defined by concentric circles of humanity. The Holy of Holies might be entered by the High Priest, and on the Day of Atonement only; the Sanctuary, solely by the clean, ministering priests of the clan of Sadoq. Within the Court of Israel, the site of the altar, only clean, male Israelites and the ministering priests might circulate. (Even this court was subdivided, limiting the mingling of priests with clean, Israelite males.) Beyond the space housing the altar was the space of (clean Israelite) Women. Finally, outermost stood the Court of the Nations; here all, even non-Jews, might gather in undifferentiated mixture. Breached boundaries in this architectonic ordering of humanity dissolved sacred cosmos. For divine power had no loci in this earthly realm outside this (singular) socio-systemic organization. And in this taxonomy of the sacred through maintenance of social boundaries, all beings, objects, or states of affairs in correlative taxonomies, in addition to the dead, will meet with comparable evaluation. So, for example, not only the dead but also charismatic, holy men, persons who straddle the boundary between ordinary human and divine being, as do prophets and inspired "judges," cease during the Second Commonwealth to find a legitimate social role. And later in the Greco-Roman period, the Temple system will find no role for itinerant Holy Men who by their semi-divine character appropriate the benefits of heaven for this earthly realm.

Jews in the Greco-Roman diaspora found themselves widely dispersed across numerous locales and living as a minority within a larger non-Jewish society with which they had seriously to deal. Diaspora Jews, then, could not avail themselves of a unique, socio-systemic creation of sacred place, whatever their loyalties to Torah and Temple. Indeed in the latter's terms, diaspora Jews were consigned to the realm of undifferentiated mixture, the anomalous territory of the demons.[8] For them, loci of the sacred must remain diverse and diffuse. They must posit a host of means and persons who in each locale might mediate the sacred (and, above all, exorcise the demonic), *just as* they themselves must maintain ethnic solidarity by mediating across wide geographical distances with their co-religionists and have meaningful dealings with their Gentile and Christian neighbors. Concomitantly they posit and value intermediaries in their various taxonomic systems, while professing loyalty to the Deuteronomic-priestly rule of the Torah. Greco-Roman Jewry in the diaspora not only elevate the dead to the status of semi-divine intermediaries, but also have recourse to Holy Men who make available the sacred life-giving power of heaven on earth. These Jews, moreover, welcome into their synagogues (and courts) Gentiles and Christians, who, while having no intention formally of converting to Judaism, selectively practice Judaic ritual and participate in the liturgy of the synagogue. Again the homologous evaluation of those who straddle boundaries, including the dead and their remains, holds throughout.

IV. TORAH AND SYNAGOGUE IN THE GRECO-ROMAN DIASPORA

The pattern of diaspora piety, replicating the configuration of their social universe, not only affects the status of the dead or Holy Men but also imposes itself on "less exotic" aspects of Judaic life, such as the synagogue and the "Torah of Moses" inherited from Jerusalem.

Synagogues in themselves are not holy places; they can become holy places only by bringing within them some sacred object that itself is a portable locus of the sacred and link between the realms. The Scrolls of the Law themselves constitute for Greco-Roman Jews just such a holy object, a relic. As the word of God, the Torah was not only canonical and authoritative, but also shared in the sacred power of the word (*debar* or *logos*) of the deity (as, to be sure, did the prophets in their performance of "miracles"). If one understands the Torah scroll as a relic, as well as Yahweh's authoritative teaching, then the taboos that apply to its preparation and handling (but not to codices of the text for study) make eminent sense. Both the Scroll and the codex contain the same text; only the scroll functions as a relic in the formal synagogue liturgy; it is paraded, like a relic, through the congregation, and is venerated, like a relic, during that procession. The presence of the Torah scrolls makes the portal of the Torah-niche in the synagogue a gate to heaven, as do the martyrs' remains in the tomb.

The Life of Torah, as defined by Greco-Roman Jewry, also plays its part in decentralizing the locus of sacredness and denationalizing it. Holy stuff may be made available, apart from Holy Men offering mediation of the extraordinary kind, not only where the sacred Scrolls of the Law and Prophets are located, but also where the members of the priestly caste dress in their traditional vestments and attempt to replicate (as best they can) ancient rites, where the sacred cycle of Sabbaths and Festivals enjoined by Yahweh are celebrated. The praxis of Torah, as a decentralized, denationalized, ethnic rite, remains distinct from the cult of Torah as expressed in the Herodian Temple. That cult produces not loci of sacred power, but a single, unique order with respect to which the entire world is oriented. And the Torah of Moses in its entirety functions in that Jerusalemite milieu as a paradigm for an Israel-centric universe. For Jewry in the Greco-Roman diaspora, the life of Torah cannot define such a comprehensive "system" of cosmic order; rather the Torah serves as an authoritative source book of divine rulings (*nomoi*) for feasts, a lay asceticism of fasting and taboos appropriating an ethnic past (as depicted in traditional stories), mediating the power of their deity, and reinforcing a religio-ethnic identity in a highly varied Hellenistic society. But as a source book, not an Israel-centric paradigm of world, it serves as well for some Gentiles and Gentile-Christians in their commerce with the sacred and in the social commerce across group boundaries, between Jew and Gentile.

V. ENTER THE RABBIS

The earliest rabbis after 70 and before circa 200 stand in the interstices between these two Judaic worlds, the shamanistic and that defined by human-orderings about the cultic center. In Mishnah they recreate in the realm of discourse and logic what before 70 existed (or should have existed) on earth about the Temple site. Mishnah allows no major legislative-administrative role for its own rabbinate, and gives it no sacral function in linking heaven and earth. Only beyond Mishnaic religion do rabbis define themselves as persons who mediate in themselves the power of heaven, this due to their knowledge of Torah. They offer their services as more efficacious than that of competing shamans. These rabbis claim expertise in demon avoidance and related prophylaxis. And in asserting their authority they appeal not only to knowledge of Torah but also to mystical prowess. That is, only after Mishnah, or outside the parameters of the world defined by Mishnah, do the rabbis enter the dispersion and evince the shamanistic pattern of sacred world characteristic of that milieu. Post-Mishnaic Rabbinism, then, some 130 years after the destruction of the Temple cult, enters at last the diaspora and, for centuries, only east of the Greco-Roman dispersion. By the middle of the eighth century, they would, with the help of Islam, come to displace virtually all other Judaic shamans in the Middle East and the Mediterranean basin. They would then control the commerce of the sacred for Jewry.

Appendix
Philo and Philosophic Mysticism

To have begun this book with a discussion of Philo Judaeus would for many have appeared most appropriate. In terms of documentary evidence for Judaism in the Greco-Roman diaspora, Philo, of course, provides the lion's share. And, traditionally, most handbooks of early Christian origins and background virtually reduce their treatment of "Hellenistic" (in contrast to "Palestinian") Judaism to a synopsis of Philonic literature.[1] This state of affairs stems less from the nature of the data for diaspora Judaism in the Greco-Roman world than from the scholarly pedigree of the authors in question. Most "historians" of early Christianity and of Late Antique Judaism have been theologians and exegetes not only by training but also by vocation. Bultmann, here, stands as a perfect example. His theological and exegetical agenda remain everywhere integral to his historical task. But theology and especially exegesis find their object of analysis in texts (usually canonical ones). Other types of evidence, such as art, artifacts, inscriptions, and the like, prove indigestible. And a whole range of questions that lead beyond literary analysis and exegesis seem beyond the conditioned interests of these scholars. Since Philo provides the sole (or most extensive) body of Hellenistic-Judaic literature of "theological" content, the study of the religion of diaspora Jewry often begins and ends with his writings.

Various methodological problems, however, devolve not only from limiting one's data to the Philonic corpus but also from the limited relevance of that literature. (Of course the two problems are related.) Were there no other evidence for Hellenistic Jewry—which, of course, is not the case—for how many Yahwehists, might we surmise, could Philo's writings legitimately speak? No doubt for few. I cannot see that this point requires much argument. Philo remains the elitist par excellence, intellectually and socially. He himself says so, as we shall see below. Nor have his modern exegetes wished to argue with him. And still, "Hellenistic Judaism" undergoes reduction to Philonism, as Philo is made to speak for the general allegorization of Scripture among Western diaspora Jewry and the widely accepted (supposedly) Stoic-Neo-Platonic understanding of Torah-practice. That Philo represents much more than himself, for example, has resulted in such curiosities as the hypothesis of a Philonic "school" so pervasive in the diaspora that ultimately a Christian in Asia Minor writes the Epistle to the Hebrews under Philo's influence. How many steps of cultural diffusion and contact must one posit to bring a Philonist to Hebrews? While Williamson[2] has laboriously proven the thesis wrong, even he cannot see its improbability *ab initio*.

E. R. Goodenough too sees Philo as representative of Hellenistic Judaism, but in a far more subtle manner.[3] Philo, for him, provides an elitist expression of a widespread popular movement characteristic of Yahwehism in the Greco-Roman diaspora. That movement, for Goodenough, has left us data in the fragmentary evidence of Yahwehistic artifacts and art (apart from Philo), but in Philo's writings it comes to us in its more comprehensive version, beyond the ken, to be sure, of the ordinary pious Yahwehist. We begin, then, our survey of the data with both Philo and Goodenough. Specifically, our point of departure is the thirty-five-year debate concerning the existence of a Judaic mystery religion, a debate ensuing upon E. R. Goodenough's interpretation of Philo in his *By Light, Light*.

Goodenough, much like this work, believed that the Judaic context of early (Gentile) Christianity ought to be sought not in Pharisaic-rabbinic Judaism, nor immediately in Hellenistic religions, but rather in a Hellenistic Judaism that provided early Christianity with an antecedent model for syncretizing biblical and Hellenistic religious constructs. That argument, of course, is entirely a priori as it stands, since Christianity should just as easily have been able to produce such a hybrid, if diaspora Judaism could. And if its Judaic (Old Testament) roots made the task difficult for early, Gentile Christianity, then all the more so for Jews in the Hellenistic world. Still, Goodenough's reading of Philo does not rest on his *a priori* statement of the problematic, and an assessment of that reading will help us toward our own ends.

Goodenough formulates his basic position as follows:[4]

I do not profess to be able to trace the process in detail. But what shreds of literature we have from Greek Judaism before Philo, and the full achievement recorded by Philo's time, indicate that here again the Jews were captivated by their neighbour's religion and thought. Yet since a Jew could not now simply become an initiate of Isis or Orpheus and remain a Jew as well, the amazingly clever trick was devised, we do not know when or by whom, of representing Moses as Orpheus and Hermes-Tat, and explaining that the Jewish "Wisdom" figure, by translation "Sophia," was identical with that "Female Principal in nature" which Plutarch identified as Isis. All that now needed to be done was to establish sufficient skill in allegory and the Torah could be represented as the *hieros logos* par excellence, whereby Judaism was at once transformed into the greatest, the only true, Mystery. Moses became priest and hierophant as well as lawgiver. The door was wide open, and the Jews, without the slightest feeling of disloyalty, or the abandonment of their cult practices, could and did take over the esoteric ideology of the mystic philosophers about them, especially and inevitably the Pythagorean-Platonism of Alexandria. Indeed they early claimed, not that they had borrowed it from the Greeks, but that the Greeks had taken it from them.

A great mystic conception of Judaism and of life was thereby developed. The stages by which all this occurred are very uncertain. Moses had become Orpheus and Hermes-Tat possibly two centuries before Philo did his writing, certainly not much later than a century and a half before him. But the intermediate steps are lost, and in Philo, while the Jewish Mystery is fully developed, all traces of the process by which the Jews came to ascribe extraordinary powers to the Patriarchs is lost. Moses now has the power of Hermes, but the explicit comparison is no longer made . . .

The objective of this Judaism was salvation in the mystical sense. God was no longer the God presented in the Old Testament; He was the Absolute, connected with phenomena by His Light-Stream, the Logos or Sophia. The hope and aim of man was to leave created things with their sordid complications, and rise to incorruption, immortality, life, by climbing the mystic ladder, traversing the Royal Road, of the Light-Stream.

A number of separate issues fall in the wake of Goodenough's claims. First, it remains problematic so readily to ascribe these beliefs to "the

Jews," as opposed to "Philo" only (or primarily). Second, one may well call into question the two centuries of pre-Philonic development posited by Goodenough for this Jewish Mystery. Third, has Goodenough in fact appropriately interpreted even Philo as the proponent of such a Jewish Mystery? As concerns the former two, Goodenough's own remarks convict him. To say that "the process by which" this popular Jewish Mystery arose "is lost" amounts to an admission that no relevant evidence exists at all. To be sure, if Goodenough properly has understood Philo as the proponent of a Jewish *mysterion*, then one may well hypothesize about pre-Philonic antecedents. But such speculation would not take us far in any case. In essence, then, the entire weight of what remains of Goodenough's theories must be borne by his exegesis of Philo.

To summarize Goodenough's position, the religious goal for Philo was to loose one's ties to this physical world of corruption through the rejection of worldly cares and pursuits, and allow one's intellect or spirit to receive into itself divine incorporeal ("intelligible") light, which flows as if on a stream from the deity through his Logos and the lesser powers of the incorporeal world to this earthly realm. On this stream the eternal (rational) soul may ascend from the world to the locus of incorporeal "things" whence it came. Here one may attain a vision of divine entities, "bask" in the light stream, and join with and contemplate eternal entities. This ascent may be accomplished in life, and in so doing prepares the soul in death to rest eternally in these blessed origins.

What now of the praxis by which this is to be accomplished? Here, as Goodenough points out, Philo is replete with the terminology of a *mysterion*. The way of Torah represents a "mystery" into the "secrets" of which one is "initiated" by such cultic officiants as the Patriarchs and principally Moses, portrayed as both divine man and hierophant. Without a doubt the image of the mystery cult seems blatant and intended by Philo. But the presence of terminology from the mysteries in itself hardly seems probative, at least not without evidence of an actual *mysterion*.

If by the term *mysterion* Philo alludes to such cults as Isis and Osiris, Dionysus, and the like, then the terminology in Philo can be nothing more than metaphorical. A *mysterion* in the context of Hellenistic mystery religions refers to a secret rite administered by a hierophant to a society of initiates; by means of the *mysterion* the initiate is transformed (sometimes in several stages) in nature, usually through union or identification with a savior figure, in whose death and resurrection to eternal life the initiate thereby participates.[5] In spite of its "otherworldliness," the mysteries did not involve a rigorous asceticism by which the "believer" rejected normal social roles and the like.[6] Quite the contrary, such societies were, so to speak, extracurricular, designed to allow the adherent to live the normal life of the householder and family provider. Nor, for the same reason, did the praxis of the mysteries tend to involve a contemplative life and discipline. The rites worked more *ex operato operandi* (with perhaps the requisite degree of "faith"). Initiation, furthermore, entailed the ministerings of a human priest and esoteric rituals, revealed and administered to the members of the society only. They were not exoteric practices understood according to some inner meaning hidden to others. Finally, a *mysterion* ever remains a group activity, not an individual vocation or discipline.

Measured by these standards Philo's mystery is no *mysterion* at all, as A. D. Nock has remarked.[7] In Philo the mysteries of Judaism seem primarily the very much exoteric life of Torah, its festivals, dietary laws, and the like. Such practices are open and known to all. So too his initiates include the entire Jewish "nation"; to be a Jew was at once to be an "initiate." Philo's hierophants are no living priests, but the great men of Israel's past. In short, the Jewish Mystery in much of the Philonic corpus is the public life of Judaism as he knows it in Alexandria and in the Pentateuch, no secret rites at all.

For Philo there does appear to be a deeper "mystery," one that transcends the public life under the Law. And here too his language seems replete with catchwords of the *mysterion*. But even here the likeness of Philo to mystery cults remains more apparent, even if deliberate, than real. Philo posits a meaning to the Law and the practices of the Judaic life beyond the "plain sense" of the text. Both sacred text and sacred act become allegories for truths about the incorporeal world and the contemplative discipline by which the individual, so gifted, may ascend to the eternal realms.[8] Here again, nevertheless, we face no *mysterion*, but the contemplative life, thought, and personal goals of a middle Platonic philosopher who by means of such philosophic contemplation may attain, as an individual, a religious goal unavailable to the vast majority of his co-"initiates" in the life of Torah.

In sum, Goodenough has accurately described Philo's religious views and praxis but, duped by Philo's own mystery terminology, failed to classify and interpret them accurately. Whence the source of

Appendix

Goodenough's error and the counterpart to Philo's deliberate misuse of mystery-language? Ironically, Goodenough himself has identified both in Plutarch's *Isis and Osiris*. The error stems from interpreting even Plutarch as representing accurately a real *mysterion*. Nock states:[9]

> The similarities of Philo to Plutarch are striking. But there is no reason to believe that initiates of Isis and Osiris were taught anything like what Plutarch says. . . . Jewish allegory [like Philo's] was in all probability drawing on Greco-Egyptian learning rather than on Greco-Egyptian religious tradition. The mysteries, like Judaism and Christianity, were [on the other hand] in themselves non-philosophical and, if they were to be intellectually acceptable at the time, had a like need of the application of terms and concepts.

To put matters simply, Philo reflects not the cult of Isis and Osiris or any other mystery; rather he anticipates Plutarch who in his *Isis and Osiris* does for that group's rituals and myths what Philo does for Moses and Torah.

If Philo evinces no Jewish Mystery in the cultic sense of the word, the data cited by Goodenough does, however, aptly paint a picture of a Hellenistic philosophic mysticism in a Jewish mode. Seen in this light one may profitably return to those passages in Philo highlighted by Goodenough.

Philo, we must remember, remains in the main an allegorist, bound in his writings to his text, the Pentateuch. As a literary genre allegorical exegesis does not lend itself well to a systematic account of a religious world-view or philosophy. Any attempt so to construct one for Philo will of necessity warrant cautionary qualifiers. Contradictory statements will rightly abound by strict philosophic standards. Still, in a number of passages, as Goodenough points out, Philo appears to give voice to his more basic (personal) religious goals and to the view of the universe upon which they depend.

Thus, to begin with, Qu. Ex. II, 39:[10]

> (Ex. xxiv 11b) What is the meaning of the words, "They appeared to God in the place and they ate and drank"?
>
> Having attained to the face of the Father, they do not remain in any mortal place at all, for all such (places) are profane and polluted, but they send and make a migration to a holy and divine place, which is called by another name, Logos. Being in this place through the Steward

they see the Master in a lofty and clear manner envisioning God with keen sighted eyes of the mind. But this vision is the food of the soul, and true partaking is a cause of a life of immortality.

Philo here seems to contrast pilgrimage to and participation in the earthly sacrificial cult to a higher form of peregrination and sustenance. Not the body migrates, but the incorporeal soul. Not to a material locus, but leaving the body and the corporeal world behind, the soul ascends to an otherworldly immaterial realm identified as the Divine Logos. Here the soul may attain a vision of the incorporeal realities, the ideas. For as Philo states elsewhere, the ideas of phenomena are situated in the idea of ideas, the Logos.[11] Here too, Philo insists, the migratory soul sees God. (I suspect some lesser hypostasis is the object of the vision.) Whereas earthly meats, even sacrificial flesh, feed only the body destined for corruption, the vision of eternal "things" sustains the soul eternally, ensuring its immortality.

This vision of the Divine attained by being situated in the Logos seems for Philo no mere metaphor, as was the case with his mystery language. For he continues in Qu. Ex.II, 40:

> (Ex. xxiv 12a) What is the meaning of the words, "Come up to Me to the mountain and be there"?
>
> This means that a holy soul is divinized (Armenian: *astouacanal*) by ascending not to the air or to the ether or to heaven (which is) higher than all but to (a region) above the heavens. And beyond the world there is no place but God. . . . For those who have a quickly satiated passion for reflection fly upward for only a short distance under divine inspiration and then immediately return. . . . But those who do not return from the holy and divine city, to which they have migrated, have God as their chief leader in the migration.

Here we face explicit language of ascent. As with later "gnostic" mystical praxis, among Jews and non-Jews, the soul, disembodied temporarily, may journey upward through various distinct strata.[12] The implication seems that each region is successively less corporeal than the former. The "altitude" of the ascent remains directly proportional to the prowess of the practitioner in philosophic contemplation. The more reflective upon things incorporeal, the more ethereal the region to which the soul may travel. But the ascent envisioned by Philo and the discipline that effects the journey differ substantially from other types of mystical "flight" known to us from Late Antique documents. Paul's ascent to the "third heaven" was not the result of any praxis (to his mind), but a virtual kidnapping.[13] He seems to have been wrenched out of this plain of existence by the divine (Christ), in his words, "caught up." The experience seems akin to prophetic ecstasy as reported in the Hebrew Bible. Other Late Antique travelers of the heavens and beyond, like Philo, sought the experience by means of some active discipline. The *merkabah* mystics among the early rabbis used, it seems, mantra-like litanies to induce trances, preparatory rites of purification, and they taught their disciples the requisite passwords that would safely allow passage past the angelic guards of successive heavenly "palaces."[14] Philo, like these *merkabah* masters, propounds a discipline that actively seeks ascent of the incorporeal soul. His praxis accords, of course, with his philosophic sensitivities and predilections—as does what he "sees" on such journeys. Not mantras and incantation-passwords, but contemplation of the immaterial realm effects the soul's ascent to the incorporeal. Again his counterparts no doubt are the Greco-Egyptian philosophers, of whom Plutarch (several decades after Philo) is characteristic.

More startling in this passage appears the clear reference to apotheosis. The one who ascends not only attains a vision unavailable to his lessers but also, if we are to take Philo's language at face value (and I see here no reason not to), has undergone a change in nature, passing from human to divine status. Far from being atypical of Hellenistic Judaism, however, Philo reflects here a notion one confronts many times over in Jewish theurgic ("magical") documents.

Qu. Ex. II, 40 alludes to the praxis by which, for Philo, this divinization and ascent are achieved, namely, reflection. But as other passages demonstrate, there remains more to the discipline of Philonic mysticism than either philosophic contemplation or the same coupled with the "mystery" of the life of Torah. In the autobiographical passage in Special Laws III, 1ff, Philo adds an ascetic dimension.

> There was a time when I had leisure for philosophy and for the contemplation of the universe and its contents, when I made its spirit my own in all its beauty and loveliness and true blessedness, when my constant companions were divine themes and verities, wherein I rejoiced with a joy that never cloyed or sated. I had no base or abject thoughts nor groveled in search of reputation or of wealth or of bodily comforts, but seemed always to be borne aloft in the heights with a soul possessed

by some God-sent inspiration, a fellow traveler with the sun and moon and the whole heaven and universe. And when I gazed down from the upper air, and straining the mind's eye beheld, as from some commanding peak, the multitudinous worldwide spectacles of earthly things, and blessed my lot in that I had escaped by main force from the plagues of mortal life.

The philosophical quest of ascent appears to involve ascetic requisites. Abject thoughts, reputation, wealth, and bodily comforts remain antagonists to the contemplative goal. Here Philo may be interpreted to have espoused a rather circumspect ascetic discipline, rather more a life according to a Golden Mean than a rejection of world and body, of emotions and bodily needs. But still other passages express more clearly a radical opposition of things true and divine and matters earthly and fleshy, an opposition bordering in tone upon gnostic and encratic sensibilities.

In Qu. Ex. II, 51 Philo calls for the elimination of emotions, among other things, which mitigate the contemplative task.

For if, O mind, thou dost not prepare thyself of thyself, excising desires, pleasures, griefs, fears, follies, injustices and related evils, and dost (not) change and adapt thyself to the vision of holiness, thou wilt end thy life in blindness, unable to see the intelligible sun. If, however, thou art worthily initiated and canst be consecrated to God and in a certain sense become an animate shrine of the Father, (then) instead of having closed eyes, thou wilt see the First (Cause) and in wakefulness thou wilt cease from the deep sleep in which thou hast been held. Then will appear to thee the manifest one, who causes incorporeal rays to shine for thee.

This passage moves far beyond calling for the requisite emotional equanimity, which allows the mind effectively to think, a kind of "normal" asceticism in the Weberian sense. The language again opposes this-worldly functions of the mind to that state required for contemplation of the intelligible realm. The one seems the enemy of the other. In concerning itself with matters and normal emotions of this world the mind really remains asleep; "closing ones eyes," that is, falling asleep to this world, effects true wakefulness (to the intelligible one). The result is one with the discipline. The mind, in dying to this world, becomes a shrine (a temple) for God, replacing the earthly sanctuaries.

This entrapment of the mind in sleep Philo relates to subjection to the senses, a function of possessing a body: "It is when the mind has gone to sleep that perception begins, for conversely when the mind wakes up perception is quenched" (Allegorical Interpretations II, 8, 25ff).

In part due to his mystical understanding of Judaism, Philo, then, makes a number of correlative distinctions: the plain sense of scripture he opposes with its inner meaning; so too the life of Torah-ritual, with the "mystery" of contemplation of the intelligible realm; the earthly Temple, with the disembodied soul in contemplative "flight"; the mind, with sense perception; wakefulness of the excarnate soul, with soporific entrapment in the flesh.[15]

These distinctions place Philo far indeed from pharisaic and early rabbinic tradition. All three ostensibly are founded in Torah. For Philo, moreover, distance from the Temple cult and the "national" life of the Jewish "homeland" makes Torah the sole basis upon which to build a legitimate sacred Jewish world in the diaspora. On the other hand, Philo empties, perhaps must empty, Torah of its content. Faced with a situation where much of Scripture's prescriptions have no point of reference beyond proximity to the cult and homeland, Philo and indeed other diaspora Jews—cannot, as do pharisees and rabbis, effectively fall back upon national custom conceived as Oral Law. For as L. Rothkrug has hypothesized,[16]

> Pharisees and, later, rabbis participated in divine revelation because oral law permitted them ostensibly to derive each and every ruling from the code revealed to Moses. Outside of Palestine Jews, however numerous, remained a predominantly urban minority ignorant of their ancestral tongue and continuously exposed to the cultural influences of the cities they inhabited. To be sure no documentation known to survive seems able to confirm or deny their possession of an oral law. But since most Jewish communities in the Dispersion, unlike their counterparts in Palestine, were deeply involved in the alien law of their cities, it seems unlikely that commentary on the Mosaic code could significantly affect judicial processes involving both Jews and Gentiles.

Philo, and his diaspora co-religionists, will have assumed an ambivalent stance toward Scripture. They remain cut off from the "native" social context in which convention and tradition—along with Scripture to be sure—may bear a large part of the burden of social cohesion and solidarity perceived as sacred order. They themselves will have maintained an "ethnic" identity as widely scattered minority communities subject to numerous modulations of the larger Greco-Roman culture. Such "loyalty at a distance" demands less shared experiences than abstract commitments and ideologies. Here the Torah, conceived in abstract terms as a constitution, might fulfill the requisites of cohesion and traditional legitimation of group identity. It should little surprise us, then, that Philo expresses himself in the exegesis of Scripture, on the one hand, but ideologizes its message, on the other—this latter endeavor in conformity with the sensitivities of his Greco-Egyptian peers and in response to the blatantly problematic character in a diaspora context of much of Scripture's content. Indeed his predilection for Greco-Egyptian Platonic mysticism effectively undermines the plane of Torah-ritual altogether. These remain matters occupying the senses and the body, and as such militate against that wakefulness of the mind which leads to apotheosis. If for Maimonides Torah-ritual ultimately is irrelevant to the philosophic life, for Philo these rites will have proven a hindrance. To be sure, neither will have been able to openly admit to such positions, to themselves or to their co-religionists.

Philo represents a particular type of Jewish Holy Man in the Greco-Roman world. Through an asceticism and philosophic contemplation the Philonic mystic might either ascend to the incorporeal world, there to join the Logos, or, alternatively, attract to himself God's incorporeal light. Both routes achieve for the practitioner self-divinization and immortality. There seems no way to determine whether Philo remained one of a kind among Hellenistic Jewry. And there is no indication that *qua* philosophic mystic he assumed a particular social role within the Jewish community or some subgroup thereof. He held communal offices; by his own admission, however, they militated against his religious goal, rather than stemming from his mystical prowess. Wealth and aristocratic ties, not divine status, suited him for public responsibility and office. Such is the not the case with other types of Jewish Holy Men in the Hellenistic milieu.

Notes

FOREWORD

1. *Footsteps*, trans. Max Lane (New York: Morrow, 1994), p. 133.

2. "God Save This Honourable Court: Religion and Civic Discourse," in *Relating Religion: Essays in the Study of Religion* (Chicago: University of Chicago Press, 2004), p. 389.

3. *Wonderful Life: The Burgess Shale and the Nature of History* (New York: Norton, 1989), 276. See also Jonathan Z. Smith's remark in *Drudgery Divine: On the Comparison of Early Christianities and the Religions of Late Antiquity* (Jordan Lectures in Comparative Religion 14; London: School of Oriental and African Studies, University of London; Chicago: University of Chicago Press, 1990), p. viii: "progress [within the human sciences] is made not so much by the uncovering of new facts or documents as by looking again with new perspectives on familiar materials. For this reason matters of method and models ought to be central."

4. See also p. 1: "Our contribution lies not in uncovering new evidence."

5. "Ethnocentrism" condenses features of a familiar mode of representing social identities in the past: asymmetrical evaluations of historical social identities (e.g., Greeks versus Barbarians, Christians versus Jews or Pagans, Us versus Them); monocentric and monogenetic origins; historical continuity that is often combined with a failure to respect the distinction between "then" and "now"; a preference for teleological history over contingent history. For elaboration see Jörn Rüsen, "How to Overcome Ethnocentrism: Approaches to a Culture of Recognition by History in the Twenty-First Century," *History and Theory* 43 (2004): 118–29; on the "synchrony of now and then" see Eviatar Zerubavel, *Time Maps: Collective Memory and the Social Shape of the Past* (Chicago: University of Chicago Press, 2003), pp. 46–48. In the historiography of early Judaisms and Christianities this ethnocentrism is often

explicitly linked to the rhetoric of uniqueness, in which comparison is ruled by "an overwhelming concern for assigning value, rather than intellectual significance, to the results of comparison," as Jonathan Z. Smith has demonstrated (*Drudgery Divine*, p. 46). See also, profitably, Smith, "Differential Equations: On Constructing the Other" (The University Lecture in Religion 13; Tempe, Arizona: Arizona State University, March 5, 1992); reprinted in Smith, *Relating Religion*, pp. 230–50; Smith, "What a Difference a Difference Makes," in Jacob Neusner and Ernest S. Frerichs, eds, *"To See Ourselves as Others See Us": Christians, Jews, "Others," in Late Antiquity* (Scholars Press Studies in the Humanities; Chico, CA: Scholars Press, 1985), pp. 3–48; reprinted in Smith, *Relating Religion*, pp. 251–302.

6. See Terry Godlove, Jr., "Religious Discourse and First-Person Authority," *Method and Theory in the Study of Religion* 6 (1994): 147–61.

7. Wilfrid Sellars, "Empiricism and the Philosophy of Mind," in H. Feigl and M. Scriven, eds, *Foundations of Science and the Concepts of Psychology and Psychoanalysis* (Minnesota Studies in the Philosophy of Science 1; Minneapolis: University of Minnesota Press, 1956), p. 298. On the "myth of the given" as a trenchant epistemological and category-defining force in the study of religion, along with a critique of this myth, see Hans H. Penner, "Interpretation," in Willi Braun and Russell McCutcheon, eds, *Guide to the Study of Religion* (London: Cassell, 2000), pp. 66, 69–70.

8. See, for example, the view taken by Matthew W. Dickie in his major recent book, *Magic and Magicians in the Greco-Roman World* (London: Routledge, 2001), on a topic that Lightstone treats with care in *Commerce of the Sacred* (chap. 2) but that Dickie does not cite. Although Dickie admits that "it has to be granted that there are some situations in which it would be crippling to confine our descriptions of an alien culture to the categories that the culture examined has at its disposal" (p. 19)—he mentions medical categories and certain "higher level concepts peculiar to modern Western society" such as the "Marxist notion of a false consciousness" (pp. 19–20)—he defends the view that it is possible "for a stranger to understand an alien society from within" and that, therefore, "the emic approach to the study of culture should not be abandoned in favour of the etic" (p. 19). On what grounds it is appropriate selectively to impose alien categories ("false consciousness") now and then, but just as apparently arbitrarily to insist on native terms ("magic") here and there is not cogently clarified. So we are stuck with the curious position of knowing that the ancients' knowledge concerning abortion is unreliable but that their knowledge of magic is trustworthy. Preferable is H. S. Versnel's methodological principle, which Lightstone would undoubtedly endorse: "Magic does not exist, nor does religion.

What do exist are our [scholars'] definitions of these concepts. Scholars in earlier decades of this century were luckier: they knew both what magic was and how to find it. They simply opposed its characteristics to those of either science or religion, which they knew as well" ("Some Reflections on the Relationship Magic–Religion," *Numen* 38 [1991]: 177); see also Jonathan Z. Smith, "Towards Interpreting Demonic Powers in Hellenistic and Roman Antiquity," *Aufstieg und Niedergang der römischen Welt* 2.16.1 (1978): 425–39; Smith, "The Temple and the Magician," in *Map Is Not Territory: Studies in the History of Religions* (Studies in Judaism in Late Antiquity; Leiden: Brill, 1978), pp. 172–89 (both of which Lightstone uses as important assists). On category definition as a first principle of scholarship in the study of religion see Jonathan Z. Smith, *Imagining Religion: From Babylon to Jonestown* (Chicago Studies in the History of Judaism; Chicago: University of Chicago Press, 1982), pp. xi–xii (cited by Lightstone, *Commerce of the Sacred*, n. 2 to ch. 1); and Willi Braun, "Religion," in *Guide to the Study of Religion*, pp. 6–14.

9. Fitz John Porter Poole, "Metaphors and Maps: Toward Comparison in the Anthropology of Religion," *Journal of the American Academy of Religion* 54 (1986): 413. If the provocation should not be recognized, one might state it in the more truculent terms of Bruce Lincoln, "Theses in Method," *Method and Theory in the Study of Religion* 8 (1996): 227: "When one permits those whom one studies to define the terms in which they will be understood . . . or fails to distinguish between 'truths', 'truth-claims', and 'regimes of truth', one has ceased to function as historian or scholar. In that moment, a variety of roles are available: some perfectly respectable (amanuensis, collector, friend, and advocate), and some less appealing (cheerleader, voyeur, retailer of import goods). None, however, should be confused with scholarship." Readers will find this scholarly axiom persistently intoned and demonstrated, often with startling conclusions, in Jonathan Z. Smith's work, in which Lightstone's *Commerce of the Sacred* takes solid anchorage. E.g.: "The cognitive power of any translation, model, map, or redescription . . . is a result of its difference from the phenomena in question and not its congruence. . . . For this reason, a paraphrase, perhaps the commonest sort of weak translation in the human sciences, nowhere more so than in biblical studies, will usually be *insufficiently different* for purposes of thought. To summarize: a theory, a model, a conceptual category, *cannot be simply the data writ large*" ("Bible and Religion," in *Relating Religion*, p. 209, emphasis in original).

10. See especially Lightstone, "Whence the Rabbis? From Coherent Description to Fragmented Reconstruction," *Studies in Religion/Sciences Religieuses* 26 (1997): 275–95; Lightstone, *Mishnah and the Social Formation*

*of the Early Rabbinic Guild: A Socio-Rhetorical Approach (Studies in Chris-
tianity and Judaism/Études sur le christianisme et le judaïsme* 11; Waterloo,
Ontario: Wilfrid Laurier University Press, 2002), pp. 10–29.

11. "Whence the Rabbis?," p. 278. Mack's assist, including the "Catch-
22" descriptor in Lightstone's posing of the problem, is in "On Redescribing
Christian Origins," *Method and Theory in the Study of Religion* 8 (1996):
247–69; reprinted in Burton L. Mack, *The Christian Myth: Origin, Logic,
and Legacy* (New York: Continuum, 2001), pp. 59–80.

12. On the "mirage" of "normative Judaism" see especially Jonathan Z.
Smith, "Fences and Neighbors: Some Contours of Early Judaism," in *Imagining Religion*, 1–18. On the rhetoric of authenticity: It should be noted that in
the current affective conditions of the academy (but hardly only or especially
in the academy), often imprecisely intoned in terms of "postmodernism" or
"postcolonialism" and associated with "experience" or "indigeneity" as a
privileged epistemological stance, the myth of authenticity is enjoying a robust
and celebrated life a quarter century after Lightstone tried to head if off at the
pass, especially, perhaps, in the study of religion. See Russell T. McCutcheon,
"The Jargon of Authenticity and the Study of Religion," in *The Discipline
of Religion: Structure, Meaning, Rhetoric* (New York: Routledge, 2003), pp.
167–88; McCutcheon, "The Tricks and Treats of Classification: Searching for
the Heart of Authentic Islam," in Bryan Rennie and Philip L. Tite, eds, *Underlying Terror: Religious Studies Perspectives on the War on Terrorism* (Albany:
State University of New York Press, forthcoming); cf. S.M.A. Sayeed, *The
Myth of Authenticity: A Study in Islamic Fundamentalism* (Karachi: Royal
Book Co., 1995). On the myth of authenticity in late modern discourse, in
scholarly circles greatly influenced by M. Heidegger, see Theodor W. Adorno,
Jargon der Eigentlichkeit: Zur deutschen Ideologie (Frankfurt: Suhrkamp,
1964; English trans. 1973); and generally, Gareth Griffiths, "The Myth of
Authenticity: Representation, Discourse and Social Practice," in Chris Tif-
fin and Alan Lawson, eds, *De-Scribing Empire: Postcolonialism and Empire*
(London: Routledge, 1989), pp. 70–85.

13. Lightstone does not develop the skewing-effect on the study of Greco-
Roman Judaisms when it was co-opted for the Christian origins problematic, but his observation is brilliantly vindicated by Smith, *Drudgery Divine*, esp. pp. 81–84. Nor does Lightstone more than imply that "whence
early Christianity?" scholarship has itself been fantastically beholden to
mythic and apologetic agenda, and driven by interests in authoritative
transmission of an "authentic" and "unique" originary Christianity. The
ground-breaking work is that of Mack (*Myth of Innocence*; "Redescribing
Christian Origins"; *The Christian Myth*); Smith (*Drudgery Divine*); Ron

Cameron, "Alternate Beginnings—Different Ends: Eusebius, Thomas, and the Construction of Christian Origins," in Lukas Borman, Kelly Del Tredici, and Angela Standhartinger, eds, *Religious Propaganda and Missionary Competition in the New Testament World: Essays Honoring Dieter Georgi* (Novum Testamentum Supplements 74; Leiden: Brill, 1994), pp. 501–25. See now especially the first volume of published results of the Society of Biblical Literature's seminar on "Ancient Myths and Modern Theories of Christian Origin" in Ron Cameron and Merrill P. Miller, eds, *Redescribing Christian Origins* (SBL Symposium Series 28; Atlanta: Society of Biblical Literature, 2004).

14. Eric Hobsbawm, *On History* (London: Weidenfeld and Nicolson, 1997), p. 5; on the complex relations between past and present, fiction and historical narrative, and make believe and "make-belief," see Willi Braun, "The Past as Simulacrum in the Canonical Narratives of Christian Origins," *Religion and Theology* 8 (2001): 213–28, and the literature cited there, including the statement that "history" is, among other things, "a catchment of the social, political, or religious interests of those who 'do history' " (p. 220).

15. For a discussion of this late modern tendency, in the academy and in popular culture, see Jean Baudrillard, "La réversion de l'histoire" in *L'Illusion de la fin: ou La greve des evenements* (Paris: Galilée, 1992), pp. 23–27; Baudrillard, *Simulacres et Simulation* (Collection Débats; Paris: Galilée, 1981). Lightstone's frequent advice not to confuse "map" with "territory" is dependent on Jonathan Z. Smith, "Map Is Not Territory," in *Map Is Not Territory: Studies in the History of Religions* (Chicago: University of Chicago Press, 1978), pp. 289–309.

16. Burton L. Mack, "The Historical Jesus Hoopla," in *The Christian Myth*, pp. 25–50; William E. Arnal, "Making and Re-Making the Jesus-Sign: Contemporary Markings on the Body of Christ," in William E. Arnal and Michel Desjardins, eds, *Whose Historical Jesus?* (*Studies in Christianity and Judaism/Études sur le christianisme et le judaïsme* 7; Waterloo, Ontario: Wilfrid Laurier University Press, 1997), pp. 308–19; Arnal and Desjardins, *The Symbolic Jesus: Historical Scholarship, Judaism and the Construction of Contemporary Identity* (Religion in Culture; London: Equinox, 2005).

17. Morton Beckner, *The Biological Way of Thought* (New York: Columbia University Press, 1959); Rodney Needham, *Against the Tranquility of Axioms* (Berkeley: University of California Press, 1983); Needham, "Polythetic Classification: Convergence and Consequences," *Man* n.s. 10 (1975): 349–69; Smith, "Fences and Neighbors" (and the bibliographic information in nn. 2–15, pp. 135–36); the brilliant comment on Smith's article by Arnal, *The Symbolic Jesus*, pp. 31–37. Generally instructive is Geoffrey C. Bowker

and Susan Leigh Star, *Sorting Things Out: Classification and Its Consequences* (Cambridge: MIT Press, 1999).

18. In the classic statement where Beckner distinguishes monothetic and polythetic taxonomies he writes: "A class is ordinarily defined by reference to a set of properties which are both necessary and sufficient (by stipulation) for membership in the class. It is possible, however, to define a group K in terms of a set G of properties $f_1, f_2, \ldots f_n$ in a different manner. Suppose we have an aggregate of individuals (we shall not yet call them a class) such that: (1) each one possesses a large (but unspecified) number of the properties in G; (2) each f in G is possessed by a large number of individuals; and (3) no f in G is possessed by every individual in the aggregate" (*The Biological Way of Thought*, p. 22); see also Smith, "Fences and Neighbors," p. 4.

19. Arnal, *The Symbolic Jesus*, p. 31.

20. The last point has been increasingly argued in recent scholarship as a significant rectification of the old "separation of the ways" model. See, e.g., Stephen G. Wilson, *Related Strangers: Christians and Jews, 70–170 C.E.* (Minneapolis: Fortress, 1995); Daniel Boyarin, *Dying for God: Martyrdom and the Making of Christianity and Judaism* (Stanford: Stanford University Press, 1999). Generally, however, Lightstone's picture of Greco-Roman Diaspora Judaism remains highly eccentric (in the most complimentary sense of the term) as a scholarly representation. Note in contrast, for example, Erich S. Gruen's recent foray into the same topic, *Diaspora: Jews Amidst Greeks and Romans* (Cambridge: Harvard University Press, 2002), a work that does not refer to Lightstone even once, and thus where tombs, theurgists, relics, and Christians, for example, do not appear, and where the Synagogue is seen as "sui generis" (p. 123).

21. Readers would do well to adjudicate Lightstone's rather laconic description of the "anthropology of knowledge" with reference to Fredrik Barth's 2000 Sidney W. Mintz Lecture, "An Anthropology of Knowledge," *Current Anthropology* 43 (2002): 1–18.

22. The reader must get over the ambiguities and unclarities in the "homology" language and recognize that Lightstone is using this term not in the technical sense it has in biology or comparative physiology, nor aligning himself with the dubious work that "homology" has performed in the history of comparing religions. See, for example, Luther H. Martin ("Comparison," in Braun and McCutcheon, eds, *Guide to the Study of Religion*, p.52): "Comparativists who explain similarities among the diversity of religious data in terms of homologies tend to presume some essential 'religiosity' common to these data."

23. Readers may consider an alternate, but congenial, vocabulary, Nelson Goodman's "world" and "worldmaking." See *Ways of Worldmaking* (Indianapolis: Hackett, 1978). "World" has been elucidated for a comparative

study of religion by William E. Paden,"World" in Braun and McCutcheon, eds. *Guide to the Study of Religion*, pp. 334–47.

24. "Proximate other" is Smith's term ("What a Difference a Difference Makes," p. 48). On Lightstone's influence on recent attempts to rethink the categories for a redescription of Christian origins, for example, see Merrill P. Miller, "Antioch, Paul, and Jerusalem: Diaspora Myths of Origins in the Homeland," in Cameron and Miller, eds. *Redescribing Christian Origins*, 182–84; Willi Braun, "The Schooling of a Galilean Jesus Association (The Sayings of Gospel Q)," in Cameron and Miller, eds. *Redescribing Christian Origins*, pp. 63–65

CHAPTER I: INTRODUCTION

1. See M. Douglas, "Self-Evidence," in M. Douglas, *Implicit Meanings* (London: Routledge, 1975); M. Douglas, *Cultural Bias* (London: Royal Anthropological Society, 1981).

2. See J.Z. Smith, *Imagining Religion* (Chicago: University of Chicago Press, 1981).

3. See M. Smith, "Terminological Problems," in P. Slater and D. Wiebe, eds., *Religions in Contact and Change: Proceedings of the 14th Congress of the International Association of the History of Religions* (Waterloo: Wilfrid Laurier, 1983).

4. See S. Safrai and M. Stern, *History of the Jewish People in the First Century*, 2. vols. (Assen: Van Gorcum, 1974–80); E.E. Urbach, *The Sages: Their Beliefs and Concepts* (Jerusalem: Magnes, 1976); S. Zeitlin, *The Rise and Fall of the Judean State* (Philadelphia: JPS, 1968).

5. As argued by G.G. Scholem in his introduction to *Major Trends in Jewish Mysticism* (New York: Schocken, 1941), pp. 1–49.

6. See, for example, W.D. Davies, *Paul and Rabbinic Judaism* (New York: Harper and Row, 1967); G.F. Moore; *Judaism in the First Several Christian Centuries*, 3 vols. (Cambridge: Harvard University Press, 1958–59); with regard to these and the immediately preceding points, a useful discussion may be found in J. Neusner's "Bibliographical Essay" at the conclusion of his *Rabbinic Traditions about the Pharisees before 70*, 3 vols. (Leiden: Brill, 1971), and in E.P. Sanders' introduction to his *Paul and Palestinian Judaism* (London: SCM, 1976).

7. The work of Ismar Schorch is instructive in this regard; see his *Jewish Reactions to German Anti-Semitism* (New York: Columbia University Press, 1972); See also J. Stern, *Claude Q. Montefiore on the Early Rabbis* (Missoula: Scholars, 1977).

8. M. Douglas, "Self-Evidence."

9. Ibid.

10. Ibid.

11. See M. Smith, "Nehemiah," in his *Palestinian Parties and Politics that Shaped the Old Testament* (New York: Columbia University Press, 1971).

12. A. T. Kraabel, "The Diaspora Synagogue," in *ANRW* series II, 19:502.

13. B. Goldman, *The Sacred Portal* (Detroit: Wayne State University Press, 1966).

14. Goldman, *Portal*; E. R. Goodenough, *Symbols*, vol. 2, pp. 70–99.

15. Goodenough, *Symbols*, vol. 12; Goldman, *Portal*.

CHAPTER 2: MAGICIANS AND DIVINE MEN

1. See M. Douglas, "Self-Evidence," in M. Douglas, *Implicit Meanings* (London: Routledge, 1975), pp. 276–77; J. Z. Smith, *Imagining Religion* (Chicago: University of Chicago Press, 1981).

2. E. E. Evans-Pritchard, *Witchcraft, Oracles and Magic Among the Azande* (London: Oxford, 1937); see also M. Douglas, ed., *Witchcraft, Confessions and Accusations* (London: Tavistock, 1970); M. Douglas, *Evans-Pritchard* (Brighton: Harvester, 1980); M. Douglas, *Cultural Bias* (London: Royal Anthropological Inst., 1979).

3. M. Douglas accounts for this tendency among modern scholars in terms of the operations of the "purity rule," that is, the tendency to see ourselves as outside the "natural"; see her "In the Nature of Things," in M. Douglas, *Implicit Meanings*.

4. J. Z. Smith, "Towards Interpreting Demonic Powers in Hellenistic and Roman Antiquity," *ANRW* series II, 16.1:425–39; see also A. F. Segal, "Hellenistic Magic: Some Questions of Definition," in R. Van Den Broek and M. J. Vermaseren, eds., *Studies in Gnosticism and Hellenistic Religion* (Leiden: Brill, 1981).

M. Douglas has pointed to witchcraft accusations among some groups as functioning to define group boundaries; see M. Douglas, *Natural Symbols*, 2nd ed. (London: Barrie and Jenkins, 1973) pp. 136ff.

Methodological perspectives regarding magic in Late Antiquity may be found as well in: J. Z. Smith, "Temple and Magician" in his *Map Is Not Territory* (Leiden: Brill, 1978); M. Smith, *Jesus the Magician* (San Francisco: Harper and Row, 1978); P. Brown "Rise and Function of the Holy Man in Late Antiquity," reprinted in P. Brown, *Society and the Holy in Late Antiquity* (New York: Faber, 1982); J. Neusner, *History of the Jews in Babylonia*,

2. Magicians and Divine Men

vol. 5 (Leiden: Brill, 1970); D. Aune, "Magic In Early Christianity," *ANRW*, series II 23.2:1507–57; W. S. Green,. "Palestinian Holy Men," *ANRW*, series II 19.2:619–47.

5. John Chrysostom, *Homily I: Against the Jews*, *Patrologia Graeca* 48:843–56; English translation by W. Meeks and R. Wilken, *Jews and Christians in Antioch in the First Four Centuries of the Common Era* (Missoula: Scholar's Press, 1978), pp. 85–104; *Homily 8: Against the Jews*, *Patrologia Graeca* 48:927–42, pp. 105–26 in Meeks and Wilken. Cited hereafter as Chrysostom, *Homily 1* (or *8*); See also M. Smith *Jesus*, pp. 114ff.

6. Justin Martyr, *First Apology*, 26, 56; Iranaeus, *Against the Heresies*, II.27, III.4; Eusebius, *Ecclesiastical History*, II.

7. See A. D. Nock, "Paul and the "Magus," reprinted in Z. Stewart, ed., *A.D. Nock: Essays*, vol. 1 (Cambridge: Harvard University Press, 1972).

8. Were it not for this latter fact, I should have more readily attributed their appeal to Jesus and Paul to Luke-Acts' apologetic designs.

9. Goodenough, *Symbols*, 2:164ff.

10. This in no way intends to deny the syncretism well documented for the Hellenistic period; see M. Avi-Yonah, *Hellenism and the East* (Jerusalem: Magnes, 1978); F. Cumont, *Oriental Religions in Roman Paganism* (New York: Dover, 1956); M. Hadas, *Hellenistic Culture* (New York: Norton, 1972); A. Momigliano, *Alien Wisdom* (Cambridge, 1975).

11. For this typology I am indebted to M. Smith's *Jesus*, pp. 68ff.

12. To be discussed in chapter 3.

13. As opposed to its Talmudic usage in which it falls into the category of name theurgy; see J. Trachtenberg, *Jewish Magic and Superstition* (New York: Behrman, 1939), pp, 78ff.

14. W. S. Green, "Palestinian Holy Men" *ANRW*, Series II, 19.2:628.

15. S. Lieberman, *Greek in Jewish Palestine* (New York: Jewish Theological Seminary of America, 1942), p. 108, n.85.

16. This in no way implies that *Sefer HaRazim* has been redacted (in the usual technical sense) in Late Antiquity. We imply only that this "exploration" of successive levels of heaven provides, in all probability, the "enduring" motif providing the basic structure to which discrete theurgic units might accrue or from which they might be excised. A similar state of affairs, for example, entails with Hekalot Rabbati, as Peter Schaefer has convincingly argued in a paper delivered to the meetings of the European Association for Jewish Studies, Oxford, July 1982.

17. Indeed it is not inappropriate to note that the Hekalot-Merkavah texts are replete with incantations intended to facilitate the journey of the ecstatic visionary through the successive Heavenly Palaces. See Appendix, n.14.

18. See again remarks in n.16 above.

19. As I am confident that a careful study of the manuscripts would indicate.

20. Goodenough, *Symbols*, 2:174ff.

21. See Ezekiel 1.

22. See Isaiah 6.

23. See *Sefer HaRazim*, chapters 1–2.

24. Goodenough, *Symbols*, 2: 200.

25. Some invoke the name of Jesus ben Pantera, for many scholars the Jesus of the Gospels, as indeed the nonrabbinic magical bowls of Nippur invoke the Pharisaic master, Simeon ben Shetah; see T. Hullin 2:24 (b. Avodah Zarah 16b–17a); T. Yebamot 2:3 (b. Yoma 66b); see M. Smith, *Jesus*, pp. 46–50; J. Neusner, *A History of the Jews in Babylonia*, (Leiden: Brill, 1970), 5: 218ff; see J. Lauterbach, "Jesus in the Talmud," in J. Lauterbach, *Rabbinic Essays* (Cincinnatti: Hebrew Union College, 1951); see also T. Shabbat 11:15 (b. Shabbat 104b; y. Shabbat 12:4; b. Sanhedrin 67a); T. Hullin 2:22 (y. Shabbat 14:4; y. Avodah Zarah 2:2; b. Avodah Zarah 27b).

26. In this regard, it may not prove insignificant that Margolioth in his introduction to his edition of *Sefer HaRazim* identifies the provenance of the materials as either Egypt or the primarily pagan coast of Palestine.

27. Mark 1; Matthew 3; Luke 3; John 1.

28. Romans 6.

29. As in John Chrysostom's *Addresses to the Catechumen, Patrologia Graeca*; but the same is already implied in Paul in, for example, Galatians 4:3, 8–9.

30. Goodenough, *Symbols*, 2: 195.

31. Ibid. 2: 194.

32. See Josephus, *Antiquities*, 12:261.

33. See the Honi tradition cited above, pp. 25f: "I swear by your Great Name that I shall not move."

34. The authority of the Holy Man as the marked characteristic of this specialist over against the magician-protagonist receives considerable treatment in patristic literature, as my colleague L. Rothkrug has pointed out to me in conversation and spells out in greater detail in his article on the origins of the Christian cult of relics to appear in the new *Encyclopaedia of Religion*, C. Long, et al., eds.; cf. Justin Martyr's *Second Apology* and Iranaeus' *Against Heresies*, II.

35. On demons and dealings with them, see numerous references in P. Brown, *The Making of Late Antiquity* (Cambridge: Harvard University Press, 1978); see also references in n. 34 above.

2. Magicians and Divine Men

36. See nn. 34 and, 35 above.

37. For a comprehensive treatment of the early rabbinic traditions about Honi, see W. S. Green "Palestinian Holy Men" *ANRW*, Series II 19.2:619–47.

38. In this I extend to insights of J. Z. Smith (in "Towards Interpreting Demonic Powers") to embrace the concerns of M. Douglas (nn. l and 3 above); namely, I would see the phenomenon in question as an instance of what Douglas calls the "purity rule" helping to map out and maintain homologous cosmological and social boundaries.

39. See M. Smith, *Jesus*, pp. 101ff.

40. M. Smith, *Jesus*, pp. 74–75.

41. PGM 14:784ff; XXI, trans., M. Smith, *Jesus*, p. 102.

42. PGM 2:148-49; see Goodenough, *Symbols*, 2:203.

43. M. Smith, *Jesus*, p. 114.

44. Ibid.

45. See John Chrysostom's *Homily 1: Against the Jews* and his *Homily 8: Against the Jews*; see our more lengthy treatment below, chapter 6.

46. See J. Neusner, *From Politics to Piety* (Garden City: Prentice-Hall, 1973); see Josephus, *Wars*, 2:162ff; *Antiquities* 13:171ff; 18:11ff.

47. See J. Neusner, *A History of the Jews in Babylonia*, 5:185ff. See also J. Trachtenberg, *Jewish Magic*.

48. See b. Berakot 6a, 43a–b, 63b; see also J. Trachtenberg, *Jewish Magic*, pp. 44ff; see J. Neusner, *A History of the Jews in Babylonia*, 5:334ff.

49. See above, n.25.

50. J. Neusner, *Judaism: the Evidence of the Mishnah* (Chicago: University of Chicago Press, 1981).

51. Or its relegation to the realm of mind, utopia.

52. See M. Douglas, *Purity and Danger* (London: Routledge, 1966); M. Douglas, "Polution," *Encyclopaedia of the Social Sciences* (1968).

53. J. Z. Smith, "Towards Interpreting Demonic Powers in Hellenistic and Roman Antiquity," *ANRW*, Series II 16.1.

54. See above, nn. 47 and 25.

55. With reference to our typology of shamanistic versus anthropo-systemic modes of sacred place, I here make no claims that systems of uncleanness correlate with the latter, although laws of uncleanness may be put to good use within anthropo-systemic contexts. Indeed this seems the case in the Deuteronomic-Priestly cult of the Second Commonwealth. But this is not to suggest either that systems of uncleanness in Ancient Israel arose within that context. Uncleanness is equally consistent with a cult conceived in shamanistic terms, as our discussion in chapter 3 will indicate.

56. In chapter 5.

3. The Dead and Their Tombs

1. L. Rothkrug, "The Odour of Sanctity and the Hebrew Origins of Christian Relic Veneration," *Historical Reflections* 8 (1981): 95–142; throughout I am ever again indebted to Prof. Rothkrug's insightful comments in numerous conversations.

2. See S. Spiegel, *The Last Trial* (New York: Schocken, 1969) for a treatment of the history of exegetical-midrashic traditions pertaining to the binding of Isaac (Genesis 18).

3. See A. F. Segal, "Heavenly Ascent in Hellenistic Judaism," *ANRW*, series II 23:2.

4. See M. Stone, *Scriptures, Sects and Visions* (Philadelphia: Fortress, 1981); see especially his bibliography of recent scholarship on the early Enochic literature.

5. See the Appendix.

6. See Josephus, *Wars* 5:18–19 f; Antiquities XV 280 f; see also Josephus, *Wars* 4:532 and M. Middot. The architectural similarity of the Herodian Temple and the Mausoleum at Hebron was demonstrated by M. Avi-Yonah on the basis of archaeological finds *cum* available literary evidence; See S. Safrai and M. Stern "The Temple," *EJ* 15:959ff; M. Avi-Yonah, *Sefer Yerushalayim*, 1 (Jerusalem, 1956) and Avi-Yonah's article in J. Neusner, ed., *Religions in Antiquity: Essays in Memory of E. R. Goodenough* (Leiden: Brill, 1968).

7. See J. Braslavi, "The Cave of Mahpela," *EJ* 11:670ff; M. HaKohen, *The Cave of Mahpela in Text and Traditions* (in Hebrew) (Tel Aviv, 1965); O. Avisar, ed., *Sefer Hevron* (Jerusalem, 1970).

8. See M. Hadas, *Hellenistic Culture* (New York: Columbia University Press, 1959); J. Z. Smith, "Map Is Not Territory," in J. Z. Smith, *Map Is Not Territory* (Leiden: Brill, 1978); See also J. E. Stambaugh; "The Function of Roman Temples," *ANRW*, series II 16.1:610–54.

9. b. Sanhedrin 47b; See J. Neusner, *A History of the Jews in Babylonia*, 2:143–44.

10. See J. Neusner, *A History of the Jews in Babylonia*, 2:147–48; 3: 102–25; and 5:169–89.

11. See b. Sanhedrin 47a–47b; see also b. Avodah Zarah 29b.

12. See E. Bickerman, "Les Maccabees de Malalas," in *Studies in Jewish and Christian History*, vol. 2 (Leiden: Brill, 1980).

13. As in the narrative of I Samuel 1.

14. See above, n.12.

15. D. Zlotnick, ed., *Maseket Semahot, the Tractate Mourning* (New Haven: Yale University Press, 1966).

16. See P. Brown, *The Cult of Saints* (Chicago: University of Chicago Press, 1981); L. Rothkrug, "Religious Practices and Collective Perceptions: Hidden Homologies in the Renaissance and Reformation," *Historical Reflections* 7 (1980).

17. See P. Brown, *The World of Late Antiquity* (New York: Harcourt, 1971), p. 62; H. Lietzmann, *A History of the Early Church: The Era of the Church Fathers*, vol. 5 (London: Lutterworth, 1951), p. 128; E. Rhode, *Psyche* (London: Kegan Paul, 1925), p. 196, n.87; M. Avot 3:3; J. M. C. Toynbee, *Death and Burial in the Roman World* (Ithaca: Cornell University Press, 1971).

18. See Exodus 30:22ff: Leviticus 2:1–2, 4–5; 6:19–20; 7:11–12: Numbers 28:29: See J. Neusner, *A History of the Mishnaic Law of Holy Things*, vol. 5 (Leiden: Brill, 1980); See also J. Neusner, *From Politics to Piety* (Englewood Cliffs, N.J.: Prentice Hall, 1973). See also J. Neusner, "Emergent Rabbinic Judaism in a Time of Crisis," *Judaism* 21.3 (1972): 313–27.

19. See, for example, F. Cumont, *Oriental Religions in Roman Paganism* (New York: Dover, 1956), pp. 68–69. See also R. Reitzenstein, *Hellenistic Mystery Religions* (Pittsburgh: Pickwick, 1978); A. D. Nock, "Early Gentile Christianity," in Z. Stewart, ed., *A. D. Nock: Essays on Religion and the Ancient World* (Cambridge: Harvard University Press, 1972).

20. See S. Lieberman, "Some Aspects of the Afterlife in Early Rabbinic Literature," in *H. A. Wolfson Jubilee Volume* (Jerusalem, 1965), p. 11.

21. In line with Judah's dictum in 8:2, the latter half of 8:2 lists foods "unfit for food," which may be hung from the canopy of the deceased young adults. The "general rule," cited at the end of 8:2, presumably is intended by the redactor to express the principle operative in the immediately foregoing statements; one may not derive benefit from the foodstuffs so hung on the canopy of the deceased (and thereby rendered unclean). Zlotnick (following the traditional exegetes) accordingly reinterprets Judah in light of the general rule; Judah would not have usable food deliberately rendered forbidden by having it hung on a funeral canopy. Judah, presumably, does not condone waste.

Judah's ruling and the subsequent lists, however, in no way appear instances of the general rule. How one may deduce the use of only foodstuffs unfit for food directly from the general rule seems unclear at best and impossible at worst. If, moreover, the foodstuffs will have been rendered unclean (as the commentators maintain), then one need not be told that it is forbidden to derive benefit from the food, if one's intentions are to limit matters to what is "unfit as food" and so avoid wanton waste. In sum, the appeal of Zlotnick and others to the notion of not (deliberately) wasting commodities essentially provides an alternative general rule to that in the text, and thus logically tightens up the pericope. In point of fact Judah's ruling and the subsequent lists appear independent of the general rule, the substance of which stands as a separate injunction. The phrase "and the general rule is" functions as joining language. But the reason for using only foodstuffs unfit for food now seems once more an open question. In this regard, 8:3 taken in conjunction with Judah and the lists will prove enlightening.

According to Zlotnick (again following classical commentators), the brides and bridegrooms of 8:3 are now living persons, not deceased young adults. He is forced into this position because so wasting foodstuffs by strewing them on the open ground, as 8:3 permits, contravenes 8:2 as generally interpreted. But 8:3 bears considerable resemblance to Judah and the lists of 8:2, with issues of waste, derivation of benefit and uncleanness aside. Just as food strewn on the ground during the dry season will not quickly spoil, so unripened food will not quickly decompose. 8:2 (Judah and the lists) and 8:3 may be seen as one in intention.

22. B. Goldman, *The Sacred Portal* (Detroit: Wayne State University Press, 1966).

23. E. M. Meyers, *Jewish Ossuaries: Reburial and Rebirth* (Rome: Pontifical Institute, 1971); Semahot 12, 13; Matthew 27:55ff; Mark 16:46; Luke 24:53ff; John 19:38ff; see also E. R. Goodenough, *Symbols*, vols. 1, 6, 12 and 2: 3–69.

24. M. Ohalot 1:1ff; J. Neusner, *A History of the Mishnaic Law of Purities*, parts 4, 5 (Leiden: Brill, 1975).

25. See M. Avot 2:7; and in somewhat later sources: Tanhuma Bereshit 38, ed. Buber; see also W. D. Davies, *Paul and Rabbinic Judaism*, 2nd edition (London: SPCR, 1955), pp. 17–36; see also Avot deR. Nathan 2:16, ed. Schechter, version A.

26. H. Lietzmann, *History of the Early Church, Vol. 5, Era of the Church Fathers*, pp. 128–29; F. Cumont, *Oriental Religions*, pp. 40–41, 50–51, 157; P. Brown, *World of Late Antiquity*, pp. 96–109.

27. See the Appendix and chapter 2.

28. In this regard some significance, no doubt, accrues to sprinkling herbs on the bones at ossilegium, a practice well attested in Late Antique rabbinic circles. (See Semahot 12:13, ed. Zlotnick.) Whatever the function or significance of anointing the corpse immediately before the first burial with spices and the like, in the case of ossilegium, attempting to deodorize the remains cannot be the issue. One is tempted to see in this rite a symbolic statement that the excarnate deceased is now acceptable to God. This follows in the long-established tradition in Israelite circles that sacrifices were acceptable to the deity, when properly performed, because of their "pleasant odor." Indeed by

later biblical times (circa the 5th century BCE) the syllogism was effectively reversed, and having a "pleasant odor" simply meant "performed appropriately so as to be an efficacious sacrifice." This appears not unrelated to notions in early medieval Christianity in which the sign of sainthood was the sweet odor of the saint's bones, as Rothkrug remarks in his "Odour of Sanctity," *Historical Reflections*, 8 (1981).

29. See E.M. Meyers, *Jewish Ossuaries*; B. Goldman, *Sacred Portal*; E.R. Goodenough, *Symbols*, 12 and 2:3–69.

30. See Goodenough, *Symbols*, 12.

31. See again A.F. Segal, "Heavenly Ascent," and our discussion of Philo in the Appendix.

CHAPTER 4: THE LIFE OF TORAH IN THE DIASPORA

1. Such is the background assumed by Cicero in Pro Flaccum.

2. As, for example, in Epistle to the Hebrews.

3. See M. Hadas' discussion in *Hellenistic Culture: Fusion and Diffusion* (New York: Columbia University Press, 1939), pp. 114–29.

4. Seneca, *De Superstitione*, cited in M. Stern, *Greek and Latin Authors*, 1:431ff.

5. See below, pp. 105–6. Further remarks regarding Sabbath observance are attributed to Meleager (Stern, *Greek and Latin Authors*, 1:140), Agatharchides of Cnidus (Stern, *Greek and Latin Authors*, 1:107), and Apion (Stern, *Greek and Latin Authors*, 1:396).

6. Such as II Mac. 1–4.

7. For example, Acts, Romans, Galatians, to name just a few.

8. Timagenes (Stern, *Greek and Latin Authors*, 1:225); Diodorus (Stern, *Greek and Latin Authors*, 1:169, 171); Ptolemy the Historian (Stern, *Greek and Latin Authors*, 1:356); Apion (Stern, *Greek and Latin Authors*, 1:415); Strabo of Amaseia (Stern, *Greek and Latin Authors*, 1: 12); Horace (Stern, *Greek and Latin Authors*, 1: 325); Martial (Stern, *Greek and Latin Authors*, 1:525).

9. See the discussion of the evidence and of the confusion arising therefrom in M. Smallwood, *The Jews under Roman Rule* (Leiden: Brill, 1976), pp. 465ff.

10. See I Mac. 1:15; Jubilees 15:33f.

11. See above, n.7.

12. On the "pagan" practice of "Judaism," see as well remarks by Valerius Maximus (Stern, *Greek and Latin Authors*, 1:359).

13. As intimated in our introduction these issues will receive more sustained treatment in chapters 7 and 8.

14. Stern, *Greek and Latin Authors*, 1:441.

15. See above, n.7.

16. See above, n.3.

*17. See Chrysostom's *Homily 1, Against the Jews, Patrologia Graeca* 48.843–56; see W. Meeks and R. Wilken, *Jews and Christians in Antioch in the First Four Centuries of the Common Era* (Missoula: Scholars, 1978), pp. 85–104.

18. In chapter 6.

19. See J. Neusner, "Emergent Rabbinic Judaism in a Time of Crisis," *Judaism*, 1972; M. Black, *Temple and Community at Qumran* (London: Oxford, 1965).

20. See with regard to the priestly "Watches" the summary article by J. Liver and D. Sperber, "Mishmarot and Ma'amadot," *EJ*, 12:89ff.

21. Cited above in chapter 2, pp. 19–20.

22. An issue discussed more fully below, chapter 5, pp. 115ff.

23. M. Hadas, *Aristeas to Philocrates* (New York: Harper, 1951), reprinted (New York: Ktav, 1973).

24. See not only Josephus' introduction to his *Antiquities* but also his summary version of the same at the beginning of *Against Apion*.

25. See M. Berakot 2:1; M. Megilah 3:4ff; 4:4–10.

26. Again, we shall discuss these issues at length in our consideration of the nature and role of the synagogue (chapter 5).

27. For example, see Esther 7; Megilat Ta'anit, ed. Lewin; M. Ta'anit certainly assumes considerable use of fasting prior to its own earliest (Yavnean) stratum.

28. Cited in M. Stern, *Greek and Latin Authors*, 1:521ff. Without ruling out the possibility that Martial refers to some "non-Jewish" Yahwehistic cult and not to the practice of Jews, the passage still attests to the association of Jews and their Sabbath with fasting in the minds of Greek and Latin authors. On a cult of the Sabbatians or Sambations, see the essay by the latter title by V. Tcherikover in V. Tcherikover and A. Fuks, *Corpus Papyrorum Judaicarum*, vol. 3 (Cambridge: Harvard University Press, 1964).

29. See above, n.28.

30. See above, n.27.

31. In the later Amoraic document by the same name, Megilat Ta'anit, ed. Lewin.

32. *Homily 1, Against the Jews, Patrologia Graeca* 48:844–45; *Homily 8, Against the Jews, Patrologia Graeca* 48:928, 935; in Meeks and Wllken, *Jews and Christians in Antioch*, pp. 86, 115.

33. As to their meaning within the larger picture of things, we wait until our consideration of the Synagogue, below in chapter 5.

34. To be treated at greater length in chapters 7 and 8.

35. See below, chapter 5, pp. 79ff.

36. Again these distinctions will be more fully discussed and defended below in chapter 8.

37. In conversation with the author.

CHAPTER 5: THE SYNAGOGUE

1. J. Gutmann, ed., "The Synagogue: Studies in Origins," in his *Archaeology and Architecture* (New York: Ktav, 1975); see also J. Gutmann, *Ancient Synagogues* (Chico: Scholars, 1981).

2. In inscriptions cited by V. Tcherikover and A. Fuks, *Corpus Papyrum Judaicarum*, vol. 3 (Cambridge: Harvard University Press, 1964).

3. For the midrashic tradition on Ezekiel 11:16, see A. Hyman, *Torah Ha-Ketuvah VeHamesorah* (Tel Aviv: Dvir, 1936), 2:228; b. Megilah 29a.

4. The first clear references are those of Philo concerning the *proseuche*; see *Legatio*, 132; Contra *Flaccum*, 48–53.

*5. Throughout the New Testament (e.g., Gospels and Acts) and patristic literature (e.g., John Chrysostom, *Homily 1, Against the Jews, Patrologia Graeca* 48:846ff; trans. in Meeks and Wilken, *Jews and Christians in Antioch*, pp. 88–89).

6. See J. B. Frey, *Corpus Inscriptionum Judaicarum*, 2 vols. (Rome: Pontifical Institute, 1936–52), reprinted with addenda, ed. B. Lischitz (New York: Ktav, 1975) .

7. See A. T. Kraabel, "The Diaspora Synagogue: Archaeological and Epigraphic Evidence," *ANRW*, series II 19.1:477–510.

8. See A. T. Kraabel, "The Diaspora Synagogue."

9. See J. Gutmann, *Ancient Synagogues*; Philo as cited above, n.4; inscriptions in Frey, n.6; See also M. Smallwood, *The Jews Under Roman Rule* (Leiden: Brill, 1975).

10. On the issue of the Jewish community and *politeuma*, see, for example, V. Tcherikover, *Hellenistic Civilization and the Jews* (New York: Atheneum, 1970), pp. 296ff; M. Smallwood, *The Jews Under Roman Rule*, pp. 138ff. See also V. Tcherikover, *HaYehudim-BeMizrayim Le'Or HaPapyrusim* (Jerusalem: Hebrew University, 1945).

11. Equally attested by evidence from early Christian sources, among others, referred to above, n.5.

12. See above, n.4.

13. See discussion in previous chapter, cf. chapter 4, n.25.

14. See references in Acts as given in chapter 1, n.22.

15. Again, both in *Homily 1, Against the Jews* and *Homily 8, Against the Jews*.

16. See chapter 4, pp. 70ff.

17. The separation of men and women, if it transpired in the early synagogues at all, is in no way sufficient to effect such an anthropo-systemic order.

18. A. T. Kraabel, "The Diaspora Synagogue," p. 502.

19. B. Goldman, *The Sacred Portal* (Detroit: Wayne State University Press, 1966).

20. See above, chapter 3, pp. 60ff.

21. See B. Goldman, *The Sacred Portal*, pp. 69–100. See also E. R. Goodenough, *Symbols*, 2:70–99.

22. A conclusion shared by Goldman, *Sacred Portal*; Goodenough, *Symbols*, 12.

23. A virtually uncontested claim, to my knowledge. Goodenough, however, has expressed some doubts in particular cases; see Goodenough, *Symbols*, 12:194ff. I am inclined to view his objections as tendentious, for the cult objects that at times he would rather place in the niches seem to come from no evidence, but rather from his own particular hypothesis regarding a Hellenistic Jewish mystery.

*24. John Chrysostom, *Homily 1, Against the Jews, Patrologia Graeca* 48:847–48; trans. in W. Meeks and R. Wilken, *Jews and Christians in Antioch* (Missoula: Scholars Press, 1978), pp. 90–91.

*25. John Chrysostom, *Homily 8, Against the Jews, Patrologia Graeca* 48:935ff; trans. in, Meeks and Wilken, *Jews and Christians*, pp. 116 f.

26. See passage cited above, chapter 4, pp. 72f.

27. E. Bickermann, "Les Maccabees de Malalas," in E. Bickermann, *Studies in Jewish and Christian History*, vol. 2 (Leiden: Brill, 1980).

28. See above, n.5.

29. The actual text of Pentateuchal injunctions being, of course, the major exception; see the introduction in J. Neusner, *Judaism: The Evidence of the Mishnah* (Chicago: University of Chicago Press, 1981).

30. See T. Zahavy, *History of the Mishnaic Law of Agriculture: Berakot* (Chico: Scholars Press, 1982).

31. For exemplars of the method applied elsewhere in the Mishnaic corpus, see J. Neusner, *Judaism: Evidence of the Mishnah* and J. Neusner, *A History of the Mishnaic Law of Purities*, 22 (Leiden: Brill, 1978). Cf. J. Heinemann, *Prayer in the Talmud* (Berlin: De Gruyter, 1981).

32. See above, chapter 4, pp. 72f.

33. As the discussion in M. Berakot 1 and related *gemarot* of b. and y. Berakot show, whether or not the evening *shema*ʿ needed to be recited was not a moot issue in early rabbinic literature.

34. In chapter 2.

CHAPTER 6: THE SYNAGOGUE AND THE CHURCH

1. I do not wish to overstate my qualifiers either. In showing, as I hope to do, that considerable interaction at various levels transpired between Gentile Christianity and Hellenistic Judaism from the first to fourth centuries, there seems a strong *prima facie* case for maintaining some causal relationship between the groups where close parallels of structure and content exist. Nevertheless, the same sociological facts make plausible a rather more complex view of "borrowings" than is normally supposed. Given the close, almost symbiotic, relationship between the two groups, our models of mutual influence ought to be open to equally complex tradental processes. Each group, moreover, shared a common cultural milieu in the larger Hellenistic context, reacting to that context no doubt with an eye to how its "sister" group managed the same. It is this complexity of cultural fusion and diffusion that Goodenough implicitly failed to recognize in seeing the necessity of an antecedent Judaic mystery as a precursor to Christianity. See E.R. Goodenough, *Symbols*, vol. 12, Introduction. In reality, while I cannot assent to Goodenough's thesis—as indeed I have explained at the beginning of chapter 2—the dependence of Christianity upon Hellenistic Judaism probably obtained considerably longer than Goodenough would have supposed and in ways he has not spelled out, a dependence of two closely related groups whose sociological boundaries were often blurred along their common boundaries.

2. See Galatians, Romans and Acts 15 concerning the Pauline-Jerusalem controversy over circumcision.

3. Acts 15; Galatians 2.

4. John Chrysostom, *Homily 8, Against the Jews, Patrologia Graeca* 48:940–41; trans. in W. Meeks and R. Wilken, *Jews and Christians in Antioch in the First Four Centuries of the Common Era* (Missoula: Scholars Press, 1978), pp. 123–24.

5. See above, chapter 2, pp. 13ff.

6. T. Hullin 2:221; see also M. Smith, *Jesus the Magician* (New York: Harper and Row, 1977), p. 48; J. Lauterbach, "Jesus in the Talmud and Midrash" in his *Rabbinic Essays* (Cincinnati: Hebrew Union College, 1951), reprinted (New York: Ktav, 1975).

6. *The Synagogue and the Church*

7. E. R. Goodenough, *Symbols*, 2:138.

8. *Didaschalia Apostolorum*, ed. and trans., R.H. Connolly,

9. Ibid.

10. One might extend our evidence to include Barnabas; Revelations 2:9; 3:9; *Apology of Aristides*; Justyn Martyr's *Dialogue with Trypho*.

11. See H. Lietzmann, *Mass and the Lord's Supper* (Leiden: Brill, 1979).

12. Acts 12:26. See W. Meeks and R. Wilken, *Jews and Christians*, pp. 13ff.

CHAPTER 7: CHRISTIANS, JEWS, AND RABBIS

1. See G. F. Moore, "The Definition of the Jewish Canon and the Repudiation of Christian Scriptures," in C.A. Briggs, ed., *Testimonial: Essays in Modern Theology* (New York, 1911), reprinted in S.D. Leiman, ed., *Canon and Masorah in the Hebrew Bible* (New York: Ktav, 1974); L. Ginzberg, "Some Observations on the Attitude of the Synagogue Towards Apocalyptic-Eschatological Writings," *Journal of Biblical Literature* 41 (1922), reprinted in Leiman, *Canon and Masorah*; J. Bloch, "Outside Books," *M. Kaplan Jubilee Volume* (New York, 1953), reprinted in Leiman, ed., *Canon and Masorah*; J. Lauterbach, "Jesus in the Talmud," in J. Lauterbach, *Rabbinic Essays* (Cincinnati: Hebrew Union College, 1951), reprinted (New York: Ktav, 1975).

2. E. Bickermann, "Les Maccabees de Malalas," in E. Bickermann, *Studies in Jewish and Christian History*, vol. 2 (Leiden: Brill, 1980), pp. 200ff

3. See H. Lietzmann, *Mass and the Lord's Supper* (Leiden: Brill, 1979).

4. Again, see Lietzmann, *Mass*; see also the editor's introduction to the *Didaschalia Apostolorum*, ed. Connolly.

5. See, for example, P. Brown, *The Cult of the Saints* (Chicago: University of Chicago, 1981). Further on the organization of the early Church, see H. Lietzmann, *A History of the Early Church*, Vol. 5, *The Era of the Church Fathers* (London: Lutterworth, 1951).

6. See *Didache* 8:1, ed. C. Richardson, p. 174; *Didaschalia Apostolorum*, ed. Connolly. See also *The Apostolic Tradition of Hippolytus*, 1:11, ed. B.S. Easton (London: Cambridge University, 1934), p. 40. See also Ibid. 3:25, 29.

7. *Didaschalia Apostolorum*, ed. Connolly.

8. See P. Brown, *Cult of the Saints* and L. Rothkrug, "Odour of Sanctity," *Historical Reflections*, 8 (1981).

9. Thus, as Brown argues in his introduction to *Cult of the Saints*, the episcopate assimilated to itself the power of the relics in order to consolidate and enhance power in the hands of the bishops.

10. See my discussion and notes in "The Culture of the Study of Cultures," in W. S. Green, ed., *Approaches to the Study of Ancient Judaism*, vol. 5 (Chico: Scholars Press, 1984).

11. See J. Neusner, *There We Sat Down* (New York: Abingdon, 1972), pp. 72–97; see also J. Neusner, *A History of the Jews in Babylonia*, vols. 4–5 (Leiden: Brill, 1968–70).

12. See previous note and also J. Neusner, "Rabbi as Holy Man," in J. Neusner, *Early Rabbinic Judaism* (Leiden: Brill, 1977).

13. See Appendix, n.14.

14. I Corinthians 12:1ff.

15. See Chapter 3, n.9.

16. See J. Z. Smith, "Map Is Not Territory," and "Temple and Magician," in J. Z. Smith, *Map Is Not Territory* (Leiden: Brill, 1978).

17. Or, alternatively, failed as of yet to define its rabbis as Holy Men in the Late Antique mode.

18. See J. Neusner, *From Politics to Piety* (Englewood: Prentice-Hall, 1972).

19. See J. Neusner, *The Rabbinic Traditions about the Pharisees Before 70*, vol. 1 (Leiden: Brill, 1971).

20. See S. Lieberman, *Greek in Jewish Palestine* (New York: Jewish Theological Seminary of America, 1947).

21. See Leiman, *Canon and Masorah* (New York: Ktav, 1973), and his *Canonization of Hebrew Scriptures* (New York: Ktav, 1973); see also my "Development of the Biblical Canon in Late Antique Judaism: Prolegomenon to a General Reassessment," *Studies in Religion* 8 (1979).

22. See J. Neusner, *Judaism: The Evidence of the Mishnah* (Chicago: University of Chicago Press, 1981). With respect to the observations about Mishnah adduced below, see also J. Neusner, *A History of the Mishnaic Law of Purities*, Part 21 (Leiden: Brill, 1978).

23. J. Neusner, *A History of the Mishnaic Law of Holy Things*, vol. 5 (Leiden: Brill, 1979), introduction.

24. b. Berakot 8a; see also b. Berakot 7b and J. Neusner, "Transcendence and Worship Through Learning: The Religious World-View of Mishnah," *Journal of Reform Judaism* 25 (1978): 15–29.

25. See S. Lieberman, *Greek in Jewish Palestine* and M. Smallwood, *The Jews Under Roman Rule* (Leiden: Brill, 1975).

26. For a more detailed discussion in this regard see my "Form as Meaning, Structure as Ethos: The Case for the Halakic Midrashim," *Semeia* 25 (1983).

27. In J. Z. Smith's "Map Is Not Territory."

28. See, for example, my *Yose the Galilean: Traditions in Mishnah-Tosefta* (Leiden: Brill, 1979), introduction.

CHAPTER EIGHT: CONCLUSIONS

1. See P. Brown, *The Cult of the Saints* (Chicago: University of Chicago Press, 1981).

2. See J. Z. Smith, "Temple and Magician," in J. Z. Smith, *Map Is Not Territory* (Leiden: Brill, 1978); see also J. Z. Smith's "Map Is Not Territory" in the same.

3. E. Bickermann, "Les Maccabees de Malalas," in E. Bickermann, *Studies in Jewish and Christian History*, vol. 2 (Leiden: Brill, 1980).

4. M. Douglas, "Self-Evidence," in M. Douglas, *Implicit Meanings* (London: Routledge, 1975).

5. M. Douglas, *Purity and Danger* (London: Routledge, 1966); see also P. Berger and H. Luckmann, *The Social Construction of Reality* (New York: Penguin, 1966).

6. See Douglas, "Deciphering a Meal" and "Self-Evidence" in *Implicit Meanings*. This notion of the plausibility of cultural knowledge as based in homologous relationships across subsystems of a culture seems not unrelated as well to claims by C. Geertz in "Religion as a Cultural System," M. Banton, ed., *Anthropological Approaches to the Study of Religion* (London: Tavistock, 1966). Geertz talks about religions providing a "way of life" rendered "reasonable" in the light of a particular world-view, while the latter is made "emotionally convincing" in that it is an "image" of a state of affairs "peculiarly well arranged to accommodate such a way of life" (p. 3).

7. And, I would add, which finds a more elaborated justification in M. Douglas, *Natural Symbols* (London: Barrie and Jenkins, 1970; 2nd ed., 1973).

8. On demons as anomalous creatures see numerous references in P. Brown, *The Making of Late Antiquity* (Cambridge: Harvard University Press, 1978); J. Z. Smith points out that demons in Late Antiquity were believed to inhabit graveyards, wild places, crossroads, ruins, and the like, all areas of ambiguous character; see his "Toward Interpreting Demonic Powers," *ANRW* series II, 16.1:425–39.

APPENDIX: PHILO

1. See, for example, C. K. Barrett, *The New Testament Background* (New York: Harper and Row, 1961); R. Bultmann, *Primitive Christianity in Its Contemporary Setting* (New York: Meridian, 1956).

2. J. Williamson, *Philo and the Epistle to the Hebrews* (Leiden: Brill, 1971).

3. Goodenough, *Light.*

4. Ibid., p. 7.

5. See A.D. Nock, "The Question of Jewish Mysteries," *Gnomon* 13 (1937): 156–65.

6. See R. Reitzenstein, *Hellenistic Mystery Religions* (Philadelphia: Pickwick, 1978); A.D. Nock, *Conversion* (Oxford: Clarendon, 1933); A.D. Nock, "Hellenistic Mysteries and Christian Sacraments," *Mnemosyne* 5 (1952).

7. Nock, "The Question of Jewish Mysteries."

8. See Philo, *On Creation; Allegorical Interpretations; Special Laws*; all of the former, virtually in their entirety, evince this endeavor.

9. Nock, "The Question of Jewish Mysteries," p. 157.

10. This and all subsequent citations from Philo are rendered from the Loeb Classical Library edition, H. Colson, et al., trans. and eds. (Cambridge and London: Harvard University Press and Heinneman, 1929–62), or from R. Marcus, trans. and ed., *Philo: Questions and Answers on Exodus* (Cambridge and London: Harvard University Press and Heinnemann, 1953).

11. See the account of H. A. Wolfson, *Philo* (Cambridge: Harvard University Press, 1947), 1: 226–52.

12. See A.F. Segal, "Heavenly Ascent in Christianity, Judaism and Hellenistic Religions," *ANRW* series II, 23:2.

13. II Corinthians 12:1ff

14. See G.G. Scholem, *Major Trends in Jewish Mysticism* (New York: Schocken, 1941), chapter 2; G.G. Scholem, *Jewish Gnosticism, Merkabah Mysticism and the Talmudic Tradition* (New York: Jewish Theological Seminary of America, 1965); M. Smith, "Some Observations on *Hekalot Rabbati*," in A. Altman, ed., *Biblical and Other Studies* (Cambridge: Harvard University Press, 1963), pp. 142–60; Peter Schaefer, *Hekalot Rabbati: Introduction and Synoptic Text* (Leiden: Brill, 1982); I. Gruenwald, *Apocalyptic in Merkavah Mysticism* (Leiden: Brill, 1980).

15. See discussion of Philo's attitude to flesh vs. excarnate bones in L. Rothkrug, "Odour of Sanctity and the Hebrew Origins of Relic Worship," *Historical Reflections* 8 (1981): 95–142.

16. Ibid., p. 111.

Selected Bibliography

UPDATED BY HERBERT W. BASSER WITH FURTHER ADDITIONS
FROM THE FOREWORD BY WILLI BRAUN

Adorno, Theodor W. *Jargon der Eigentlichkeit: Zur deutschen Ideologie.* Frankfurt: Suhrkamp, 1964. English translation, *The Jargon of Authenticity.* Trans. by Knut Tarnowski and Frederic Will. Evanston: Northwestern University Press, 1973.

Arnal, William E. "Making and Re-Making the Jesus-Sign: Contemporary Markings on the Body of Christ." In William E. Arnal and Michel Desjardins, eds., *Whose Historical Jesus?* pp. 308–19. Studies in Christianity and Judaism/Études sur le christianisme et le judaïsme, vol. 7. Waterloo, Ontario: Wilfrid Laurier University Press, 1997.

——. *The Symbolic Jesus: Historical Scholarship, Judaism and the Construction of Contemporary Identity.* Religion in Culture. London: Equinox, 2005.

Aune, D. E. "Magic in Early Christianity," *ANRW* series II, 23.2 (1980): 1507–57.

Avisar, O., ed. *Sefer Hevron.* Jerusalem, 1970.

Avi-Yonah, M. *Bimei Roman U-Bizantiyum.* Jerusalem: Mosad Bialik, 1970.

——. *Hellenism and the East: Contacts and Interrelations from Alexander to the Roman Conquest.* Jerusalem: Magnes, 1978.

——. *Sefer Yerushalayim.* Vol. 1. Jerusalem: Magnes, 1956.

——. "The Temple." In *EJ* 15:959 ff.

Barrett, C. K. "Jews and Judaizers in the Epistles of Ignatius." In R. Hamerton-Kelly and R. Scroggs, eds., *Jews, Greeks, and Christians: Religious Cultures in Late Antiquity.* Leiden: E. J. Brill, 1976.

Barth, Fredrik. "An Anthropology of Knowledge." *Current Anthropology* 43 (2002): 1–18.

Baudrillard, Jean. "La réversion de l'histoire." In *L'Illusion de la fin: Ou la greve des evenements*, pp. 23–27. Paris: Galilée, 1992; English translation, *The Illusion of the End*. Trans. by Chris Turner. Stanford: Stanford University Press, 1994.

——. *Simulacres et Simulation*. Collection Débats. Paris: Galilée, 1981; English translation, *Simulacra and Simulation*. Trans. by Sheila Faria Glaser. Ann Arbor: University of Michigan Press, 1994.

Beckner, Morton. *The Biological Way of Thought*. New York: Columbia University Press, 1959.

Betz, H.D., ed. *The Greek Magical Papyri*. Vol. 1: *Texts*. Chicago: University of Chicago Press, 1986.

Bickerman(n), Elias. *The Jews in the Greek Age*. Cambridge: Harvard University Press, 1988.

——. *Studies in Jewish and Christian History*. 2 Vols. Leiden: E.J. Brill, 1980.

Bloch, J. "Outside Books." In *Mordecai M. Kaplan Jubilee Volume*. New York, 1953. Reprinted in S.D. Leiman, *Canon and Massorah of the Hebrew Bible*. New York: Ktav, 1974.

Bowker, Geoffrey C. and Susan Leigh Star. *Sorting Things Out: Classification and Its Consequences*. Cambridge: MIT Press, 1999.

Boyarin, Daniel. *Dying for God: Martyrdom and the Making of Christianity and Judaism*. Stanford: Stanford University Press, 1999.

Braslavi, J. "The Cave of Mahpelah." In *EJ* 11:670 ff.

Braun, Willi. "Religion." In Willi Braun and Russell McCutcheon, eds., *Guide to the Study of Religion*. London: Cassell, 2000, pp. 3–18.

——. "The Past as Simulacrum in the Canonical Narratives of Christian Origins." *Religion and Theology* 8 (2001): 213–28.

——. "The Schooling of a Galilean Jesus Association (The Sayings Gospel Q)." In Cameron and Miller, eds., *Redescribing Christian Origins*, pp. 43–65.

Brown, P. *The World of Late Antiquity*. New York: Harcourt, 1971.

——. *The Cult of the Saints*. Chicago: University of Chicago Press, 1981.

——. *Society and the Holy in Late Antiquity*. New York: Faber, 1982.

Burkert, Walter. *Greek Religion*. Translated from the German by John Raffan, 1977. Cambridge: Harvard University Press, 1985.

Cameron, Ron. "Alternate Beginnings—Different Ends: Eusebius, Thomas, and the Construction of Christian Origins." In Lukas Borman, Kelly Del Tredici, and Angela Standhartinger, eds., *Religious Propaganda and Missionary Competition in the New Testament World: Essays Honoring Dieter Georgi* Novum Testamentum Supplements 74. Leiden: Brill, 1994, pp. 501–25.

Cameron, Ron and Merrill P. Miller, eds., *Redescribing Christian Origins*. SBL Symposium Series 28. Atlanta: Society of Biblical Literature, 2004.

Bibliography

Chadwick, H. *The Early Church* (London: Penguin-Pelican, 1967).

Charlesworth, James H., ed. *Old Testament Pseudepigrapha*. Vol. 1. Garden City: Doubleday, 1983.

Childs, B. S. *Introduction to the Old Testament as Scripture*. Philadelphia: Fortress, 1979.

Cohen, Shaye. *The Beginnings of Jewishness: Boundaries, Varieties, Uncertainties*. Berkeley: University of California Press, 1999.

Collins, John J. *Seers, Sibyls, and Sages in Hellenistic-Roman Judaism*. Leiden: Brill, 2001.

——. *The Apocalyptic Imagination: An Introduction to Jewish Apocalyptic Literature*, 2nd ed. Biblical Resource Series; Grand Rapids: William B. Eerdmans, 1998; [1984].

Conzelmann, Hans. "Part I. The Political Background," "Part II. The Evaluation of Judaism in Greco-Roman Literature," and "Part III. The Debate of Hellenistic Judaism Within the Hellenistic-Roman World." In *Gentiles, Jews, Christians: Debates in the Literature of the Hellenistic-Roman Era*. Trans. M. Eugene Boring, Minneapolis: Augsburg Fortress, 1992; German original Tübingen: J.C.B. Mohr [Paul Siebeck] 1981.

Court, John M. and Dan Cohn-Sherbok, eds., *Religious Diversity in the Greco-Roman World: A Survey of Recent Scholarship*. Sheffield: Sheffield Academic Press, 2001.

Cumont, F. *Oriental Religions in Roman Paganism*. New York: Dover, 1956.

Davies, W. D. *Paul and Rabbinic Judaism*. 2nd ed. London: SPCK, 1955.

Dickie, Matthew W. *Magic and Magicians in the Greco-Roman World*. London: Routledge, 2001.

Douglas, M. *Purity and Danger*. London: Routledge, 1966.

——. *Natural Symbols*. 2nd ed. London: Barrie and Jenkins, 1973 [1970].

——. *Implicit Meanings*. London: Routledge, 1975.

——. *Cultural Bias*. London: Royal Anthropological Society, 1981.

Feldman, Louis H. *Jew and Gentile in the Ancient World: Attitudes and Interactions from Alexander to Justinian*. Princeton: Princeton University Press, 1993.

Frey, Jean-Baptiste. *Corpus Inscriptionum Judaicarum*. 2 Vols. Rome: Pontifico Instituto di Archeologia Cristiana, 1936-52. Reprinted with Addenda by B. Lifschitz. New York: Ktav, 1975.

Gallagher, Eugene V. *Divine Man or Magician? Celsus and Origin on Jesus*. SBL Dissertation Series, no. 64. Missoula: Scholars Press, 1982.

Ginzberg, L. "Some Observations on the Attitude of the Synagogue Towards the Apocalyptic-Eschatological Writings." *Journal of Biblical Literature*

41 (1922). Reprinted in S.D. Leiman, ed., *Canon and Hassorah of the Hebrew Bible*. New York: Ktav, 1974.

Godlove, Terry, Jr. "Religious Discourse and First-Person Authority." *Method and Theory in the Study of Religion* 6 (1994): 147–61.

Goldenberg, R. "The Jewish Sabbath in the Roman World up to the Time of Constantine the Great." *ANRW* series II, 19.1 (1979): 414–47.

Goldman, B. *The Sacred Portal*. Detroit: Wayne State University Press, 1966.

Goodenough, E.R. *By Light, Light*. New Haven: Yale University Press, 1935.

——. *Religious Tradition and Myth*. New Haven: Yale University Press, 1937.

——. *Jewish Symbols in the Greco-Roman Period*. 13 vols. New York: Pantheon-Bollingen, 1956–1968.

Goodman, Nelson. *Ways of Worldmaking*. Indianapolis: Hackett, 1978.

Gottwald, N.K. *The Tribes of Yahweh*. New York: Orbis, 1979.

Gould, Stephen Jay. *Wonderful Life: The Burgess Shale and the Nature of History*. New York: Norton, 1989.

Green, W.S. "Palestinian Holy Men." *ANRW* series II, 19.2 (1979): 619–47.

Griffiths, Gareth. "The Myth of Authenticity: Representation, Discourse and Social Practice." In Chris Tiffin and Alan Lawson, eds., *De-Scribing Empire: Postcolonialism and Empire*. London: Routledge, 1989, pp. 70–85.

Gruen, Erich S., *Diaspora: Jews Amidst Greeks and Romans*. Cambridge: Harvard University Press, 2002.

Gruenwald, Ithamar. *Apocalyptic in Rabbinic Literature*. Leiden: E.J. Brill, 1978.

——. *Apocalyptic and Merkavah Mysticism*. Arbeiten zur Geschichte des antiken Judentums und des Urchristentums, vol. 14. Leiden: E.J. Brill, 1980.

Gutmann, Joseph. *The Dura Europos Synagogue: A Re-evaluation*. Missoula: University of Montana Press, 1973.

——. "The Synagogue: Studies in Origins." In Joseph Gutmann, ed., *Archaeology and Architecture*. New York: Ktav, 1975.

——. *Ancient Synagogues*. Chico: Scholars, 1981.

Gutmann, Joshua. *HaSifrut HaYehudit-Helenistit*. 2 vols. Jerusalem: Mosad Bialik, 1963.

Hadas, M. *Hellenistic Culture: Fusion and Diffusion*. New York: Columbia University Press, 1959.

HaKohen, M. *Me'arat HaMahpelah BeMeqorot U-Mesorot*. Tel Aviv, 1955.

Hanson, J.S. "Dreams and Visions in the Greco-Roman World and Early Christianity." *ANRW* series II, 23.2 (1980): 1395–1427.

Hawthorne, Gerald F. "Canon and Apocrypha of the Old Testament." In F.F. Bruce, ed., *International Bible Commentary*. Grand Rapids MI: Zondervan, 1986, pp. 34–35.

Bibliography

Heinemann, J. *Prayer in the Talmud*. Berlin; de Gruyter, 1980.

Hengel, M. *Judaism and Hellenism: Studies in their Encounter in Palestine During the Early Hellenistic Period*. 2 vols. Philadelphia: Fortress, 1974.

——. *Property and Riches in the Early Church*. Philadelphia: Fortress, 1974.

——. *Jews, Greeks, and Barbarians*. Philadelphia: Fortress, 1980.

Hobsbawm, Eric. *On History*. London: Weidenfeld and Nicolson, 1997.

Hoenig, S. B. "The Ancient City-Square: The Forerunner of the Synagogue." *ANRW* II 19.1 (1979): 448–76.

Hornung, Erik. *The Valley of the Kings: Horizon of Eternity*. Trans. David Warburton. New York: Timken, 1990; German original, Zürich: Artemis, 1982.

Kennedy, Charles A. "Dead, Cult of the." In David Noel Freedman et al., eds., *Anchor Bible Dictionary*, 2:105–8. New York: Doubleday.

Kloner, A. "A Tomb of The Second Temple Period at French Hill, Jerusalem." *IEJ* 30 (1980): 99–108.

Kraabel, A.T. "Jews in Imperial Rome: More Archaeological Evidence from an Oxford Collection." *JJS* 30 (1979): 41–58.

——. "The Diaspora Synagogue: Archeological and Epigraphic Evidence." *ANRW* series II, 19.1 (1979): 477–510.

Kraemer, Ross Shepard. *Maenads, Martyrs, Matrons, Monastics: A Sourcebook on Women's Religions in the Greco-Roman World*. Philadelphia: Fortress, 1988.

——. *Her Share of the Blessings: Women's Religions Among Pagans, Jews, and Christians in the Greco-Roman World*. New York: Oxford University Press, 1992.

Krause, M., ed. *Gnosis and Gnosticism*. Leiden: Brill, 1977.

Lauterbach, J. "Jesus in the Talmud." In J. Lauterbach, *Rabbinic Essays*. Cincinnati: Hebrew Union College, 1951.

Leca, Ange-Pierre. *The Egyptian Way of Death: Mummies and the Cult of the Immortal*. Trans. Louise Asmal. Garden City: Doubleday, 1981

Levi, Y. '*Olamot Nifgashim: Mehaqarim 'Al Ma'amadah shel HaYahadut Be'Olam HaYevani-Roma'i*. Jerusalem: Mosad Bialik, 1969.

Levine, L. *Caesarea Under Roman Rule*. Leiden: E.J. Brill, 1974.

Lieberman, S. "Some Aspects of Afterlife in Early Rabbinic Literature." In *H. A Wolfson Jubilee Volume*. Jerusalem, 1965.

Lietzmann, H. *The Era of the Church Fathers: A History of the Early Church*. Vol. 5. London: Lutterworth, 1951.

Lightstone, Jack N. *The Commerce of the Sacred: Mediation of the Divine Among Jews in the Greco-Roman Diaspora*. Brown Judaic Studies 59. Chico: Scholars Press, 1984.

——. "Whence the Rabbis? From Coherent Description to Fragmented Reconstruction." *Studies in Religion/Sciences Religieuses* 26 (1997): 275–95.

——. *Mishnah and the Social Formation of the Early Rabbinic Guild: A Socio-Rhetorical Approach.* Studies in Christianity and Judaism/Études sur le christianisme et le judaisme 11. Waterloo, Ontario: Wilfrid Laurier University Press, 2002.

Lincoln, Bruce. "Theses on Method." *Method and Theory in the Study of Religion* 8 (1996): 225–27. Reprinted in Russell McCutcheon, ed., *The Insider/Outsider Problem in the Study of Religion: A Reader.* London: Cassell, 1999, pp. 395–98.

Mack, Burton L. *A Myth of Innocence: Mark and Christian Origins.* Philadelphia: Fortress, 1988.

——. "The Historical Jesus Hoopla." Reprinted in *The Christian Myth: Origin, Logic, and Legacy.* New York: Continuum, 2001, pp. 25–50.

——. "On Redescribing Christian Origins." *Method and Theory in the Study of Religion* 8 (1996): 247–69. Reprinted in *The Christian Myth*, pp. 59–80.

Margolioth, M. ed. *Sefer HaRazim.* Jerusalem: Yediot, 1966

McCutcheon, Russell T. "The Jargon of Authenticity and the Study of Religion." In *The Discipline of Religion: Structure, Meaning, Rhetoric.* New York: Routledge, 2003, pp. 167–88.

——. "The Tricks and Treats of Classification: Searching for the Heart of Authentic Islam." In Bryan Rennie and Philip L. Tite, eds., *Underlying Terror: Religious Studies Perspectives on the War on Terrorism.* Albany: State University of New York Press, forthcoming.

McKay, Heather A. *Sabbath and Synagogue: The Question of Sabbath Worship in Ancient Judaism.* Leiden: Brill, 2001.

Martin, Luther H. "Comparison." In Willi Braun and Russell McCutcheon, eds., *Guide to the Study of Religion.* London: Cassell, 2000, pp. 45–56.

Meeks, A.W. and R. L. Wilken. *Jews and Christians in Antioch in the First Four Centuries of the Common Era.* Missoula MT: Scholars Press, 1978.

Meyer, Marvin and Paul Mirecki, eds. *Ancient Magic and Ritual Power.* Leiden: Brill, 2001.

Meyers, C. L. *The Tabernacle Menorah: A Synthetic Study of a Symbol from the Biblical Cult.* Missoula MT: Scholars Press, 1976.

Meyers, E. M. *Jewish Ossuaries: Reburial and Rebirth.* Rome: Pontifical Institute, 1971.

——. "The Cultural Setting of Galilee: The Case of Regionalism and Early Judaism." *ANRW* II 19.1 (1979): 686–702.

Meyers, E. M., A.T. Kraabel, and J. F. Strange. *Ancient Synagogue Excavations at Kirbet Shema.* Durham: Duke University Press, 1976.

Bibliography

Meyers, E. M. and J. F. Strange. *Archaeology, the Rabbis and Early Christianity*. Nashville: Abingdon, 1981.

Miller, Merrill P. "Antioch, Paul, and Jerusalem: Diaspora Myths of Origins in the Homeland." In Cameron and Miller, eds., *Redescribing Christian Origins*, pp. 177–235.

Moore, G. F. "The Definition of the Jewish Canon and the Repudiation of Christian Scriptures." *C. A. Briggs Testimonial: Essays in Modern Theology*. New York, 1911. Repr. in S.D. Leiman, ed., *Canon and Massorah of the Hebrew Bible*. New York: Ktav, 1974.

Murnane, William J. "Taking It With You: The Problem of Death and Afterlife in Ancient Egypt." In Hiroshi Obayashi, ed., *Death and Afterlife: Perspectives of World Religions*. New York: Greenwood, 1992, pp. 35–48.

Needham, Rodney. *Against the Tranquility of Axioms*. Berkeley: University of California Press, 1983.

——. "Polythetic Classification: Convergence and Consequences." *Man* n.s. 10 (1975): 349–69.

Neusner, J. *A History of the Jews in Babylonia*. 5 vols. Leiden: Brill, 1965–70.

——. *The Idea of Purity in Ancient Judaism*. Leiden: Brill, 1973.

——. *Judaism: Evidence of the Mishnah*. Chicago: University of Chicago, 1981.

——. "The Symbolism of the Ancient Synagogue: Interpreting the Evidence of the Synagogue." In *Method and Meaning in Ancient Judaism*. 3rd Series. Chico: Scholars Press, 1981.

——, ed. *Christianity, Judaism and Other Greco-Roman Cults*. 4 vols. Leiden; E. J. Brill, 1975.

Nickelsburg, George W. E., Jr., *Resurrection, Immortality, and Eternal Life in Intertestamental Judaism*. Harvard Theological Studies, vol. 26. Cambridge: Harvard University Press, 1972.

Nilsson, Martin. *Greek Piety*. Trans. J. J. Rose. New York: Norton, 1969.

Nock, A.D. *Conversion*. Oxford: Clarendon, 1933.

——. "Paul and the Magus." In Jackson-Lake, ed., *The Beginnings of Christianity*, 5:164–88. Reprinted in Z. Stewart, ed., *A. D. Nock: Essays on Religion in the Ancient World*. 2 vols. Cambridge: Harvard, 1972.

——. "The Question of Jewish Mysteries." Gnomon 13 (1937): 156–65. Reprinted in Z. Stewart, ed., *A. D. Nock: Essays on Religion in the Ancient World*. 2 vols. Cambridge: Harvard University Press, 1972.

Ogden, Daniel. *Greek and Roman Necromancy*. Princeton: Princeton University Press, 2001.

Oppenheimer, A. *The Galilean Am Ha'Aretz*. Leiden: Brill, 1979.

Paden, William E. "World." In Willi Braun and Russell McCutcheon, eds. *Guide to the Study of Religion.* London: Cassell, 2000, pp. 334–47.

Pagels, E. *The Gnostic Jesus and Early Christian Politics.* Tempe: Arizona State University Press, 1981.

——. *The Gnostic Gospels.* New York: Penguin-Pelican, 1982.

Penner, Hans H. "Interpretation." In Willi Braun and Russell McCutcheon, eds. *Guide to the Study of Religion.* London: Cassell, 2000, pp. 57–71.

Pitigliani, L. "A Rare Look at the Jewish Catacombs of Rome," *BAR* 6 (1980): 32–43.

Poole, Fitz John Porter. "Metaphors and Maps: Toward Comparison in the Anthropology of Religion." *Journal of the American Academy of Religion* 54 (1986): 411–57.

Preisendenz, K. and A. Henrichs, eds. *Papyri Graecae Magicae.* 2nd ed. (Stuttgart: Teubner, 1973–74).

Rajak, Tessa. "Jews and Christians as Groups in a Pagan World." In Jacob Neusner and Ernest S. Frerichs, eds., *"To See Ourselves as Others See Us": Christians, Jews, "Others" in Late Antiquity.* Scholars Press Studies in the Humanities; Chico: Scholars Press, 1985, pp. 247–62.

Reeves, J. S. *Jewish Lore in Manichaean Cosmogony: Studies in the Book of Giants Traditions*, Hebrew Union College Monographs 14. Cincinnati: Hebrew Union College Press, 1992.

Reitzenstein, Richard. *Hellenistic Mystery-Religions: Their Basic Ideas and Significance.* Translated from the German by John E. Steely, 1925. Pittsburgh Theological Monograph Series, no. 15. Pittsburgh: Pickwick Press, 1978.

Richards, Kent Harold. "Death, Old Testament." In David Noel Freedman et al., eds., *Anchor Bible Dictionary*, 2:108–10. New York: Doubleday.

Richardson, C. C. *Early Christian Fathers.* New York: MacMillan, 1970.

Robinson, C. E. *Everyday Life in Ancient Greece.* New York: AMS, 1977 [1933].

Robinson, J. M., ed. *The Nag Hammadi Library.* Leiden; E. J. Brill, 1977.

Rohde, Erwin. *Psyche: The Cult of Souls and Belief in Immortality Among the Greeks.* Translated from the German by W. B. Hillis, 1892. 8th ed. New York: Harcourt, 1925.

Rothkrug, L. "The Odour of Sanctity, and the Hebrew Origins of Christian Relic Veneration." *Historical Reflections* 8 (1981): 95–142.

Rüsen, Jörn. "How to Overcome Ethnocentrism: Approaches to a Culture of Recognition by History in the Twenty-First Century." *History and Theory* 43 (2004): 118–29.

Rutgers, Leonard Victor. *The Jews in Late Ancient Rome: Evidence of Cultural Interaction in the Roman Diaspora.* Leiden: Brill, 2000.

Bibliography

Safrai, S. and M. Stern. *A History of the Jewish People in the First Century. Compendium Rerum Judaicarum ad Novum Testamentum.* 2 vols. Assen: Van Gorcum, 1974–1980.

Sanders, E. P. *Paul and Palestinian Judaism.* Philadelphia: Fortress Press, 1978.

——. *Paul, the Law, and the Jewish People.* Philadelphia: Fortress Press, 1983

——. *Jesus and Judaism.* Philadelphia: Fortress Press, 1985.

——, A. Baumgarten, and A. Mendelson, eds. *Jewish and Christian Self-definition.* 2 vols. London: SCM, 1980–81.

Sanders, J. A. *Torah and Canon.* Philadelphia: Fortress Press, 1972.

Sanders, J. T. "Dionysus, Cybele and the 'Madness' of Women." In Rita M. Gross, ed., *Beyond Androcentrism: New Essays on Women and Religion,* pp. 125–37. Missoula MT: Scholars Press, 1977.

Sayeed, S. M. A. *The Myth of Authenticity: A Study in Islamic Fundamentalism.* Karachi: Royal Book Co., 1995.

Scholem, G. G. *Major Trends in Jewish Mysticism.* New York: Schocken, 1941.

——. *Jewish Gnosticism, Merkabah Mysticism, and the Talmudic Tradition.* 2nd. ed. New York: Jewish Theological Seminary of America, 1960.

Schuerer, E. Revised and edited by G. Vermes, F. Millar, and M. Black. *The History of the Jewish People in the Age of Jesus Christ.* 2 vols. Edinburgh: T. and T. Clark, 1975–79.

Segal, Alan F. "Heavenly Ascent in Hellenistic Judaism, Early Christianity and their Environment." *ANRW* series II, 23.2 (1980): 1333–94.

——. "Hellenistic Magic: Some Questions of Definition." In R. Van Den Broek and M. J. Vermaseren, eds. *Studies in Gnosticism and Hellenistic Religion.* Leiden: Brill, 1981.

Sellars, Wilfrid. "Empiricism and the Philosophy of Mind." In H. Feigl and M. Scriven, eds. *Foundations of Science and the Concepts of Psychology and Psychoanalysis.* Minnesota Studies in the Philosophy of Science 1. Minneapolis: University of Minnesota Press, 1956, pp. 253–329.

Smallwood, E. Mary. *The Jews Under Roman Rule from Pompey to Diocletian: A Study in Political Relations.* Leiden: Brill, 2001.

Smith, Jonathan Z. "Hellenistic Religions." *The New Encyclopedia Britannica* 8:749–51. Macropaedia. 15th ed. Chicago, 1975.

——. "Map Is Not Territory." In *Map Is Not Territory: Studies in the History of Religions,* pp. 289–309. Chicago: University of Chicago Press, 1978.

——. "The Temple and the Magician." In *Map Is Not Territory,* pp. 172–89.

——. "Towards Interpreting Demonic Powers in Hellenistic and Roman Antiquity." *ANRW* series II, 16.1 (1978): 425–39.

Bibliography

——. *Imagining Religion.* Chicago: University of Chicago Press, 1982.

——. "Fences and Neighbors: Some Contours of Early Judaism." In *Imagining Religion: From Babylon to Jonestown.* Chicago Studies in the History of Judaism. Chicago: University of Chicago Press, 1982, pp. 1–18.

——. "What a Difference a Difference Makes." In Jacob Neusner and Ernest S. Frerichs, eds. *"To See Ourselves as Others See Us": Christians, Jews, "Others," in Late Antiquity.* Scholars Press Studies in the Humanities. Chico: Scholars Press, 1985, pp. 3–48. Reprinted in *Relating Religion: Essays in the Study of Religion.* Chicago: University of Chicago Press, 2004, pp. 251–302.

——. *Drudgery Divine: On the Comparison of Early Christianities and the Religions of Late Antiquity.* Jordan Lectures in Comparative Religion, 14. London: School of Oriental and African Studies, University of London; Chicago: University of Chicago Press, 1990.

——. "Why Compare Religions?" Unpublished Paper, Princeton University Conference in Honor of John F. Wilson, October 2003.

——. "Differential Equations: On Constructing the Other." The University Lecture in Religion, 13. Tempe, Arizona State University, March 5, 1992. Reprinted in *Relating Religion*, pp. 230–50.

——. "The Bible and Religion." In *Relating Religion*, pp. 197–214.

——. "God Save This Honourable Court: Religion and Civic Discourse." In *Relating Religion*, pp. 375–90.

Smith, Morton. "Observations on Hekhalot Rabbati." In Alexander Altman, ed., *Biblical and Other Studies.* Cambridge: Harvard University Press, 1963, pp. 142–60.

——. "Goodenough's *Jewish Symbols* in Retrospect." *Journal of Biblical Literature* 80 (1967).

——. "Prolegomena to a Discussion of Aretologies, Divine Men, the Gospels and Jesus." *Journal of Biblical Literature* 90 (1971): 174–99.

——. *Palestinian Parties and Politics that Shaped the Old Testament.* New York: Harper, 1974.

——. *Jesus the Magician.* (San Francisco: Harper, 1978).

——. "Terminological Problems in the Study of Late Antique Judaism and Christianity." In P. Slater and D. Wiebe, eds. *Proceedings of the 4th Congress of the International Association for the History of Religions.* Waterloo: Wilfrid Laurier University Press, 1983.

Starnbaugh, J.E. "The Function of Roman Temples," *ANRW* series II, 16.1 (1978): 610–54.

Stemberger, Gunter. *Jews and Christians in the Holy Land: Palestine in the Fourth Century.* Edinburgh: T and T Clark, 2000.

Bibliography

Stern, Menahem. *Greek and Latin Authors on Jews and Judaism*. 2 vols. Jerusalem: Academic Press, 1974–78.

———. *HaYehudim VeYahadut Be'Einei Ha'Olam HaHelenisti*. Jerusalem: Hammad, 1964.

Stevenson, J. *Creeds, Councils and Controversies*. London: SPCK, 1973.

Strange, J.F. "Archaeology and Religion of Judaism in Palestine." *ANRW* series II, 19.1 (1979): 646–85.

Stuckenbruck, Loren T. "The 'Angels' and 'Giants' of Genesis 6:1–4 in Second and Third Century BCE Jewish Interpretation: Reflections on the Posture of Early Apocalyptic Traditions." *DSD* 7 (2000) 354–77.

Tabor, James D. *Things Unutterable: Paul's Ascent to Paradise in Its Greco-Roman, Judaic, and Early Christian Contexts*. Studies in Judaism. Lanham MD: University Press of America, 1986.

Tcherikover, Victor. *HaYehudim BeMitsrayim BiTequfah HaHelenistit-Romit Le'Or HaPapyrologiyah*. Jerusalem: Hebrew University of Jerusalem, 1945.

———. *HaYehudim Be'Olam HaYevani-Romi*. Tel Aviv: Neuman, 1964.

———. *Hellenistic Civilization and the Jews*. New York: Atheneum, 1970.

——— and Alexander Fuks. *Corpus Papyrorum Judaicarum*. 3 vols. Cambridge: Harvard University Press, 1957–64.

Toer, Pramoedya Ananta. *Footsteps*. Trans. with an introduction by Max Lane. New York: Morrow, 1994.

Toynbee, J. M. C. *Death and Burial in the Roman World*. Ithaca: Cornell University Press, 1971.

Tripolitis, Antonía. *Religions of the Hellenistic-Roman Age*. Grand Rapids: Eerdmans, 2002.

Turcan, Robert. *The Cults of the Roman Empire*. Trans. Antonia Nevill. Ancient World. Oxford: Blackwell, 1996.

Urbach, Ephrayim E. *The Sages: Their Beliefs and Concepts*. Jerusalem: Magnes, 1976.

Vermes, Geza. *Jesus the Jew*. London: Collins, 1973.

Versnel, H.S. "Some Reflections on the Relationship Magic–Religion." *Numen* 38 (1991): 177–97.

Widengren, George. *The Ascension of the Apostle and the Heavenly Book*. Uppsala Universitets Arsskrift, no. 7. Uppsala: A. B. Lundequistska, 1950.

Wilson, Stephen G. *Related Strangers: Christians and Jews, 70–170 C.E.* Minneapolis: Fortress, 1995.

Winston, David. "Freedom and Determinism in Greek Philosophy and Jewish Hellenistic Wisdom." In *Studia Philonica*, 2:40–50. Chicago: The Philo Institute, 1974.

——. "Hellenistic Jewish Philosophy." In Daniel H. Frank and Oliver Leaman, eds. *History of Jewish Philosophy.* Routledge History of World Philosophies 2. London: Routledge, 1997, pp. 38–61.

Wolfson, Harry A. *Philo.* 2 vols. Cambridge: Harvard, 1947.

Zaidman, Louise Bruit and Pauline Schmitt Pantel. *Religion in the Ancient Greek City.* Trans. Paul Cartledge. New York: Cambridge University Press, 1992; French original, Paris: Armand Colin, 1989.

Zerubavel, Eviatar. *Time Maps: Collective Memory and the Social Shape of the Past.* Chicago: University of Chicago Press, 2003.

Zlotnick, Dov, ed., *The Tractate Mourning.* New Haven: Yale University Press, 1966.

Index